D062702

◄ AIMING FOR PENSACOLA ►

AIMING FOR PENSACOLA

FUGITIVE SLAVES ON THE ATLANTIC

AND SOUTHERN FRONTIERS

MATTHEW J. CLAVIN

Harvard University Press

Cambridge, Massachusetts

London, England

2015

First Printing

Library of Congress Cataloging-in-Publication Data
Clavin, Matthew J.
Aiming for Pensacola : fugitive slaves on the Atlantic
and Southern frontiers / Matthew J. Clavin.
pages cm
Includes bibliographical references and index.
ISBN 978-0-674-08822-1
1.   Fugitive slaves—Florida—Pensacola—History. 2.   Fugitive
slaves—United States—History. 3.   Fugitive slaves—South
Atlantic States—History. 4.   Antislavery movements—Florida—
Pensacola—History. 5.   Underground Railroad—Florida—
Pensacola. 6.   Pensacola (Fla.)—Race relations. 7.   Pensacola
(Fla.)—Social conditions. 8.   Pensacola (Fla.)—History.   I. Title.
E450.C55 2015
305.8009759'99—dc23
2015002553

For the loves of my life:

Gladys

Madeline

Joseph

and

Joshua

◁| CONTENTS |▷

◁ AIMING FOR PENSACOLA ▷

INTRODUCTION

IN JUNE 1838, a central Alabama cotton planter placed a classified advertisement in a newspaper published nearly 150 miles away in Pensacola, Florida, a small seaport on the northern edge of the Gulf of Mexico. In the notice, Thomas Barnett offered fifty dollars for the return of Bill, Frank, and Virgil, three bondsmen who fled from his plantation. The text described Bill as "a chunky, well-set, yellow (though not a mulatto) fellow, about 23 years old"; Frank as "a black fellow, of middle size 29 years old"; and Virgil as "a black fellow, of middle size, 27 years old." Barnett hoped to repossess all three runaways, but he seemed particularly interested in the capture of Virgil, "a notorious run-away and villain" who "always aimed for Pensacola in his run-away trips, and once succeeded in getting to that place, where he remained many months before I got him." Barnett was certain of the destination of the three fugitives, adding, "I have no doubt all the above Negroes will aim for Pensacola." He then concluded with a cryptic comment, of the sort found commonly in runaway slave advertisements published throughout the region: "There is reason to believe, that the above negroes have been stolen, if so, I will give ONE THOUSAND DOLLARS for the thief, with proof that will lead to conviction."[1]

Bill, Frank, and Virgil were not alone in fleeing bondage and heading south toward Pensacola. For more than a century, the frontier city's multiethnic and multiracial population, its proximity to the Gulf Coast, and the number of industries and public works projects that employed both free and enslaved black men and women made it both a launch and a landing for runaway slaves. Evidence abounds in the letters and correspondence of slaveowners and public officials as well as the advertisements for fugitive slaves that appeared in regional newspapers published from the colonial period through the American Civil War. There were two types of notices that appeared in these sheets. Slaveowners offering cash rewards for the return of their prized possessions placed the first type, while city officials announcing the imprisonment of suspected runaways in the local jail placed the second. Many of the bondspeople described in these announcements lived and worked in Pensacola or adjacent communities as carpenters, masons, fishermen, lumberjacks, stevedores, shipwrights, and servants. Others originated from adjacent colonies and states along the Gulf Coast, including present-day Louisiana, Mississippi, Alabama, and Georgia. Some came from as far away as Virginia. The frequency with which bondspeople fled to Pensacola by both land and sea often led slaveowners to inform readers that their bondsperson had "made for Pensacola," "is endeavoring to get to Pensacola," or "will no doubt try to get to Pensacola."[2]

Accounts of bondspeople fleeing south toward Pensacola counter the popular image of enslaved men and women escaping from the Upper South to the Northern United States and Canada in the decades before the Civil War. The image, which derives from the legendary tales of the Underground Railroad and its heroic conductors, is rooted in fact. As some of the most widely read and respected studies of the railroad demonstrate, the small group of bondspeople who managed to escape from slavery permanently and about whom much is known almost always traveled in a northerly direction, often with the assistance of others.[3] Among them are the most celebrated figures in the history of American slavery, including Frederick Douglass, Henry "Box" Brown, William Wells Brown, Harriet Jacobs, Harriet Tubman, and Josiah Henson. Even Eliza, the most iconic fugitive slave in American literature whose dramatic flight across the icy Ohio River and into the arms of a kindly Good Samaritan moved the readers of *Uncle Tom's Cabin*, meets the criteria of the archetypal fugitive slave.[4]

Despite its veracity, the prevailing narrative of the Underground Railroad is illusory and requires revision for a number of reasons. First, the limited focus on time and place—the Upper South before the Civil War—slights the efforts of bondspeople in the Lower South who over the course of several generations tried to escape from bondage despite truly incredible odds. This chronological and regional slight is extraordinary given the number of bondspeople in the Lower South eventually dwarfed that of bondspeople in the Upper South. Indeed, a demographic

$50 Reward.

RAN AWAY from the Subscriber, living near Moun Meigs, Montgomery County Alabama, the following described Negroes: BILL, a chunky, well-set, yellow (though not a mulatto) fellow, about 23 years old ; FRANK, a black fellow, of middle size 29 years old ; VIRGIL, a black fellow, of middle size, 27 years old. He is a notorious run-away and villain, and has always aimed for Pensacola in his run-away trips, and once succeeded in getting to that place, where he remained many months before I got him. He likewise became well acquainted about Brooklin.

I have no doubt all the above Negroes will aim for Pensacola. The above reward will be given for their apprehension and lodgment in Jail, so that I get them ; or in proportion for any one of them. Any information concerning them, by letter, directed to me at Mount Meigs, or otherwise, will be thankfully received.

There is reason to believe, that the above negroes have been stolen, if so, I will give **ONE THOUSAND DOLLARS** for the thief, with proof that will lead to conviction. **THOS. M. BARNETT.**

As this advertisement demonstrates, fugitive slaves often aimed for Pensacola from hundreds of miles away. *Pensacola Gazette* (1838). Courtesy of the Library of Congress.

transformation begun in the eighteenth century meant that in the antebellum era more bondspeople lived closer to the Gulf of Mexico than the Ohio River and the Mason-Dixon Line, the two most recognized boundaries between the slave and free states.[5] Second, emphasis on the assistance free Northerners provided bondspeople not only obscures the incredible efforts of fugitive slaves who seldom received assistance from an organized group of antislavery radicals, but it ignores the role of native and foreign-born Southerners in assisting enslaved people in their efforts to become free. Third and lastly, a nationalist framework denies the internationalism of fugitive slaves and their allies in various times and places. Bondspeople who fled from the colonies and territories that became part of the United States, or tried to escape from the republic itself, routinely exploited international rivalries and crossed international boundaries to be free.[6] Especially in the towns and small cities along the southern Atlantic Coast and the Gulf of Mexico that

maintained their international character well into the nineteenth century, bondspeople benefited from a diverse and dynamic urban culture
that never fully adopted the traits of a complete slave society.

By widening the definition of the Underground Railroad and providing a more holistic approach to the study of fugitive slaves, *Aiming for
Pensacola* arrives at the intersection of three distinct historical conversations. First among them is the Atlantic world. Developed by scholars
desirous of applying a global framework to the study of the early modern
world, this analytical concept depicts the universality of societies that
developed on and along the perimeter of the Atlantic Ocean in the centuries following the commencement of European and African colonization of the Americas.[7] When applied to the study of slavery, the Atlantic
world model establishes the centrality of Africans and their descendants
in the making of the nations, cultures, and economies on both sides of
the Atlantic, from the first days of the Atlantic slave trade to its abolition four centuries later. Pointing to the shared maritime experiences
of enslaved people, specialists of the Black Atlantic see the vessels that
crossed the Atlantic and the towns and cities along the ocean's shores
where they docked as places of contestation and negotiation where free
and enslaved black men and women, often alongside their poor white
contemporaries, exercised economic, social, and cultural authority in
the face of the tremendous obstacles placed before them by European
and American merchants and masters.[8] Even in the United States, with
slavery embedded deeply in the nation's core, racial distinctions and
barriers washed away frequently in the coastal communities that joined
the early American republic to the Atlantic world. Numerous studies of
black sailors on the New England and mid-Atlantic shores prove this
in the North and Upper South through the middle of the nineteenth
century.[9] Heeding the clarion call for a more cosmopolitan rendering of
America's past, *Aiming for Pensacola* does similarly for the Deep South by
exploring the long-standing tradition of slave flight in one small seaport
on the outer edge of the Atlantic world.[10]

Colonial Pensacola occupied the Atlantic frontier, but by the turn
of the nineteenth century the city drifted increasingly into the outer
orbit of the American South and what scholars have long referred to as
the Southern frontier, the second historiography this study engages.[11]
The transition stemmed from the emergence of the Southern United
States in an increasingly modern international capitalist system and the

emergence of "second slavery."[12] Throughout this transitional period, Pensacola stood at the intersection of a dynamic system of global exchange and the United States' expansive slave society, making it a cockpit of social and political conflict. This was especially the case during the American Revolution and the War of 1812, when the city was the site of major military battles involving combatants from Europe, Africa, and the Americas.[13] Following the United States' acquisition of Florida in 1821, Pensacola integrated into a regional economy ruled by King Cotton and acquired many of the trappings of a proper Southern city. Among them was a white supremacist culture in which free people of European descent—regardless of class, religion, and ethnicity—considered all people of African descent inferior and all those who were enslaved as chattel. Still, the remote seaport never integrated fully into the economy and culture of the South.

Antebellum Pensacola remained on the margins of Southern society where racially divisive institutions and cultural traditions developed slowly and unevenly. While neighboring seaports along the Gulf Coast like New Orleans, Louisiana, and Mobile, Alabama, and distant Atlantic ports such as Savannah, Georgia, and Charleston, South Carolina, experienced explosive population growth and rapid economic development, Pensacola remained an isolated frontier village.[14] "The old town of Pensacola had one of the finest harbors in all Florida, but was of no commercial importance whatever," is how some early historians described the city. "The inhabitants were chiefly West India traders, smugglers, privateersmen, Indians, half-breeds, runaway negroes, and white men who had fled from American territory for good cause."[15] Pensacola's liminality posed significant challenges for slaveowners who endeavored to build a plantation complex on the twin pillars of slavery and white supremacy; consequently, the city remained an interracial enclave of slaves, sailors, soldiers, and civilians.

The phenomenon of such diverse people cooperating across clearly demarcated racial lines, which social scientists refer to as interracialism, is the third academic discourse this book joins.[16] In the last generation, historians have depicted both the social and cultural construction of race as well as its deconstruction at certain times and in various places. On ships and in seaports along the Atlantic littoral, for example, African Americans and European Americans who lived and worked together often enjoyed lives that were relatively free of racial conflict.[17] Studies of interracial amity in these and other times and places are dangerous enterprises, as they risk understating or even romanticizing the terrible history of racial hatred and violence that characterized and sometimes defined societies that emerged during the era of American slavery; nevertheless, they prove history's contingency by offering an important counternarrative to the presumptive story of the triumph of white supremacy. In the case of Pensacola, an interrogation of interracial interaction reveals a dynamic world in which peoples of African, European, and American descent not only competed and clashed but also cooperated and collaborated with each other daily.

Joining the historiographies of the Atlantic world, the Southern frontier, and interracialism, *Aiming for Pensacola* illuminates the long tradition of slave flight across the southeastern borderlands and later the Deep South as generations of fugitive slaves and a disparate collection of Indians, outlaws, and abolitionists resisted slaveowners' efforts to dominate the region and its people. Over the course of a century, Pensacola was a beacon for enslaved people who sought refuge on the city's waterfront, which verged on a boundless world of ocean and sea, and the surrounding villages that opened into a vast expanse of forests, swamps, and streams. In times of peace, fugitive slaves encountered freemen and freewomen of various races, ethnicities, and nationalities— including farmers, laborers, mechanics, and seamen—who subsisted on the margins of society and had no vested interest in maintaining slavery or white supremacy. In times of war, they confronted soldiers and sailors who tried to destroy the institution of slavery entirely. As a result, interracial resistance to slavery survived in Pensacola in the century before the Civil War and, when the shock waves of that revolutionary sectional conflict reverberated across the city, proved vital to the institution's destruction.

COLONIAL PERIOD

"IT IS THE most miserable place that I have beheld since I crossed the Atlantic," declared Karl Bernhard after visiting Pensacola, Florida, shortly after its transfer from Spain to the United States formally in 1821. As part of an exhaustive North American tour, the German aristocrat traveled through much of the American republic and recorded his experiences in *Travels through North America*. The natural landscape awed Bernard as did the small towns and burgeoning cities he visited from the Atlantic coastline to the banks of the Mississippi River, but the tiny village along Pensacola Bay at the western edge of the Florida Territory left him utterly disappointed. Though captivated by the exotic plants and wildlife, including cactuses, palm trees, and a flock of pelicans, he described Pensacola as a backwater. Wooden houses and a dilapidated Catholic Church on the shore of the Gulf of Mexico appeared "in a forlorn condition," while piles of white sand covered unpaved streets and made travel nearly impossible. At the center of the "ancient Spanish town" the charred remains of an old English barracks testified to the city's stagnancy. Worst of all, the Duke of Saxe-Weimar Eisenach pointed out as he looked beyond the banks of a ready and navigable harbor, there was "not a single ship in the port."[1]

What happened following Bernhard's departure from Pensacola amplified his antipathy. Several miles west of the city, he and his associates met a black riverboat pilot who ferried them across the Perdido River from the Florida Territory into the state of Alabama. Upon disembarking, the enslaved ferryman spotted his master and quickly darted out of sight. He was, Bernhard recorded, "no more to be seen." The fugitive's owner, who lived on a plantation on the banks of the Alabama River several miles away, enjoined Bernhard and his fellow travelers

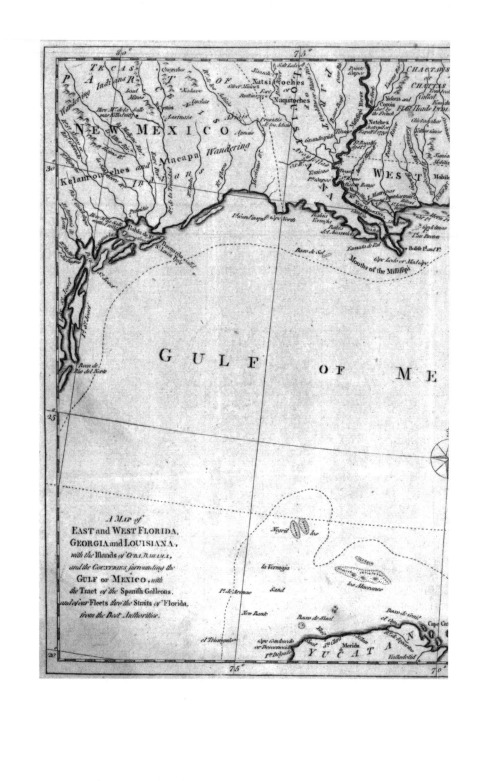

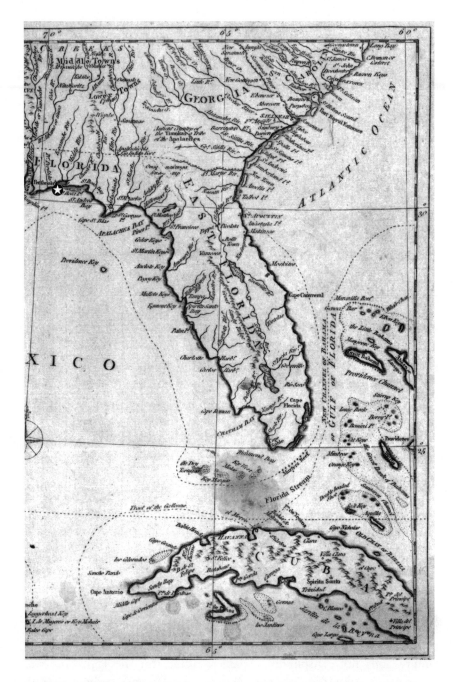

An 1781 map shows Pensacola's location (star on map) on the Gulf Coast roughly halfway between the western and eastern boundaries of colonial West Florida. Courtesy of the Library of Congress.

to assist him in his effort to regain his human property. They stead-fastly refused. Bernhard explained, "The gentleman asked us to assist him in arresting and detaining his negro, but we unanimously rejected his proposal with disgust." The motivation behind the duke's refusal to assist the planter in tracking the runaway was clear. "Some days before, the negro had pleased me much by his lively and agreeable disposition, while his master and tormentor appeared to me, in every respect, highly the reverse."[2]

Bernhard's brief account of a rough and undeveloped frontier town, transient European Americans, and an African American who refused to accept his enslaved status indicates some of the major obstacles slaveowners would face when they tried to transform Pensacola into a bona fide antebellum Southern city. But these obstacles were neither recent nor temporary developments. They were, in fact, several centuries in the making. To understand the enduring tradition of slave flight in Pensacola and the surrounding frontier, it is essential to start at the beginning, for the seeds of resistance planted by Africans, Europeans, and Native Americans would prove difficult to uproot.

Pensacola first attracted the attention of European colonizers in the sixteenth century, when Spain sought to expand the northern boundary of its American empire. Spanish imperialists early recognized the strategic importance of Pensacola, or what they referred to as Ochuse, and its deepwater bay. With water access to the interior and a narrow entrance bounded by land on two sides, the inlet offered an easily defensible position to whoever controlled it. Little is known of the Panzacola Indians, the area's native inhabitants, other than their name, which translates in the Choctaw language as "long-haired people."[3] The first documented encounter between Pensacola's indigenous people and the Spanish occurred in 1528, when Pánfilo de Narváez and Álvar Núñez Cabeza de Vaca arrived with some fifty men aboard five crudely built ships after a disastrous journey that lasted several months and took them from Spain, through the West Indies, and along Florida's Gulf Coast. De Vaca wrote favorably of the Panzacola, noting their physical stature as well as their impressive homes, canoes, and abundant food supply. First impressions notwithstanding, Spanish affinity for the Panzacola was short-lived. After dinner in the home of a local cacique, tribesmen with rocks and arrows attacked the explorers, killing several. The following morning, the entire party departed Pensacola to continue their ill-fated expedition. Only four of the explorers survived the journey from Florida to Mexico.[4]

Among them was Estévanico, a black conquistador who touched down in Pensacola nearly a century before the first African captives landed in Jamestown, Virginia.[5] A West African native, Estévanico came to Florida as the personal servant of a Spanish captain. After finally reaching Mexico City, he came into the possession of the viceroy of New Spain Antonio de Mendoza, who, after learning of Estévanico's talent for converting Indians, ordered him and a collection of Spanish, African, and Indian pioneers to explore northern Mexico. Estévanico traveled ahead of the rest of his party toward Cibola and its famed cities of gold, sending back white crosses of various sizes to indicate the significance of his discoveries. The dark-skinned, bearded man from Islamic Africa who discovered new territory for Spain in parts of present-day Texas, Arizona, and New Mexico struck a remarkable figure. Besides adorning himself with a colorful drinking gourd and bells and feathers around his arms and ankles, he traveled with an entourage consisting of some three hundred Indian men and women. Estévanico's hubris led to his demise at the hands of enraged Zuni chieftains; nevertheless, his success serves as an important reminder of the capacity for Africans to transcend their bonded status on the Atlantic frontier.[6]

The treatment Estévanico and his fellow travelers received from America's indigenous people failed to deter Spanish ambitions. In August 1559, more than fifteen hundred soldiers, settlers, and slaves disembarked at Pensacola from Vera Cruz, Mexico, in an effort to establish a permanent Spanish settlement under the leadership of Governor Tristán de Luna y Arellano, a respected nobleman and soldier.[7] The expedition was a massive undertaking, consisting of thirteen ships loaded with food and livestock along with weapons and tools intended to subdue both native people and the land. The human cargo assured the extension of the tri-racial character of New Spain to Florida by including "Spanish women, negro men and women servants, other servants," and more than one hundred Aztec warriors.[8] The expedition also included members of the soldiers' entourage, whom the Viceroy of New Spain, Luis de Velasco, referred to as "halfbreeds, mulattoes, and Indians."[9]

Spain's first effort to plant a permanent Spanish colony on the northern Gulf Coast was unsuccessful. Only one month after coming ashore a hurricane destroyed the Spanish fleet and sent the colonists scurrying into the interior.[10] Four years later, the Spanish claimed Saint Augustine in East Florida as the capital of its North American empire; still, de Luna's failure discouraged the Spanish from attempting to colonize Pensacola until French and British incursions along the Gulf Coast reignited their interest more than a century later. In the 1690s, hundreds of Spanish colonists arrived at Pensacola and established Presidio Santa María de Galve, a small settlement on the coast that consisted of a fort, church, hospital, and village.[11]

This second attempt to colonize the area was only slightly more successful than the first. In addition to tropical storms, infertile soil, and a lack of resources, an unmotivated and unruly population doomed the settlement from the start. During what has become known as the First Spanish period, Pensacola's population consisted of European landowners and bureaucrats alongside soldiers of various nationalities at the top of the social pyramid with Indians, mestizos, and both free and enslaved Africans and mulattoes positioned beneath them alongside a disparate collection of convict-servants from throughout the Spanish Empire. According to historians of the presidio, the settlement was "a multicultural, multiethnic hybrid: a settlement that functioned as both a military garrison and a penal colony."[12]

Spain's tenuous hold on Pensacola came to an end after the French and Indian War, when the Treaty of Paris of 1763 ceded all the Florida territory to Great Britain. Though largely forgotten today, British Florida comprised two massive royal colonies that stretched from the Mississippi River as far north as Natchez, Mississippi, hundreds of miles eastward to the Atlantic Ocean, and then southward, covering the entire Florida peninsula. The Apalachicola River, which comes together at the confluence of the Chattahoochee and Flint Rivers in Georgia and slices through the Florida panhandle before spilling into the Gulf of Mexico, bisected Britain's fourteenth and fifteenth North American colonies: West Florida and East Florida.

Immediately after authorities chose Pensacola as the capital of West Florida, British settlers who were eager to make their mark began arriving, but they were dismayed by what they found. One officer described Pensacola as a "small Village of about one hundred huts surrounded with a stockade" that because of the "insuperable Laziness of the Spaniards remains still uncultivated, the woods are close to the village and a few paltry gardens shew the only improvements."[13] Another soldier wrote,

"Instead of the best country in the world, [we] found the most sandy, barren, and desert land that eyes could see, or imagination paint!" He presumed the land was incapable of producing a single vegetable, for it was essentially a beach, "consisting, not of earth, but of the whitest sand you ever saw."[14] A third commentator refrained from providing a detailed description of Pensacola as he considered it "impossible to describe it bad enough."[15]

Despite the views of the first Britons to arrive in Pensacola, like the Spanish before them, British officials thought the potential rewards of colonizing Florida outweighed the risks. So the project continued apace. The proponents of colonization fell into two camps. For some, Florida promised great wealth through both trade and agriculture. The leading advocate of this view was George Johnstone, West Florida's first governor, who shortly after taking office proclaimed the virtues of the new colony. Where others saw the barren land along the Gulf Coast as an impediment to colonization, Johnstone entreated skeptics to look further inland, where "the soil is rich, capable of producing wine, oil, silk, indigo, tobacco, rice, and all the fruits of southern climates, together with those of more northern latitudes." The governor predicted boldly, "Upon the whole, whether we regard the situation or the climate, *West-Florida* bids fair to be the emporium as well as the most pleasant part of the New World."[16] For others, Florida's advantage was geopolitical. Edmund Burke saw little to admire of Florida's agricultural prospects, contending, "This country indeed makes no great figure in the commercial world; and cannot be therefore put in competition with the other conquests." But what it lacked in profitability, Burke believed, it made up for "by connecting our settlements on the Mississippi with those upon the Atlantic ocean, and by enabling us greatly to distress, if not wholly to destroy the trade of the Spaniards, in case of a rupture with them."[17]

British West Florida, with its capital at Pensacola, was from its inception a royal colony, led by a Crown-appointed governor, lieutenant governor, and council, along with a democratically elected assembly. The government resembled those of Britain's thirteen original North American colonies with one major exception, an annual disbursement from the imperial treasury meant to compensate for the colony's numerous disadvantages.[18] One of the first important decisions of the colony's government was the appointment of Elias Durnford to design the city's layout, which became a rectangular gridiron covering an area of roughly one square mile. With streets running north and south from the water's edge, and a large public common with a star-shaped wood fort at the center, Pensacola's main thoroughfare extended from the bay north roughly one mile to a stone fort named after King George III. Residential lots located within the town limits were 80 by 160 feet, with landowners entitled to plots of land for farming north of the city on Garden Street. Several miles south of the capital the British built a redoubt, or defensive fortification, near the site of Spain's original fort.[19]

A decade later, the renowned naturalist and explorer William Bartram described the British capital as a small, energetic city bursting with potential. "There are several hundred habitations in Pensacola: the governor's palace is a large stone building ornamented with a tower, built by the Spaniards." Fort George was a large, tetragon shaped fortress made of wood and armed with light cannon. "Within this fortress is the council chamber; here the records are kept, houses for the officers, and barracks for the accommodation of the garrison, arsenal, magazine, &c. The secretary resides in a spacious, neat building: there are several merchants and gentlemen of other professions, who have respectable and convenient buildings in the town."[20]

This etching suggests colonial Pensacola's embryonic nature in 1781. Courtesy of the Library of Congress.

The promise of free land attracted a variety of colonists who came to British West Florida in two separate waves.[21] The first were loyalists and slaveowners attracted by the enthusiastic proclamations of Governor Johnstone and other promoters. Among the most successful of this group was David Waugh, an emigrant from Virginia who shortly after his arrival established a brickyard and "made many Improvements in and ab't Pensacola" before becoming an assemblyman.[22] The second appeared more than a decade later as news spread of fertile land opening along the Mississippi River. Consisting of ambitious landowners primarily, these settlers came from across the British Empire with dreams of large plantations and immense profits.[23] Both groups of settlers came to the Gulf Coast expecting to transform the new colony into an economic powerhouse. But not all the residents of British West Florida were politicians and planters with a vested interest in the colony's success.

To the contrary, much of the population consisted of indentured servants in urban areas and a rough collection of backwoods pioneers who squatted on unclaimed land in the surrounding wilderness. In Pensacola, economic and political elites like Governor Johnstone thought these subalterns were "scum" who could "only be held together by coercive means."[24] In response, the legislature ordered the arrest of "all persons wandering about in the several counties, districts, and places within this Province, living idle without employment, and having no visible means of subsistence but by hunting in a savage manner, and all persons wandering about or lodging in private tippling houses, barns, outhouses, or in the open air, and not giving a good account of themselves." The law recommended impressing serial offenders "in His Majesty's service either by sea or land as they shall judge proper." Additional legislation that countenanced the punishment of intoxicated workers, encouraged the apprehension of horse and cattle thieves, and required licenses for the owners of taverns and public gaming houses, indicated the variety of amusements available to those who made their home in British West Florida.[25] A published report in 1765 provides insight on one recreation that avoided legislative censure: "Since last Monday 43 nymphs of Covent-garden have been engaged to visit Pensacola, in West Florida, on high encouragement; where, it seems, there is at present a great want of the sex."[26]

The Europeans of modest means and minimal morality that Pensacola attracted helped convince colonial leaders of the necessity of transforming the entire colony into a slave society ordered along strict racial lines. With an abundance of land, water, and a seemingly unending supply of enslaved Africans via the Atlantic slave trade, there was reason to believe the colony could replicate the success of Britain's other subtropical colonies. Consequently, the colonial government took a number of steps to promote and protect slavery. First, it enacted legislation that allowed colonists to count bondspeople among their family members. This provided a powerful incentive for slaveowners as each family member entitled the head of household to an additional fifty acres of land. Second, the assembly enacted a slave code based on existing laws in South Carolina, Georgia, and the West Indies.[27] An Act for the Regulation and Government of Negroes and Slaves severely restricted the rights of black, Indian, mulatto, and mustee slaves and called for the severe punishment of any enslaved person found guilty of committing any number of crimes. In the case of serious transgressions that warranted capital punishment, the law directed the government to reimburse slaveowners the full market value of any executed bondsperson. An Act for the Order and Government of Slaves stiffened the penalties for crimes committed by bondspeople and further limited their ability to buy and sell goods or assemble in numbers after dark or on Sundays and holidays.[28]

British West Florida's slave code addressed one concern above all others—fugitive slaves. Indeed, of the seventy regulations signed into law, twenty-seven, or roughly a third, dealt with absconding slaves. The legislation regulated the distances and length of time bondspeople could travel from their homes and stated that the penalty for running away was "corporal punishment at the discretion of the owner or employer, not exceeding twenty lashes on the bare back." Any free "Negro, mulatto, or mustee" helping fugitives escape risked enslavement, while white settlers who were found guilty of committing the same crime would "suffer death."[29] Though extreme, the fear of European Americans aiding and abetting fugitive slaves in seaports throughout the Atlantic world was general. Pensacola was no exception, leading one historian of British West Florida to conclude, "It would seem certain that" bondspeople could not have escaped "without assistance from a white protector."[30]

The legislature's preoccupation with runaway slaves stemmed from Florida's history as a sanctuary for bondspeople fleeing from the British colonies just to the north. As Jane Landers has demonstrated,

Spanish authorities in Florida, in the decades before the British occupation, welcomed and encouraged slaves from South Carolina and Georgia to make their way to Florida and especially Saint Augustine, where the men joined the colonial militia, and their wives and children received safe haven.[31] The arrangement resulted in the first free black settlement in North America, known as Fort Mose, just outside the East Florida capital. The pipeline of fugitive slaves from British plantations to Spanish Florida culminated in one of the largest slave insurrections in North American history. In September 1739, scores of bondsmen from Charleston, South Carolina, and the plantations along the Stono River marched south toward Saint Augustine, leaving a trail of burnt plantations and the corpses of nearly two dozen white men, women, and children in their wake.[32] Two centuries later, the great-grandson of one of the rebels recalled the words of his ancestor who revealed the motive behind the exodus with the following: "We don't lak slavery. We start to jine de Spanish in Florida."[33]

Britain's acquisition of East and West Florida in 1763 should have spelled the end of slave flight into the two colonies, for, as Landers points out, "under British rule, black freedom in Florida became only a remote possibility."[34] Nevertheless, bondspeople continued to bolt to both colonies during the two decades of British rule. Pensacola in particular held advantages for fugitive slaves, because unlike the mature "slave societies" emerging near Saint Augustine and along the eastern edge of the Mississippi River, it remained an isolated and unstable "society with slaves."[35]

Bondspeople were not the only denizens who exploited Pensacola's liminality. The pace at which British troops abandoned their posts alarmed Brigadier General Frederick Haldimand, the colonial governor who in response issued a formal declaration, offering numerous incentives to those who returned to their post. The proclamation promised "a free Pardon to all Deserters from His Britannic Majestys Troops who shall Surrender themselves at Pensacola On or before the First Day of March Next." It then added, regarding those who came back, "they will not be sent to the Regiments from which they have Deserted, but will be put into other Regiments, And that they shall receive Pay from the day of their arrival at Pensacola, where they may come without the least difficulty." Should these incentives fail to provoke an appropriate response, Haldimand also offered to pay ten dollars to the master of any vessel "for the Passage & Provisions &c. of each Deserter upon their Disembarkation at Pensacola."[36]

Indentured servants also slipped away from their owners regularly. Among them was Kelly, who fled from the prominent Pensacola council member Daniel Clark, despite owing Clark three years of service. To better his chances of staying free, the tall, redheaded Irish native with a strong Scottish accent "stole many valuables" belonging to Clark, including a canoe, before heading toward New Orleans. Desperate to reclaim the servant, Clark offered forty dollars to whoever apprehended "this notorious villain, Ingrateful and abandoned Miscreant."[37] In another instance, a South Carolina paper reported the flight of two men from Pensacola toward South Carolina. John Brookes was a thirty-year-old sawyer from England with straight brown hair and "a downcast look in his eyes." He was missing "two teeth in the upper part of his mouth, and the nail of one of his thumbs." Harry was also thirty years old, but he was an enslaved mulatto shoemaker originally from New York. He was additionally "a remarkable good fisherman and seine maker, also very handy about any kind of work." The two men belonged to William Marshall, a wealthy landowner and magistrate, who in a gesture that indicates the comparable value of black and white labor in British Florida, offered a ten-dollar reward for anyone responsible for "securing the said servant or slave."[38]

Other than sharing the same owner, it is unknown whether the European-descended servant named John Brookes and African-descended slave named Harry worked together or in what other capacity they came to form an alliance. But such a pairing was unremarkable throughout the Atlantic world, especially in port towns where people of varying races, ethnicities, and nationalities lived and worked in close proximity. In Pensacola, bondspeople held nearly every available occupation available to freemen and freewomen of European descent.[39] Leading administrators opened their homes to black servants, waiters, and cooks, while businessmen employed bondspeople as coopers and carpenters, millwrights and shipwrights. Like the Spanish before them, British officials responsible for both developing and defending Pensacola employed enslaved labor on various public works. Brigadier General Colonel William Tayler used bondsmen as woodcutters in the place of soldiers who, in his opinion, too readily succumbed to the subtropical climate, while his successor, Haldimand, employed bondsmen in construction and dredging.[40]

A description of three fugitive slaves that Spanish authorities captured in New Orleans five months after running away from British Pensacola demonstrates the type of labor bondsmen completed in the colonial capital regularly. The three men belonged to shopkeeper James O'Neil and the planter James Kirby. Wexford, an English-speaking "carpintero" ("carpenter") between the ages of twenty-two and twenty-three, was "alto y delgado, muy atezado" ("tall and thin, very dark-skinned"). Harry was a twenty-two-year-old "sastre, delgado vien echo, color amaralada," ("lean well-built tailor of yellowish complexion"), who also spoke English well. Greenwich was a "tonelero, su estatura mediano vien echo" (well-built cooper of medium height") who struggled with the English language more than his two companions.[41] The loss of three skilled artisans threatened the economic livelihoods of O'Neil and Kirby, who enlisted a powerful associate to assist them in recovering the three captives. In a cordial letter to Bernardo de Gálvez, the Spanish governor of Louisiana, West Florida Governor Peter Chester requested "that Your Excellency will be pleased to give the necessary Orders for having them sent round by the first vessel to Pensacola—that they may be restored to their respective Owners, who will thankfully pay all expenses incurred on their account."[42]

The correspondence is illuminating as it diagnosis the epidemic of runaway slaves along the Gulf Coast at the same time it demonstrates the willingness of imperial rivals to fight the disease collectively. Besides seeking the return of Wexford, Harry, and Greenwich, Chester described a recent exchange of black prisoners between British Pensacola and Spanish New Orleans. "By the Vessel that carries this Letter," Chester informed, "Your Excellency will receive a Fugitive Slave, who hath been lately secured in this Town; and who is said to be the property of an Inhabitant of Your Province, whose name I have not been able to learn.— I am therefore to request that Your Excellency will be pleased to deliver the said Slave to his Owner, if resident in Your Colony; otherwise to return him by the first opportunity to Me." The delivery of the prisoner from Pensacola to New Orleans came in response to a similar extradition that took place in the opposite direction several weeks earlier. "The two fugitive Negroes which you were pleased to send round to me," Chester wrote of two other bondsmen who had fled from Pensacola to New Orleans, "have been delivered to Captain Lloyd, and Mr. Strother. These Gentlemen have a grateful sense of Your Excellency's politeness and generosity to them—and I thank You for your kind attention to the interests of His Majesty's subjects in my Government." Desperate to maintain the status quo regarding the capture and return of fugitive slaves across international boundaries, Chester concluded, "I flatter myself that Your Excellency will rest assured, that I shall be happy at all times to receive Your Commands."[43]

Because of the vigilance of both Spanish and English officials, fugitive slaves from Pensacola often turned away from the Gulf Coast and headed deep into the heart of Indian country, where an estimated twenty-five thousand Muscogee-speaking Chickasaw, Choctaw, and Creek Indians inhabited the forests and swamps surrounding the colonial capital.[44] Warriors of these nations fought against the British in the late war, and they resented their presence in the region; consequently, they harassed settlers and insisted the colonial government treat their representatives to lavish parties and shower them with expensive gifts. They moreover welcomed black fugitives from Florida.[45] To be sure, bondspeople who fled to Indian country risked trading a European American master for a Native American one, but those who did, in most cases experienced a form of bondage quite different from what they knew in British America. David George, a fugitive slave from colonial Virginia who escaped to the Creeks and later published a narrative of his experiences, recalled that while his Indian master required him to work assiduously, in comparison to the "rough and cruel" usage he experienced on an English plantation, the Creek "people were kind to me."[46]

Near Pensacola, Indians depended on fugitive slaves to maintain their dominance over English trade in Florida. A British agent wrote from Creek country, "The traders in this Nation excepting a very few are Composed of Deserters, Horse thieves, half breeds and Negroes." Operating without licenses or permits, "these hirelings after getting a few Skins with the Goods which the Merchant has entrusted him with, Carrys them to Pensacola where they Barter them with the Merchants for Rum; with it they buy the Horses which the Indians steal from the Settlements of the Different Provinces."[47] A French visitor to the Southern frontier at the close of the eighteenth century wrote similarly in a widely circulated travel narrative. "These Indians keep such negroes as they carry away in their petty wars, or those who desert to them. They treat them as slaves, but behave well to them; are sparing of them in labour, and share with them their own food; these carry the produce of their husbandry to Pensacola," which frustrated English settlers who were thus "deprived of considerable advantages."[48]

The residents of East and West Florida failed to publish a newspaper or obtain a printing press during the two decades of British rule; therefore, additional evidence of fugitive slaves fleeing from Pensacola into Indian country comes from runaway slave advertisements printed in Britain's other Southern colonies.[49] In the winter of 1770, an English trading company captured a runaway living among the Creek and brought him to Georgia. The twenty-year-old black fugitive was a native of the "Bumbo Country" in southern Angola. He spoke no English, but while at large for nearly a year acquired the ability to "talk Indian." Using his newly acquired language, the captive revealed that he lived in Pensacola, where his job required him "to fetch wood in a schooner for his master, who was a man with a big belly."[50] Several months later, rice planter Thomas Netherclift asked the readers of the *Georgia Gazette* to be on the lookout for a light-skinned bondsman from Pensacola named Peter whom he expected would pretend to be free. Netherclift promised to pay all "reasonable charges" for anyone who brought the runaway to the warden of the workhouse at Savannah, noting "'tis supposed may be gone toward the Creek nation."[51] When three African natives, Neptune, Bacchus, and Apollo, fled the Pensacola plantation of Robert Bradley, they were accompanied by an American-born slave named Limerick, who was "very much marked on the back, &c. by severe whipping." The quartet was most likely destined for Savannah, Georgia, as it was believed "that they may have found their way through the Creek nation."[52]

Notwithstanding the supposedly benign nature of Indian bondage, fugitive slaves from Pensacola in most cases viewed Indian country as a doorway rather than a destination. George Smith of Charleston, South Carolina, implored readers of the *South-Carolina Gazette* to be on the lookout for three bondsmen who had escaped from West Florida assemblymen Arturo O'Neill. Scipio was a "strong negro" considered "fit for the house or field." He wore a blue jacket and breeches, and he carried a militia musket and powder horn; Blackwell was a clean-shaven cook who "has been in England"; and Osmyn was a "new negro" recently arrived in America and "inclin'd to squint or looking side-ways." At least two of the runaways were in Charleston prior to living in Pensacola; thus, it was expected that all three were making their way back to South

Carolina by traveling "thro' the Indian nations."[53] Fugitive slaves passing through Indian country understood the dangers they were likely to
encounter and thus carried arms and ammunition with them frequently
on their journey. Glasgow, an eighteen-year-old "country born" bondsman who belonged formerly to the "white Indian" James M'Queen,
stole his new owner's rifle and a horse belonging to several prominent Pensacola merchants before fleeing toward Georgia from the area
"between Pensacola and the Lower Creeks."[54]

The backwoods trails that conveyed fugitive slaves from Pensacola
to Indian country ran in both directions. The deputy provost marshal
at Pensacola Alexander Macullagh announced the apprehension of a
thirty-year-old black man who wore "a large ring of iron uncommonly
well fixed" on his left leg. A jailhouse interview revealed the bondsman belonged to a man named Johnny in North Carolina, and "that he
eloped from his service four years and a half ago, since which time he
continued among the Indians, that growing tired of that life he chose to
leave their nation." If the owner failed to come forward and claim his
property, Macullagh declared, "the said negro man slave shall and will,"
according to the laws of the colony of West Florida, be "sold at publick
auction to the highest and best bidder."[55]

Slaveowners who managed to reclaim fugitive slaves often took
extreme measures to convince these rebels of the evils of running
away. While there is a dearth of evidence regarding the punishment of
captured runaways in British Pensacola, the diary of the West Florida
planter William Dunbar, who owned a substantial plantation on the
western edge of the colony, paints a disturbing picture. Shortly after
Ketty and Bessy "received a little correction" for failing to obey orders,
the pair absconded. One of Dunbar's neighbors captured Bessy the night
she escaped, while Ketty returned to Dunbar the following day. For
coming back voluntarily Ketty avoided punishment, but the "Wench
Bessy" was placed in irons for nearly a week and then "received 25
lashes with a Cow Skin as a punishment & Example to the rest." A year
later, when two other bondspeople failed to escape from Dunbar's farm,
the result was a brutal chastisement intended to break their will to resist
permanently. Dunbar recorded casually, "Condemned them to receive
500 lashes Each at Dift. times, & to carry a chain & log fixt to the ancle—
Poor Ignorant Devils." Dunbar then revealed the blissful ignorance so
common among slaveowners when he asked rhetorically, "For what do

they run away? They are well cloathed, work easy, and have all kinds of Plantation produce at no allowance."[56]

Fugitive slaves who absconded from their owners undermined Britain's efforts to establish a prosperous colony on the Atlantic frontier, but after two decades of British rule an even greater threat emerged. In the aftermath of the French and Indian War, the relationship among the thirteen colonies along the Atlantic Coast and Great Britain deteriorated rapidly. By the spring of 1775 fighting between the two sides broke out at Lexington and Concord in western Massachusetts. In East and West Florida, the annual royal subsidy supplied by the British government and the military support provided to protect against Indians and other enemies made both colonies unlikely partners in any independence movement; thus, on the eve of the American Revolution, Great Britain's fourteenth and fifteenth colonies remained faithful to the empire and offered loyalists from the thirteen rebellious colonies asylum, going so far as to offer them free land to encourage their immigration.[57] West Florida's fidelity to the British Empire put them at odds with their Spanish neighbors in Louisiana, who sided with the American patriots, and when Benjamin Franklin promised to return Pensacola to Spain if they joined the rebel cause, the Spanish seized the opportunity.[58]

Responsibility for reclaiming West Florida fell to Louisiana Governor Gálvez, who, after subduing the British at Baton Rouge in September 1779 and Mobile in March 1780, aimed for the capital.[59] The ensuing battle involved thousands of combatants who were a microcosm of the eighteenth-century Atlantic world. The British force, consisting of regular troops, Indians, and German mercenaries, counted more than sixteen hundred men, "sin incluir los muchos Negros que ayudaban á la defense" ("not including the many negroes that assisted in its defense").[60] Gálvez's eight-thousand-man army was equally diverse. It consisted of "men of all species, nations and color" from Louisiana, Alabama, Cuba, France, and French Saint-Domingue. Francisco de Miranda, who went on to play an important role in independence movements throughout Latin America, led a contingent of several hundred freemen of color and an additional force of black grenadiers and scouts.[61] The battle began with Gálvez's forces sailing into Pensacola Bay on March 9, 1781, and laying siege to the city. For two months, the invaders pounded the British defenses until a shell launched from a Spanish battery exploded the magazine at one of the British redoubts and killed eighty-five soldiers and sailors, quickly forcing a British surrender. The Siege of Pensacola was largely inconsequential to the outcome of the American Revolution. Its effect on the Gulf Coast, however, was profound. The Treaty of Paris of 1783 resulted in Spain reacquiring East and West Florida. For the second time in twenty years, Pensacola was under Spanish control.[62]

The reconquest of Pensacola was an incredible victory for Spain over its imperial nemesis. In Madrid, the popular periodical *Mercurio Histórico y Político* boasted, "Con la toma de Panzacola logró la España someter á su dominio toda la Florida Occidental, echar á los Ingleses del Seno Mexicano, y sobre todo quitarles un Puerto tan capaz y cómodo como el de Panzacola, en que caben muchos, y muy numerosas esquadras" ("With the taking of Pensacola carried out successfully Spain submitted to its dominion all of West Florida, drove the English out of the Gulf of Mexico, and, above all, took from them a port as spacious and convenient as Pensacola, one that can accommodate many and numerous squadrons").[63] There was reason to believe that Gálvez's victory would reverse the downward trajectory of the Spanish Empire by elevating Pensacola's rank among North America's greatest seaports. Instead, the city regressed during the Second Spanish period, serving the empire almost exclusively as a frontier garrison.

According to one visitor, there were upward of two hundred one-story wooden framed houses alongside unpaved streets topped with ankle-deep sand that made walking nearly impossible. Public buildings were unremarkable with the exception of a large two-story home, the former home of the British governor, which the Spanish converted into a barracks. A large warehouse functioned as a Catholic Church, while a small rotunda and attached rooms allowed residents to exhibit their "rage for excessive gaming." For travelers in need of a room, the only options were gaining admittance to a personal residence or happening upon the one American-owned home that accepted guests and was distinguished by a "sign post of which announces a tavern." Produce was inferior and manufacturing nonexistent, with the exception of one sawmill north of the city. Downtown were a handful of house carpenters and tailors, but there were no "printers, potters, tinmen, coppersmiths, watch-makers, hatters, or saddlers, and probably no silver-smiths, black-smiths, boot and shoemakers." The population consisted almost entirely of soldiers and government officials, with everyone else depending on the military and government for "their comfortable existence."[64]

Despite such unenthusiastic reports, Spanish Pensacola attracted a variety of settlers from across the Atlantic world, who, despite their modest numbers, helped the empire maintain a foothold on the northern Gulf Coast. The population, which usually numbered fewer than one thousand, included Spanish speakers from Cuba and Mexico and Spain's colonies off the coast of West Africa, along with French speakers from Louisiana, Mobile, France, and the French West Indies.[65] Also present were English-speaking frontiersmen of Scots-Irish extraction, who emerged from the woods that stretched from the Appalachian Mountains to the Louisiana Territory, which the United States acquired from France in the Louisiana Purchase of 1803.[66] Africans and African Americans who spoke Spanish, French, English, and various West African dialects comprised a significant percentage of the population throughout much of the Second Spanish period. Indeed, in the final years of Spanish rule, the colony of just under one thousand residents had a black majority, consisting of 343 enslaved and 217 free African Americans.[67]

A dynamic international and interracial community amid the inherent inchoateness of the Atlantic frontier made Spanish Pensacola, like other border towns throughout Spain's American Empire, a place where racial and social boundaries often blurred and sometimes disappeared altogether.[68] According to Virginia Gould, residents "did not exist in a world in which a strict interpretation of race and class ordered the population. Instead, their world was fraught with economic uncertainty, a reality that served to knit them together, despite their diversity." In Pensacola, "where ability and adaptability outweighed considerations of color and class, racial mixing was tolerated and even encouraged."[69]

Evidence abounded. At the city's lone Catholic Church, bondspeople received the sacraments alongside their free white neighbors, who in turn often served as the godparents of enslaved children.[70] Inside the garrison, convict prisoners of American, African, and European descent—who at times comprised nearly 20 percent of the city's population—worked as construction and maintenance workers, blacksmiths, butchers, chimney sweeps, and gardeners.[71] Watering holes were another place that revealed the leveling influences of frontier life. A traveler noted that one of the establishments he visited was "the general meeting place of everyone from the Governor down to the laborer and the humblest clerk." Here, ordinary people gathered to eat, drink, play, and in other ways socialize, and they considered themselves "as good as the highest military officer. Here, in short, equality reigns."[72]

Free people of African descent understood better than most the limits of the egalitarian ethos that seemed to permeate the West Florida capital; nevertheless, they benefited from the absence of the inflexible binary racial divide that characterized neighboring Anglo-American societies and the strictly ordered caste system that persisted throughout much of Spanish America. Free black women worked in the residences and shops of their husbands or outside the home as cooks, laundresses, servants, and seamstresses. Free black men worked as carpenters, laborers, masons, blacksmiths, bricklayers, shoemakers, sailors, tailors, and farmers. At least two people of color owned their own shops.[73] The military was the largest employer of African Americans. Following the American Revolution, Spain's regular army was desperate for volunteers and eagerly accepted black recruits, some of whom they stationed in Pensacola as part of Louisiana's Third Battalion.[74] Underfunded and undermanned, the battalion stood out for its uniforms—bright red coats left by the British after their withdrawal from the city in 1781.[75] In addition to regular troops, West Florida law required all free black men to assist in the city's defense. An order by Governor Vicente Folch y Juan in March 1805 ordered the town's militiamen to appear with their weapons in front of the Government House on Sunday morning. This included "all white men and free persons of color from the age of fourteen years to sixty, who are not employed as sailors nor by the Royal Treasury, under penalty of eight days in jail for anyone not doing so."[76] A decade later, Salvador Ruby, a free black revolutionary war veteran, commanded the Company of Mulatto and Black Urban militia, which consisted of fifty "mulattoes" and sixty-seven "blacks."[77]

Visitors to Spanish Pensacola noticed the irony of armed and uniformed black men patrolling the streets of a town so proximate to the American South. With interest in acquiring Florida spreading throughout the United States, a prejudiced army captain avowed, "Pensacola itself is, I can assure you, entirely defenceless." The garrison contained no more than one hundred men, "exclusive of a battalion of colored troops, say about 150 men, of whom the inhabitants themselves stand in constant dread." In spite of the supposed fear of black soldiers, the captain dismissed any notion that Spain's multiracial armed forces were a threat to the United States, adding, "They have about 150 serviceable muskets, about 500 musket cartridges, and not enough gunpowder to fire a salute."[78] Several years later, another American also found the Spanish troops at Pensacola ill prepared for a fight. This was, he believed, because of the lack of provisions, "and to cut them off from supplies, will be a speedy and effectual means of conquering them." Still, he noted, "A great proportion of the troops are blacks whose activity, industry and enterprise is at least equal to the poor Spaniards."[79]

Bondspeople in Spanish Pensacola shared little in common with free black soldiers other than African ancestry; nevertheless, as was often the case on the periphery of the Spanish Empire, they experienced a type of bondage that compared favorably with other systems of slavery practiced throughout the Americas for a number of reasons. First, Spanish law granted civil rights to enslaved people that, while enforced inconsistently throughout Spain's American colonies, granted slaves the right to marry, purchase their own freedom, and acquire a new master if mistreated.[80] Second, on the outer edge of the Spanish Empire, where large plantations requiring hundreds of laborers were rare, bondspeople worked in the homes of officers and bureaucrats as domestic servants, along the waterfront as stevedores and shipwrights, or on the edge of the city as cowboys and lumberjacks. Often they worked for various employers as rented labor.[81] Though enslaved, their lives contrasted sharply with those of enslaved people in the nearby plantation South.

It comes as no surprise, then, that Pensacola's largest slaveowner was not a powerful planter but a corporation. Established by British loyalists in East Florida, Panton, Leslie & Company moved its headquarters after American independence to Pensacola, where the Scottish-born trader William Panton built a massive three-story mansion, along with a store, warehouse, and tannery along Pensacola Bay. In return for the pacification of Indians who posed an existential threat to East and West Florida, the Spanish government granted Panton, Leslie & Company— and its successor companies, including John Forbes & Company—control of Indian trade throughout both colonies. Among the various goods the company exchanged for animal skins were "rum, powder, lead, guns, blankets, blue cloth, woolen ribbons, colored cloth, axes, knives and other knickknacks of apparel."[82] Through the offering of generous credit, the companies' Indian trading partners accumulated enormous debts they would eventually pay off with an astonishing 1,200,000 acres of land.[83] The result was an international firm of unprecedented wealth and power that dominated trade and dictated diplomacy between Native Americans and European Americans along the Gulf Coast for decades.[84]

Company owners owed much of the success of their various enterprises to an enslaved labor force numbering in the hundreds. In Pensacola, dozens of bondspeople hewed and hauled lumber or labored in the companies' tannery, "beating, cleaning, and packing" the hides of fox, otters, squirrels, wolves, and other wild game.[85] Many worked as guides and trackers, which took them deep into Indian country, or sailed on the companies' ships along the Gulf Coast and sometimes across the Caribbean Sea to the British West Indies. Others traveled to remote locations where they helped build and maintain trading posts, a situation that resulted in their service as farmers, ranchers, and occasionally soldiers.[86] The diverse labor opportunities available to bondspeople suggested even greater possibilities for free black men and women in Spanish Pensacola. This, combined with Florida's reputation as a refuge for runaways, helps explain why for bondspeople throughout the region the temptation to fly toward the city often proved irresistible.

The ingression of fugitive slaves into Spanish Pensacola began shortly after Gálvez's victory over the British in the Siege of Pensacola. In December 1781, four bondsmen came to the city seeking protection from the Spanish king and "Papel de libertad" ("free papers") from Governor Arturo O'Neill.[87] Several of the runaways claimed they were from the American colonies, and during the revolution "tomados a fuerza de armas por los Indios y partisanos Ingleses" ("they were taken by force of arms by the Indians and English partisans").[88] Though unable to secure permission to give the men free papers, O'Neill considered them free and put them to work as "empleados y pagados en las lanchez se la plaza" ("paid employees on the launches in the plaza").[89] Two years later, O'Neill recognized the freedom of six other runaways who came to Pensacola from Indian country. The governor explained the rationale behind his favorable treatment of the runaways, noting they were victims of a nefarious trade in black people carried on by "algunos hombres blancos casados con Indios y Domiciliado in la Nacion, y otro Criollos o Mestizos llevandos" ("some white men married with Indians and living in the Nation, and other Creoles or Mestizos traders").[90] The postwar rush of fugitive slaves led the colonial government to abandon its policy established in the seventeenth century of providing religious sanctuary for runaways from Anglo-American masters; nevertheless, as Christine

Snyder points out, Indians' black captives "continued to see Florida as their land of freedom."[91]

Before and after the Louisiana Purchase, New Orleans was a constant source of fugitive slaves to Spanish Pensacola. When officials in Pensacola apprehended one of two bondsmen who had escaped from Louisiana Governor Casa Calvo, West Florida Governor Vicente Folch y Juan informed Calvo that the fugitive named Davies was in the possession of John Forbes of John Forbes & Company, where he would remain until being returned to New Orleans. Folch was optimistic about the fate of the runaway who remained at large, adding, "espero que tambien Robin tendrá iqualmente" ("I expect that Robin will meet the same fate").[92] Several years later, after New Orleans fell into the possession of the United States, Sammy, a mulatto rope maker who spoke good English, fled to Pensacola after committing various thefts throughout New Orleans. Sammy's owner, Daniel Clark, implored an associate in Pensacola to enlist the help of his neighbors in order to "to have the fellow taken up, carefully secured with strong Irons and sent to me by a Person of Confidence who will prevent his escaping on the way."[93]

Beyond Louisiana, bondspeople throughout the Deep South saw Spanish Pensacola as a refuge in the decades after the American Revolution. When Isaac, a six-foot-tall, dark-skinned bondsman escaped from his owner in Blakely, Alabama, he avoided detection for several months until "he was shot near that place" by a potential slave catcher. Isaac survived the attempt on his life, but his owner suspected he would continue to run in a southerly direction, predicting "he will endeavor to get to Pensacola or some other place in the Spanish government for refuge."[94] Nearly a decade after Sam, Nat, and George disappeared from the plantation of John McKenzie in Washington County, Georgia, their owner continued to seek their return. The only clue to the whereabouts of the three men was the rumor that "they were in the Creek Nation and sumtime after that they were in West Floridy at Pensacola."[95]

McKenzie later claimed the bondsmen were captured and sold by Indian slave traders, but another case involving a fugitive slave McKenzie claimed ownership of illuminates the allure of Spanish Pensacola among Southern slaves over the course of more than two decades.[96] When the "likely young negro" Peter stole fifty dollars and fled with his family several days before Christmas in 1814, McKenzie apprehended the bondsman's wife and child following a brief but violent encounter. Peter suffered a bullet wound in the affray, but he avoided capture. Desperate, McKenzie reached out to the public for assistance in capturing the twenty-five-year-old bondsman, explaining, "I expect he will make for Pensacola, as he has two or three relations there who runaway about 23 years ago, and was detained by the Spaniards from my father."[97]

In many cases, slaveowners were unsure where their absconded slaves took aim, yet they believed Spanish Pensacola was among the most likely destinations. Leonard Scott offered one hundred dollars to anyone who captured Israel and returned him to his owner in Monroe County, Alabama. The short and stout bondsman was twenty-six or twenty-seven years old, "little inclined to be of a yellowish cast," and "supposed to have gone towards New Orleans or Pensacola."[98] James Johnston of Baldwin County, Alabama, promised that anyone who apprehended the "negro slave by the name of Jim" would be "handsomely rewarded" for their efforts, but locating the two-hundred-pound blacksmith and carpenter known for his "considerable aptitude" was a nearly impossible task given he took flight some five years earlier. Still, Johnston pointed any slave catchers toward the east, informing them, "It is probable he will make for Pensacola or Georgia."[99]

Few of the runaways who aimed for Spanish Pensacola were as well traveled as Billy and John Pierne. Billy was a twenty-two-year-old quadroon who wore his "very black hair" in a queue. A "Handsome and sensible fellow," he spoke English and "a very few words of French." Billy and his owner, Charles Cabell, were Virginia natives living in New Orleans; thus, Billy was likely returning home. To reach the Old Dominion, Cabell expected Billy to pass as a freeman and first seek passage on a vessel to West Florida, whose boundary had crept within a few miles of Pensacola following the United States' annexation of the Territory of Orleans several weeks earlier.[100] Pierne was a twenty-five-year-old bondsman of "yellowish complexion" who ran away from his owner, James Thomas, in Pulaski County, Georgia, and then reemerged in Mobile, Alabama, where he "passed as a free man" and worked "upon a boat or barge." With access to the Gulf of Mexico, Pierne eventually moved east to Pensacola, "where he was taken up and confined in the Barrancas, but effected his escape by knocking down the guard."[101] Pierne's travels ended after his arrest in the Alabama Territory more than a year after first running away.[102]

Pierne's case demonstrates that fugitive slaves could exit Spanish Pensacola just as easily as they entered. Adjacent settlements were a popular destination for some runaways. Ugenio Fanfan alerted the residents of Mobile of the expected arrival of a bondsman, who had recently absconded, with the following announcement: "Ran-away, From the subscriber, living in Pensacola, on the first of June, a negro man named George, 45 years of age, four feet and a half high, has a very thick beard."[103] Indian country also attracted runaways from Spanish Pensacola. A bondsman belonging to William Panton fled the city with the assistance of Cunsadiemathla, a Creek Indian who later apologized to Panton for having assisted in the man's escape. Cunsadiemathla explained that "he was very drunk and did not know what he was doing for the negro wanted to runaway." The apologetic Indian promised to do everything in his power to help Panton locate the fugitive, and he hoped in return that Panton would "forgive him for what had happened."[104]

The fate of bondspeople who fled from Spanish Pensacola is unknown in most cases, though some joined maroon communities deep within the wilds of the Atlantic frontier. Julían Carballo was a Spanish interpreter who traveled several hundred miles east on the "Camino de Pensacola" ("Pensacola Road") before coming upon a "Palenque" ("fortified settlement of fugitive slaves") in the backwoods of western Georgia. In a letter to the governor of West Florida describing the frontier colony, Carballo cautioned that its more than one hundred inhabitants consisted not only of Indians but "Negros libros y Simaronnes, de los Americanos y algunos de Penzacola" ("free and maroon negroes, from the Americans and some from Pensacola").[105] In the coming decades, the palenque known as Chiaja continued to attract fugitive slaves from American and Spanish slaveowners, becoming, in the words of Claudio Saunt, "the hub of African and Indian relations in Creek country."[106]

The central role of fugitive slaves from Pensacola in establishing the long tradition of marronage along the United States–Florida border forced trading company owners to turn to the half-blood Creek Indian chief Alexander McGillivray for assistance. Born to a Scottish father and a mother of French-Creek decent, McGillivray served as a colonel in the British army during the American Revolution and after the war helped broker an important treaty between the Creek and Spanish in 1784 that led to his appointment as a paid trade commissioner to the

Spanish government. When colonial leaders then granted the Creek exclusive trading rights throughout Spanish Florida, the directors of Panton, Leslie & Company offered McGillivray a partnership in the firm, which he accepted promptly.[107] It was a transformative moment. In the coming years, mounting Indian debts to Pensacola's trading firms led McGillivray and the Creek to pursue fugitive slaves across the southeastern borderlands with abandon. Where bondspeople once expected to find solace among the region's indigenous people, they now faced an organized and heavily armed force of professional slave catchers who gained much monetarily from their alliance with well-funded slaveowners. The machinations of these ruthless Indian mercenaries in and around Pensacola illuminate the pivotal role of Native Americans in securing slavery's expansion at the turn of the nineteenth century. Indeed, without their assistance, European Americans may have failed to spread racial slavery across the southwest.[108]

Despite the relative success of Indian slave catchers, the business of capturing fugitive slaves was a complicated and sometimes chaotic affair. It began with slaveowners or government officials alerting their Indian allies of the escape of one or more bondspersons. When Governor Arturo O'Neill forwarded a list of runaways to Alexander McGillivray, the Indian leader responded, "I will preserve the Negro list & if chance Should direct any to these parts you may be assured of them."[109] When a bondsman in Pensacola shot the nephew of William Panton and ran away, Daniel McGillivray—a Scotsman originally known as Daniel McDonald who later adopted the Creek chief's last name—promised to capture the fugitive. "The Raskally Negro Tom" had not shown up in any of the Creek settlements, but McGillivray promised Panton, "If he does you'll have him or his scalp if in my power."[110] After securing their human prey, Indians then faced the difficult task of collecting payment as two letters from Daniel McGillivray demonstrate. The first letter arrived at the doorstep of Panton, Leslie & Company in the hands of an Indian trafficker named Micko, who was returning a fugitive slave belonging to Don Pedro de Alba. The letter revealed McGillivray's fear that company officials would fail to disburse the promised reward to Micko, but McGillivray nonetheless trusted his "friend Don Pedro will not make me a lyar."[111] In the second letter, a rejoinder to John Forbes, McGillivray defended his failure to deliver a fugitive slave to Pensacola promptly. "I think I am entitled to a reward instead of reflections for my conduct,"

McGillivray asserted; then, invoking the name of the renowned U.S. Indian agent Benjamin Hawkins, he added, "When I informed Col. Hawkins of the Particulars concerning the negro he was well pleased & approved of my conduct & said I was entitled to the reward commonly given for runaway negroes."[112]

For all the problems facing slave catchers, the greatest obstacle to the successful completion of their work was runaways' absolute refusal to return to bondage. After Alexander McGillivray discovered several bondspeople from Pensacola hiding among the Creek, they resisted his efforts to make them "go peacefully" back to the city. To convince the runaways to return to their owners, McGillivray told them the Spanish government "would intercede for them" and thus "their punishment might not be very great." Still the bondsmen refused to go back, forcing McGillivray to inform the owners of the unlikelihood of their regaining their valuable possessions. McGillivray advised one of the owners that if he ever managed to regain his slaves, he "ought to dispose of them as soon as he can because they seem determined not to live with him & if they run away again they may not be soon recovered."[113]

Lucrative rewards for those who captured and returned fugitive slaves resulted in a cutthroat environment in which Indian traffickers battled slaveowners, public officials, and each other over the possession of black people. The result was that in addition to runaways, a growing number of Indian traders kidnapped bondspeople from their homes and residences and sold them for a profit at markets throughout the region. And they were not alone. White frontiersmen of various stripes also profited from the nefarious trade in black men, women, and children. Fearful of additional competition, Alexander McGillivray warned the Spanish governor of a number of these traders traveling from Georgia toward Pensacola "with some negroes," adding, "I hope Your Excellency will not receive any of the rebellious crew."[114] In another instance, a bondsman who returned to Pensacola after being kidnapped by a number of English slave traders reported the thieves had fled the city in the direction of Indian country, "llevandose esclavos y cavallos de various individuos" ("taking with them slaves and horses belonging to various individuals").[115]

The ubiquity of slave stealers often made it impossible for slaveowners and employers to determine why bondspeople disappeared from their homes and workplaces. In one instance, John Innerarity, a trading company partner, sent two men scouring the woods between Florida and Alabama in search of a group of bondspeople he had sent to work in Mobile but never reached their destination. Innerarity thought they had run away, though he considered it possible that they were "decoyed away" by the brothers Billy and Ben Marshall, who may have then hired or sold the bondsmen for "a mere trifle" to a notorious slave trader known as Loyd. Innerarity feared the slaves would end up in Loyd's possession "as he is a most dangerous character and is always laughing at lawyers." To recover his investment, Innerarity enlisted the help of some of Pensacola's prominent residents, who "promised me to spare no pains, time, or expense to trace" the slave stealers and "to have the negroes apprehended if found." He also asked his brother to advertise for the runaways in a local newspaper "to put people on their guard against buying them as I hold their titles."[116]

Not all slave stealers traded African Americans for gain. Some were sympathetic to the plight of enslaved people and tried to deliver them to freedom. Among the most notorious and certainly the most colorful in Florida during the second Spanish period was William Augustus Bowles. A Maryland-born loyalist, Bowles arrived in Pensacola from Jamaica at the start of the American Revolution a hardened war veteran. Events soon led to his dismissal from the British navy, however, and in disgust, the European American teenager threw his red coat into Pensacola Bay and fled to Indian country, where he quickly assimilated into Indian culture, learning the Muskogean language and taking an Indian wife. During the Siege of Pensacola, Bowles returned to the city alongside Alexander McGillivray at the head of a large Creek army that fought alongside the British and earned Bowles reinstatement in the British military. After the war, Bowles traveled to the British West Indies, where he worked as an actor, painter, and musician. In the Bahamas, Bowles befriended British officials who saw in the eccentric veteran a vehicle to destroy Panton, Leslie & Company's monopoly on Indian trade.[117] Between 1792 and 1802, Bowles assembled a disparate collection of "Indians, negros and vagabond white men" that twice sacked Panton, Leslie & Company's store at Fort San Marcos de Apalache, some two hundred miles east of Pensacola.[118] After the second conquest, the region surrounding the fort became a refuge for more than three hundred Indian warriors, European military deserters, "y muchos negros de los Desertados, de Panzacola, y San Agustin de Florida, con ellos" ("and many negroes with the deserters, from Pensacola and Saint Augustine in Florida, with them").[119]

Bowles's multiracial army formed the nucleus of a radical plot to create an independent nation of Indians and other forsaken people in the backwoods of Spanish Florida. Centered on a settlement on the banks of Lake Miccosukee just south of the Georgia border, the "State of Muscogee" had a central government with a national flag and a navy. More than a sanctuary for displaced Indians, the rebel colony was also home to roughneck European adventurers and free and enslaved African Americans. The Indians at Lake Miccosukee had "Negro blood in their veins," writes Bowles's biographer, "and with Bowles on the scene the percentage was increasing."[120]

The State of Muscogee threatened the plantation complex that was overflowing the American South and spilling into Spanish Florida. The partners of Panton, Leslie & Company understood this, as they lost part of their enslaved labor force to Bowles. Among them were "a mulatto and a negro boy" valued together at eight hundred dollars, who, after disembarking at Fort San Marcos from a company brig, were "carried off by Bowles" and never returned.[121] Bowles's multiracial naval force stalked the Gulf Coast in an effort to win Native American and African American recruits, and in at least one instance battled the Spanish navy on Pensacola's shore, further convincing the city's slaveowners of the incredible danger in their midst.[122] Intrigues such as these convinced William Panton, shortly before his death, to write of Bowles and his nation, "No time should be lost to stop the career of that unprincipled Vagabond—for if he is permitted to remain, that place will soon become the nest and refuge of Robbers, Pirates, and outcasts from Society who will be very troublesome Neighbors."[123] The Spanish government agreed and called on its Indian allies to bring Bowles to the authorities "muerto ó vivo" ("dead or alive").[124]

Bowles's contempt for American and Spanish slaveowners was exceptional, yet it reflected an emerging Anglo-American solution to the problem of slavery by focusing on the Atlantic frontier. Before the American Revolution, the British essayist Maurice Morgann published "A Plan for the Abolition of Slavery in the West Indies," which offered a solution to both the moral problem of slavery and the economic and military problems facing Britain's settlements in the "deserts of Florida." Impressed with the number of converted black Britons who were "sober, industrious, and intelligent" and convinced of the inability of Europeans to labor in Florida's climate, Morgann called for the importation of enslaved African children to Great Britain, where they would receive education and training in gardening, agriculture, and manufacturing. At the age of sixteen, they were to be "sent to some district near Pensacola, to be at present reserved for this purpose." In addition to land, they would receive assistance "proper to be given to new settlers." The black colonists, because of their education and maturity, would naturally become teachers and "restrainers" of the present settlers. Thus, Morgann suggested, "many of them might be vested, under English magistrates, with subordinate authority." With this talented and motivated black population in place, the need for coerced labor would disappear. Throughout the colony "no slave must be bought or employed, under any pretense whatever," Morgann insisted. An imperialist scheme modeled in part on Spain's Fort Mose, Morgann envisioned a colony of "free Negroes, united in a common interest, perfectly and affectionately attached and dependent, such as well regimented and disciplined, might act in the hot climates with unabated vigour, and thereby shake the power of Spain to its foundations."[125] Christopher Leslie Brown concludes rightly that Morgann's proposal to build a colony for former slaves on the Atlantic frontier represented "the first British publication to offer a concrete, if quixotic, emancipation scheme," but he was inaccurate when concluding that "no one took seriously Maurice Morgann's Pensacola project."[126] To the contrary, the British government adopted and implemented elements of the plan when it established a colony of black loyalists and other formerly enslaved British subjects at Sierra Leone along the West African coast the following decade.[127]

Bowles visited Sierra Leone briefly in 1798 and no doubt saw a sanctuary for American slaves that hardly resembled the paradise envisioned by Morgann and other British reformers.[128] From its inception, Sierra Leone's black colonists experienced poverty, disease, and an appalling mortality rate. Still, any visitor to the colony at the turn of the nineteenth century would have seen African Americans building houses, cultivating small gardens and farms, and attending church freely. For someone familiar with the trials and tribulation of colonial life on the Atlantic frontier like Bowles it was too early to declare the colony a failure. If the brief stopover in the black British colony had no effect on Bowles's abolitionism, his stay in the Bahamas certainly did. For here he befriended

Lord Dunmore, the Bahamian governor and former royal governor of Virginia who at the outbreak of the American Revolution promised liberty to all bondsmen who deserted their American masters and joined Britain's armed forces. Dunmore's proclamation was one of the most explosive political bombshells of the American Revolution, instantly transforming British slaveowners into American patriots and American slaves into British loyalists. Years later, Dunmore shared Bowles's dream of an independent British-American state on the Florida frontier, a refuge where black and white loyalists of the American Revolution could start their lives anew.[129]

In the end, building and maintaining a colony in the forests and swamps of Florida proved as difficult for Bowles's motley crew of Indian warriors, European deserters, and fugitive slaves as it had for Europe's imperial powers. In addition to lacking basic resources, Bowles's colony suffered from the fact that so many of his potential allies lacked his egalitarian fervor. The case of a fugitive slave claimed by Panton, Leslie & Company demonstrates. In the winter of 1803, a young American Indian agent, Wiley Thompson, encountered Bowles at a Creek village in southern Georgia controlled by two well-known mestizo traders, John and Billy Canard. Thompson recognized Bowles's aide as Jack Philips, a bondsman claimed by Panton, Leslie & Company, whom Bowles's army had "carried off" three years earlier.[130] Bowles threatened to scalp Thompson for trying to take custody of the former company slave, but Billy Canard intervened and brutally assaulted Bowles while his Indian acquaintances "sat still and did not say a word." Moments later, Bowles watched in disbelief as "the Canards took the negro and put him in Irons."[131] Several weeks after Philips's abduction, Creek mercenaries captured Bowles and immediately handed him over to Spanish authorities. The revolutionary freedom fighter died in a Spanish military fortress in Cuba two years later.[132]

Florida's return to Spain in the aftermath of the American Revolution had a profound impact on Native Americans and especially the Creek, who were powerful players in the domestic slave trade. But many Indians refused to adopt the practices of their countrymen as it related to African Americans. Dismayed by the loss of tribal lands to settlers from the United States and frustrated with the direction of their people in regard to slavery, they, in the words of Christina Snyder, "voted with their feet" and embarked for the Florida frontier, where "they joined other dissatisfied Creeks and fugitive slaves to form a new society—the Seminoles."[133] Though often misunderstood, the Seminole—whose name derived from the Spanish word *cimarrónes* (runaways)—were renegade Creeks and other Muscogee-speaking people who migrated south to Florida and after joining forces with fugitive slaves from the United States and Spanish Florida launched a violent anti-expansionist campaign against American settlers and soldiers that lasted more than a half century.[134]

The Seminole contributed significantly to the tradition of slave flight across the southeastern borderlands, for in addition to offering sanctuary to fugitive slaves, they eagerly assisted enslaved people in finding their way to Indian country; still, it is important to remember that in the era of slavery, interracial alliances among Native Americans and African Americans were always imperfect and often unequal. "Seminoles were not waging a war of liberation," Claudio Saunt reminds us. "They did not share the liberal ideology of emancipationists and did not profess special concern for the fate of black plantation slaves."[135] The Seminole, like their Creek relatives, practiced racial slavery; nevertheless, they assimilated bondspeople into their culture and welcomed some African Americans as full tribal members who were known collectively as Black Seminoles.[136]

That fugitive slaves from Pensacola predominated among the Seminole's black confederates is anticipated. The alliance began in the late eighteenth century when fugitive slaves began making the long trek from West Florida to the lands recently occupied by the Seminoles in East Florida. This included the valuable "Negro Man named Brutus" whom Alexander McGillivray learned "was roaming among the Seminole Indians."[137] But it grew precipitously during the War of 1812 when British and Native American forces along the Gulf Coast collided with the U.S. Army in the West Florida capital. The resulting Battle of Pensacola introduced the world to the talented and tenacious frontier general Andrew Jackson, whose American army crushed its combined British, Native American, and African American adversaries. At the same time, it provided an opportunity for a majority of the city's bondspeople to flee with their British and Indian allies to a recently constructed fortification deep in the Florida wilderness. What follows is an examination of the epic confrontation between Jackson's army and these runaways at what came to be known as Negro Fort—the largest maroon colony of fugitive slaves in the history of the present-day United States.

WAR OF 1812 AND NEGRO FORT

IN THE FALL of 1852, a delegation of Seminole Indians led by the legendary warrior-chief Billy Bowlegs traveled to Washington, DC, to discuss the future of Florida's remaining indigenous people. After meeting with President Millard Fillmore, the group continued on to Philadelphia and then New York City, where officials treated them to a wide variety of parties and popular entertainments. Clothed in traditional tribal garb, the Indians were a spectacle as they took to Manhattan's streets. The group visited City Hall, toured Barnum's museum, and watched performances of Christy's Minstrels and *The Barber of Seville* at the world-famous theater Niblo's Garden. While on Broadway, Bowlegs and his entourage entered the gallery of one of the nation's premier portrait studios and sat for an early black-and-white photograph. The resulting daguerreotype inspired a variety of reproductions that appeared in the United States and Europe in some of the most popular illustrated periodicals of the day.[1]

The grainy image that emerged from the Meade Brothers's studio is an archetype of the Noble Savage. Four middle-aged men sit together on a low white couch with their arms, legs, and bodies pressed close together. Their clothes are a combination of European American pants, shoes, shirts, and vests, with Native American head pieces, leg warmers, and various embroidered patterns. The men are dignified, though their crowded and awkward positioning on a cheap parlor-room couch makes them appear out of place and even absurd. Above them are two other men lacking the gravitas of the seated figures. On the left is a younger man with a gigantic ostrich feather curling out of his headband, who stares indifferently across the room. On the right, an elderly man with skin noticeably darker than his companions glares at the photographer.

His face is wrinkled and weathered, while an oversize turban and loose-fitting garments indicate a long and hard life. It moreover suggests his unique status among the other subjects.

The black man's appearance on the silver-coated copperplate is historic as it represents the only known photograph of a fugitive slave from colonial Pensacola. The Black Seminole's name was Abraham, and he fled from the city and his owner during the War of 1812. Following the first of two invasions of Florida by the U.S. Army under General Andrew Jackson, Abraham joined the British and their free black, white, and Indian allies at a heavily armed fort built during the war by the British and Indians on the Apalachicola River, which divided East and West Florida. The former Pensacola bondsman went on to fight alongside the Seminoles in the First and Second Seminole Wars, earning a distinguished reputation among both the Seminole and their adversaries as a warrior, interpreter, and diplomat. Abraham eventually migrated west with the Seminole on the infamous Trail of Tears, but, as the most famous Black Seminole, he remains a popular symbol of frontier resistance and rebellion. Still, his story is only one among many worth telling.

In one of the most extraordinary instances of collective slave flight in early American history, most of Pensacola's enslaved population absconded from the city during the War of 1812 in the aftermath of Britain's invasion and occupation of the city. Prompted by the exigency of war and aided and abetted by British soldiers, Indian warriors, and a collection of free black and white insurgents, these runaways traveled deep into the Florida wilderness, where they occupied and eventually commanded what came to be known as Negro Fort. Isolated and independent for more than a year, it was the largest maroon colony of fugitive slaves in the history of the territory that would become the United States. The potential for an all-out interracial assault on slavery always existed in colonial Pensacola; nevertheless, a study of the city's history during the War of 1812 and the subsequent battle of Negro Fort illuminates how reaching this potential became possible when fugitive slaves, British soldiers, and Indian warriors united against an American army that sought their division.

In the summer of 1813, Spanish Pensacola emerged as a battleground of the second armed contest between the United States and Great Britain in just over a generation, when an internal dispute among Creek Indians

"BILLY BOWLEGS," AND HIS SUITE OF INDIAN CHIEFS—FROM A DAGUERREOTYPE BY MEADE, BROTHERS, NEW YORK.—(SEE PRECEDING PAGE.)

Reproducing a daguerreotype of a traveling Indian delegation in New York City, this engraving depicts the famous fugitive slave and Seminole leader from Pensacola known as Abraham (back row, center). *Illustrated London News* (1853). Author's collection.

in Georgia and Alabama devolved into a bloody civil war. As a result of the internecine conflict, hundreds of Upper Creeks flew south toward Pensacola, where Spanish settlers, who were desperate for Indian allies in the face of a possible invasion of Florida by the United States, welcomed these refugees and provided them with arms and ammunition in addition to sustenance. In the coming months, the arrival of more than one thousand Indians in Pensacola inspired British military officials that were stationed along the Gulf Coast to take the city from Spain, which insisted on remaining neutral in the war, in preparation for a decisive amphibious assault on New Orleans.[2] In August 1814, a British force of one hundred Royal Marines swept into Pensacola and in a matter of hours captured the entire city, including the Spanish garrison at Fort San Miguel (the former British Fort George).[3]

No isolated incident, Britain's occupation of Pensacola was part of a revolutionary strategy to turn the tide of the War of 1812 against the United States by invading the South, arming fugitive slaves, and sending them into battle against their former masters. Long ignored by historians, Britain's abolitionist efforts in the United States during the war have become the subject of a burst of new and exciting scholarship in the area of slavery studies.[4] Though the motivations for Britain's newfound egalitarianism are several, including military necessity, Alan Taylor in his study of the war's impact on antebellum Virginia points to another significant impetus—British exceptionalism. The British saw the liberation of Southern slaves not only as a pragmatic solution to the problem of insufficient manpower but also "as a chance to highlight American hypocrisy about liberty." Taylor asserts, "By protecting runaways, the officers claimed moral superiority over the enslaving Americans."[5]

The plan took shape early in the war when bondspeople from plantations along the Chesapeake Bay escaped to British vessels and eagerly served His Majesty's Forces as "spies, guides, messengers, and laborers."[6] Several hundred African Americans enlisted in the newly created Corps of Colonial Marines and saw action immediately in Baltimore, Bladensburg, and Washington, DC, before heading south to fight on the Georgia Sea Islands. Given the success of black troops along the East Coast, Admiral Alexander Cochrane, the commander in chief of the Royal Navy in North America, expected even greater results in the Deep South given the large enslaved population. But he understood that black recruits wanted more than just freedom in return for military service. "Their bent is to obtain settlements in the British Colonies in N. America," Cochrane wrote to the British Secretary of State for War and the Colonies, "where they will be most useful subjects; from their hatred to the citizens of the United States."[7]

To attract fugitive slaves to the British standard, Cochrane published a revolutionary document that African American and Native American agents distributed along the Gulf Coast in the English, French, and Spanish languages beginning in April 1814. The proclamation promised freedom to "all those who may be disposed to emigrate from the UNITED STATES." It moreover guaranteed these fugitive slaves would, along with their families, "be received on board of His Majesty's Ship or Vehicles of War, or at the Military Posts that may be established, upon or near the Coast of the United States, where they will have their choice of either entering into His Majesty's Sea or Land Forces, or of being sent as Free Settlers to the British Possessions in North America or the West Indies, where they will meet with all due encouragement."[8]

Responsibility for organizing Britain's multiracial force along Florida's Gulf Coast fell to the Irish abolitionist Lieutenant Colonel Edward Nicolls and his coadjutor, Captain George Woodbine, a roughneck

Jamaican Indian trader well-versed in the racial politics of the Atlantic frontier.[9] Buoyed by Cochrane's radicalism, the two marines spearheaded the British invasion of Pensacola and in its aftermath hoisted the Union Jack atop the Spanish flag flying over the city and in other ways made their dominance apparent. Nicolls declared martial law, arrested all those who resisted his authority, and forced residents leaving the town to acquire a passport. He furthermore restricted outsiders from coming into town "without being brought before him to render an account of himself."[10] For his part, Woodbine "commenced collecting Indians, negroes and American deserters" in preparation for the anticipated invasion of New Orleans.[11]

Before launching the historic offensive, Nicolls gathered hundreds of troops in the city's plaza and delivered an emotional speech in front of an enthusiastic throng of Indians, soldiers, and slaves. In this touchstone of radical interracialism, the Irish egalitarian called on the European troops under his command to fight for subject people "who had robberies and murders committed on them by the Americans." He ordered the soldiers to be respectful of the "likes and dislikes" of the Indians and "be careful to offend them in nothing." He also commanded the soldiers to treat slaves sympathetically because they had been oppressed by cruel masters. Nicolls envisioned a racially integrated army in which freemen of European and African descent sacrificed for each other and the British Empire, proclaiming, "What a glorious prospect for British soldiers to set them free, how grateful will they be to you, how ready to mix their Blood with yours in so good a cause additional lustre will beam on that Standard under whose waft no slave can combat." Nicolls then addressed the fugitive slaves in the audience directly, insisting they were "men" for having struck for freedom and endeavoring to "unrivet the Chains of Thousands of your Colour now living in Bonds." Citing Cochrane's proclamation, Nicolls reminded these black volunteers that in addition to freedom they would one day receive land in one of Great Britain's colonies. Nicolls beseeched his black "Brothers" to serve their king and country honorably and show mercy toward their former masters, imploring, "Do them no other harm or violence than is necessary to put it out of their power to harm us."[12] The effect of the speech was soon apparent as at least forty fugitive slaves enlisted in the British Corps of Colonial Marines where Nicolls had delivered his electrifying address.[13]

Confident in the martial ability of his growing multiracial army, Nicolls decided to strike. In mid-September, he ordered hundreds of "Indians, negroes and British marines" to march approximately fifty miles from Pensacola toward Mobile, Alabama, where they would deal an early blow to the United States.[14] The result, however, was that a smaller army of professional American soldiers quickly dispatched the inexperienced invaders.[15] Defeated, the British limped back to Pensacola, where, in an effort to replenish their ranks and perhaps to mend their bruised egos, they tried to free nearly every bondsperson in the city and vicinity. Over the course of several weeks, slaveowners watched helplessly as British soldiers and agents liberated scores of enslaved people and clothed them in "una especie de uniforme, y gorros encarnados obligandolos á trabajar dia, y noche á nuestra vista" (a kind of uniform and red caps, obliging them to work day and night before our eyes").[16] John Innerarity, a partner in the firm of John Forbes & Company and a prominent Pensacola slaveowner, protested that once the British returned from Mobile, "they began to exert all their faculties of deceit, to set all their traps, to put all their tools to work, to catch negro Slaves." The British "visited the negro Cabins in this town, attended their meetings & by every means that the genius of seduction could invent endeavoured to entice the slaves of the Spanish citizens to join them." Bondspeople seized the moment, Innerarity continued. "The evasion of the slave was easy he had but to walk to the fort, at noon day or at night, he was sure of reception." Indians did their part as well. When one slaveowner attempted to capture a bondswoman who had fled to Fort San Miguel, "she was rescued by twelve or fifteen Indians" and taken across Pensacola Bay, where as many as three hundred of the city's slaves had taken refuge.[17]

While Nicolls and Woodbine were largely responsible for the efficient execution of Britain's radical abolitionist plot in Spanish Pensacola, their success depended on a multiracial collection of "American Renegade[s]" who served on the front lines as liberators and recruiters of enslaved people.[18] Among them was Hugh McGill, a former American soldier turned deserter Woodbine ordered to "take away all negros that could be got at."[19] During the British occupation, McGill's house in the center of the city served as British headquarters, while he guided a small band of black and Indian fighters in the woods between Pensacola and the Alabama border searching for food and other provisions in addition to runaways.[20] McGill's associates included Sergeant Thomas Dougherty,

a Bahamian shoemaker and notorious local thief once banned from
the colony, and Caldwell, a boat captain who when confronted with
angry slaveowners after conveying bondspeople across Pensacola Bay
retorted "that he would shoot any man who said he carried off the
said negroes."[21] Another successful recruiter of black troops was John
Bennett, a free black Pensacola native whose success earned him one
hundred dollars and a sergeant's commission in the Colonial Marines.[22]
According to some eyewitnesses, bondspeople were the greatest allies
of the British recruiting effort. John Innerarity recalled, "The greatest
part of the negroes were gone together with the two negroes Prince
& Lucas belonging to Dr. Eugenio Antonio Sierra who were hired &
worked in the yard."[23] Corroborating evidence confirms Innerarity's
account and indicates that Prince, like Bennett, received both cash and
rank for enlisting "all sorts of Negroes whether Freemen or Slaves" in
the marines.[24]

Black men from distant ports likewise contributed to Britain's abolitionist efforts in Pensacola. At the outset of the War of 1812, the law recognized Charles as the property of an eastern Virginia slaveowner. But
when the British appeared on the Chesapeake Bay, Charles abandoned
a life of servitude and took to the water. After enlisting in the Colonial
Marines, Charles embarked upon the HMS *Sea Horse* and set sail for the
Gulf of Mexico. After a short stop on the Apalachicola River, he continued to Pensacola, where, after disembarking from the frigate, he assisted
in the city's capture. Charles likely participated in the attack on Fort
Bowyer and after returning to Pensacola helped liberate bondspeople in
the city and surrounding areas, yet his freedom proved short-lived. After
the war, Charles fell into the hands of the U.S. Army, who arranged for
his return to Virginia; nevertheless, his actions demonstrate the revolutionary opportunities made possible by British actions on the Atlantic
frontier in the Age of Revolution.[25]

The British occupation of Pensacola terrified some in the United
States, including one Southern congressman who decried the city's
transformation into "a place of asylum, refuge, and resort for Nicholls,
for Indians, for Negroes, for Woodbine, and for the dregs of mankind,
collected together to perpetrate violence in the extreme."[26] Among those
willing to eradicate this ominous interracial enclave was Andrew Jackson,
a backwoods planter, politician, and soldier, who only months before
had vanquished the Red Sticks—the most militant and anti-American

faction of the Creek Indians—at the Battle of Horseshoe Bend in central Alabama. Still basking in the glory of his victory, Jackson descended on Pensacola in November at the head of more than four thousand troops, consisting of army regulars, militia volunteers, and hundreds of Choctaw and Chickasaw Indians. After a brief skirmish known as the Battle of Pensacola, the British, who were greatly outnumbered and afraid of suffering a second defeat at the hands of the Americans in fewer than three months, withdrew from the city and headed east to regroup, taking with them several hundred Indians and, according to one protest signed by more than thirty of the city's slaveowners or their representatives, "á los menos dos tercias de nuestros Esclavos" ("at least two-thirds of our slaves").[27]

In the coming days and weeks, hundreds of British "troops, Indians, and many negroes" arrived at Prospect Bluff, or what the Spanish referred to as "la loma de buena vista" ("the hill of good view").[28] The bluff was a steep and heavily wooded cliff that rose over the eastern shore of the Apalachicola River fifteen miles north of the Gulf of Mexico, roughly midway between Pensacola and Saint Augustine. The British and their Indian allies had begun erecting an earth-and-wood fort here on the water's edge the previous spring with the intention of creating a safe haven for their Indian allies, but the site quickly became a refuge for fugitive slaves from both Florida colonies and the Southern United States. Indeed, within a month of its construction, Woodbine reported the arrival of more than two hundred black fugitives from Southern plantations, and he had "no doubt of many hundred slaves joining our standard" subsequently.[29]

The interracial alliance of British soldiers, Indian warriors, and fugitive slaves at the British post prompted dire warnings from American officials, who predicted terrible racial violence would accompany a British invasion of the Gulf Coast. In a communication to the secretary of the navy William Jones, Daniel Patterson, the commander of the United States naval station at New Orleans, avowed, "The enemy have in contemplation an attack on this country from the formation of an establishment at Apalachicola, as well as to excite the Indian tribes to hostilities with us, I cannot doubt, and that they will also endeavor to create an insurrection among the Blacks here, is, I think no longer to be doubted, for after inducing the Savage to raise the tomahawk and draw the Scalping knife, they will descend to tamper with negroes."[30] Andrew

Jackson wrote similarly to the governor of the Mississippi Territory, which at the time included all of present-day Alabama and Mississippi. "The British are arming the indians I have no doubt," Jackson avowed before warning, "We must be prepared to act with promptness, or mobile and new Orleans by a sudden attack may be placed in the hands of our enemies, and the negroes stimulated to insurrection and massacre, may delluge our frontier in blood."[31] Jackson's use of the possessive pronoun was intentional, for he had come to believe that the borderlands between the American South and Spanish Florida were the rightful possession of the United States.

Despite the widespread fears of Jackson, Patterson, and others, the British attack on New Orleans failed to produce a racial Armageddon. To the contrary, the United States' decisive victory over the British in the Battle of New Orleans in January 1815 ensured the preservation of the racial status quo throughout New Orleans and the vicinity. Still, even in defeat, the British delivered another blow to those who claimed ownership of black people by removing several hundred bondspeople from New Orleans and the surrounding plantations to Dauphin Island at the mouth of Mobile Bay.[32] Beginning in February, American representatives, including an assortment of prominent planters, met with British leaders along the Gulf Coast to discuss the terms of peace set forth in the Treaty of Ghent, which brought the War of 1812 to a formal conclusion, and in particular the return of fugitive slaves; on this point, however, the British refused to negotiate. By the end of March, a frustrated United States major, Joseph Woodruff, reported to Jackson that British general John Lambert agreed to every article of the treaty "except that part relating to *slaves,* as it was totally incompatible with the spirit and constitution of his government to recognize *slavery* at all." Lambert promised that he would try to convince the fugitive slaves on the island to return to their owners, but "he would not use force in compelling their obedience, or permit it to be used within the British lines."[33] The British honored their promises to the fugitive slaves from New Orleans, who, with the exception of a small number who chose to return to their owners, became free British subjects in parts of Florida, the Bahamas, and Trinidad shortly after running away.[34]

This was not the first time British authorities refused to return fugitive slaves. Several weeks earlier, Spanish slaveowners demonstrated the same obsession with maintaining ownership of their human commodities as their American counterparts, when they sent a Pensacola delegation to the British post on the Apalachicola River to recover "los negros que en dicho pasage de han refugiado, y han dido llevados por las tropas Inglesas, perteneciente á habitants de este Pueblo & Provincia" ("the negroes who had fled and been carried hither by the English troops, belonging to the inhabitants of this town and province").[35] Upon their arrival at the post in December 1814, Spanish lieutenant José Urcollo and trading company overseer William McPherson met with British army captain Robert Henry, the commander of the post in Nicolls's absence, who authorized the Spaniards to take to Pensacola as many runaways as they could convince to leave the post voluntarily; in the end, however, only ten bondswomen agreed to return.[36] When the Spanish envoys persisted, presenting Henry with a list of 135 suspected runaways, he responded that he was "unable to discover those negroes who may be the property of the Inhabitants of Pensacola, as I find there are not any to answer to the names contained in the list given by Lieut. Urcollo."[37] Henry then added that "it would be dangerous and Imprudent to force those People into a vessel without a strong guard, as the moment Lieut. Urcollo's mission became public they expressed their sentiments of disapprobation in strong terms, such as to convince me of the danger which might attend those who would attempt to take them in a vessel unarmed."[38]

Despite the setback, the Spanish were undeterred and three months later sent a second delegation to the British post from Pensacola, consisting of McPherson, Vicente Sebastián Pintado, the surveyor general of West Florida, and Dr. Sierra, the respected surgeon and slaveowner. The deputation also included British captain Robert Spencer, whom Admiral Cochrane hoped would, given the terms of the Treaty of Ghent, reduce the financial liability of Great Britain by convincing as many fugitive slaves as possible to return to their owners. At the British post, Spencer tried "every art of persuasion to induce them to return"[39]; however, after conversing with some of the post's black residents he openly admitted defeat. "I strongly recommend your not interfering with the slaves," Spencer beseeched the Pensacola delegates.[40] "The blacks are very violent & say they will die to a man rather than return."[41]

The decision of more than one hundred fugitive slaves from Pensacola to remain at the British post was theirs alone, as the visitors from Pensacola would soon learn. In April, Nicolls, who had just returned, allowed McPherson, Pintado, and Dr. Sierra to meet face-to-face with the Pensacola runaways. What transpired over the next several days was extraordinary as three white men tried to convince the 128 black men and women who agreed to be interviewed to return to slavery.[42] The delegates made several arguments to convince the interviewees to accompany them back to Pensacola, including that Spanish slaveowners were more merciful than English slaveowners and thus likely to forgive their slaves for having absconded. The argument failed to convince slaves like Samson, a middle-aged artisan who insisted "Que los Españoles y Americanos eran unos mismo y que lo mataran si venia" ("that the Spanish and Americans were the same and that they would kill him if he returned"). Some of the runaways refused to leave the British post because they believed they were no longer slaves. Reuben Nelson, for example, claimed that he was a freeman, and "presentó algunos papales tendentes a probarle" ("he presented some papers intended to prove it"). Others, when asked if they wanted to return to Pensacola, informed their interrogators that "No quisieron venir" ("they did not want to go").[43]

The fugitive slaves at the British post demonstrated their yearning for freedom clearly; nevertheless, it took an incredible act of interracial fellowship by British leaders to guarantee they remained free. That this radical undertaking occurred after the conclusion of the War of 1812 suggests its inspiration was neither political nor military. When word of the Treaty of Ghent reached the British post, Nicolls provided every black man who enlisted under his command official documentation of their hard-earned freedom. Nicolls recalled years later that he "left with each soldier or head of a family a written discharge from the service, and a certificate that the bearer and family were, by virtue of the Commander-in-Chief's Proclamation, and their acknowledged faithful services to Great Britain, entitled to all the rights and privileges of true British subjects."[44] The issuance of these papers infuriated the Pensacola delegation as "cada una de estas licencias era una carta da de libertad, pues que solo los hombres libres eran admitido en el servício de las armas" ("each one of the licenses was a letter of freedom for only free men were admitted to the armed service"). Because these certificates made no mention of the bearers' "color ni estado de escalvitud" ("color or state of slavery"), the former slaves would be treated as freemen "en qualquier pasage que se presentaron con este documento" ("in whatever place that they presented themselves with this document").[45]

Nicolls's actions encouraged the fort's black residents to identify strongly with their white, red-coated allies. According to Nathaniel Millett, the author of the first book-length treatment of the British post, "The maroons of Prospect Bluff sought to achieve freedom by rejecting their prior condition of enslavement and embracing a belief that they had been granted the rights and liberties of full British subjects."[46] Still, determining the permanent status of the fugitive slaves at the post fell largely to Admiral George Cockburn, who, in a letter to Admiral Cochrane penned shortly after the Battle of New Orleans, clarified Britain's policy regarding black refugees from Florida who found refuge behind British lines. Slaveowners in Spanish Florida assumed Spain's wartime alliance with the British guaranteed the protection of their rights as slaveowners, but Cockburn disagreed. Though there was little legal precedent, he argued that since British courts were in the process of constructing a color-blind legal tradition, enslaved Floridians who ran away of their own free will deserved the protection they sought under the British Dominion. To support this controversial point of view, the admiral paraphrased Justice William Blackstone's famous impartation in his *Commentaries on the Laws of England:* "the spirit of liberty is so deeply implanted in our very soul that a slave or a negro the moment he lands in England, falls under the Protection of the laws and so far becomes a freeman." Cockburn concluded that any territory occupied by the British during the late war was a part of the empire; thus, the fugitive slaves at the British post were free people.[47]

The determination did not sit well with Pensacola's slaveowners who dreaded the loss of even one bondsperson. James Innerarity exemplified the widespread antipathy of the city's slaveowners for the British in a letter to business partner John Forbes in which he asserted, "Of all the Fiends that ever assumed the human form to disgrace it and torment mankind, some of the most atrocious and the vilest were vomited on these Coasts by England during the last summer or fall." Innerarity claimed the stress resulting from the loss of the company's property nearly drove him insane; nevertheless, he would seek reparations from Great Britain "for the unparalleled wrongs we and others have suffered from these bands of Commissioned robbers, these British Algerines, these barbarians cowardly and treacherous, who flee before their enemies and plunder their allies." Innerarity feared that "the far famed Shewy humanity of the African association, Abolition

Society and others of a like stamp" would undermine the company's efforts to recover their enslaved workers because for the British "Negro Stealing is no crime but rather the chief of virtue."[48] Despite Innerarity's hyperbole, his charge was not unfounded. From their base on the Apalachicola River, the British not only tried to destroy slavery but actively assisted Indians in their ongoing battle with the land-hungry Americans to the north.

In the end, the British were unsuccessful on both counts, yet as they set to withdraw from the Gulf Coast they prepared an interracial force of thirty-five hundred Indian warriors and as many as four hundred black soldiers to take possession of the post.[49] The history of the Southern frontier is replete with stories of tension and strife between Native Americans and African Americans, but during and immediately after the War of 1812, in the face of a common American enemy, the two groups proved strong allies first in Pensacola and then at the steep bluff on the eastern shore of the Apalachicola River. In a memo to Admiral Cochrane, Nicolls took great pride in reporting, "The Indians and Blacks are on very good terms and cooperate bravely together."[50] Additional evidence of the harmonious relationship between Indians and slaves came just prior to the British withdrawal when Nicolls informed the post's black residents that he "had not transports sufficient" to take them all to the British West Indies as Cochrane's Proclamation had promised. The former slaves took the news in stride, informing Nicolls that they and their Indian allies had already "agreed to keep together, under the protection of the Indian Chiefs, until we had an opportunity of sending for them."[51]

Despite Nicolls's optimism, the Indian–slave alliance at the British post proved short-lived. Even before the last British troops withdrew from the Apalachicola River in June 1815, large numbers of Creeks and Seminoles had begun to desert the region. During the late war, the British had made many promises to their Indian allies, including the return of "the lands of your forefathers—from the common enemy, the wicked People of the United States; and that you should hand down those lands to your children hereafter, as we hope we shall now be able to deliver them up to you, their lawful owners."[52] The outcome of the Battle of New Orleans forced the British to break their promise to return the Indians to the lands of their forefathers; consequently, the Creek and Seminoles lost faith in their European ally and decided to abandon the British post, leaving it and all of its resources to their black brothers-in-arms.[53]

With the departure of the British and Indians, the British post became known as Negro Fort, an independent colony of fugitive slaves that survived under black leadership for more than a year.[54] To help understand the significance of this extraordinary frontier settlement, a brief description of the fort and its inhabitants is necessary. At the center of the expansive military complex was an octagonal structure roughly one hundred feet in diameter with fifteen-foot-high walls made of stacked timbers filled with dirt and debris. Inside this fort were barracks, "un número considerable de Cabañas" ("a considerable number of huts"), and several solid structures made of stone.[55] The fort, which one observer claimed had "64 faces," sat on a two-acre tract of land surrounded by a small ditch and a dirt parapet beneath a wooden stockade that opened westward toward the river.[56] Throughout the entire complex were many provisions left by the British, including several large cannons, hundreds of caskets of gunpowder and cartridges, thousands of steel swords, pistols, and bayoneted muskets, "besides a large quantity of military stores and clothing."[57] Beyond the fort's stockade were villages that ran along on the banks of the river and were occupied by "American negroes" who grew corn and "every article of sustenance."[58] While the number of slave-soldiers who inhabited the fort is impossible to determine precisely, eyewitnesses put the number between 300 and 450, which is consistent with Nicolls's recollection of 350.[59] Estimates of the number of fugitives inhabiting the villages beyond the fort's perimeter are unreliable, but it was at least a comparable amount and perhaps a significantly larger number as their farms stretched some fifty miles north of the fort on both sides of the river. Moreover, according to one U.S. Army lieutenant, "their numbers were increasing daily."[60]

A rare eyewitness account from a Creek informant provides one of the first and most reliable descriptions of the residents of Negro Fort. In the summer of 1815, William McGirt came to Florida to meet his uncle who lived forty miles east of the Apalachicola River. He then made his way to the complex, where he found "no British troops there at present now but negroes." Though forbidden to enter the fort, McGirt saw at least one hundred armed black men within its confines, noting, "They Keep Sentry & the Negroes are Saucy & insolent, and say they are all Free." Equally impressive was the amount of provisions. There were "Several houses filled," McGirt wrote, along with "a vast deal of ammunition," corn, and rice. There were five large cannons visible as well, though McGirt suspected "there were a great many inside the Fort, which I could not See." As for the untold numbers of fugitive slaves who had fled from farms and plantations across the Southern frontier in recent months, McGirt revealed that the "runaway negroes are I believe nearly all down there, and they all call themselves free."[61]

Though bondspeople from the United States comprised a majority of the fort's residents, "los tres capitánes" ("the three captains") who commanded the citadel were fugitive slaves from Spanish Pensacola, highly skilled artisans who belonged to some of West Florida's most prominent colonial leaders.[62] Garçon was a thirty-year-old "carpintero" ("carpenter") owned by Don Antonio Montero, a member of the Pensacola Cabildo (council).[63] Having come of age during the Haitian Revolution, it is easy to imagine this "French negro" had intimate knowledge of the revolution. It is also possible he was a young eyewitness to the revolution, given the thousands of refugees who fled to the Gulf Coast during the upheaval or in its immediate aftermath.[64] Whether having learned of the successful slave revolution on Haiti through personal experience or what Julius Sherrard Scott III called the "common wind," Garçon displayed the militancy found commonly among Frenchmen of African descent throughout the Americas during the Age of Revolution.[65] Given the rank of sergeant major in the Colonial Marines, Garçon was responsible for drilling troops at the fort and on several occasions displayed an extraordinary level of courage and self-confidence in the face of Spanish and American opposition. Rare is the correspondence of those who came in contact with the fort and its residents that does not mention his name.

Sharing authority with Garçon were two other bondsmen about whom less is known. Cyrus's rank in the Colonial Marines is undetermined, yet the twenty-six-year-old was a highly valued "carpintero y tolenero" ("carpenter and cooper") distinguished by his ability to both "read and write."[66] Cyrus's literacy, along with the fact that he belonged to Pensacola's former governor, Don Vicente Ordozgoity, leads Millett to conclude that the bondsman "was acutely aware of the nuances of revolutionary era political debate and the Machiavellian actions required to maintain political office."[67] Evidence to support such a claim is wanting; nevertheless, it is possible that Cyrus provided much of the brains behind the brawn of the leadership at Negro Fort. A third captain was

Prince, the twenty-six-year-old "maestro carpintero" ("master carpen
ter") who, during the British occupation of Pensacola, became one of
Woodbine's chief recruiters.[68] The marine lieutenant played a crucial
role in persuading "all sorts of negroes whether Free or Slaves" to enlist
in the Colonial Marines.[69]

That the fugitive slaves who controlled the largest maroon colony in
the history of the Atlantic and Southern frontiers came from Pensacola
would not have surprised their owners, given these bondsmen held
some of the most highly skilled occupations in the colonial capital,
which often put them alongside and sometimes in positions superior
to free white men. The success of Negro Fort confirms what American
slaveowners already suspected: that the employment of bondspeople in
urban, industrial, and maritime labor subverted the racial foundations of
American slavery, especially on the Atlantic frontier, where safeguards
of the institution were wanting. The rosters provided by Pensacola's
slaveowners to the British indicating the names, ages, and occupations
of the bondspeople that inhabited Negro Fort reveal the existence of
a citywide apprenticeship system that privileged skill as well as race.[70]
Artisanal work provided enslaved men in particular access to highly
skilled careers that carried with them numerous benefits, including professional status and a powerful sense of self-worth.[71]

Despite the varying levels and types of skills they brought from
Pensacola, the soldiers at Negro Fort united first behind the British
and then their own leaders to remain free. Toward this end, they took
an oath to Nicolls "that they would never permit a white man, except
an *Englishman*, to approach it, or leave it alive" and as a consequence
refused any vessel to pass the fort.[72] Anyone who ignored these threats
put their lives at great risk. In one instance, when a small party of
Spanish traders attempted to deliver a collection of letters from Felipe
Prieto, a storekeeper at nearby Fort San Marcos, to William Hambly, a
paid British agent and former store employer known to be at Negro Fort,
they were intercepted at the shore by twenty-five armed black sentinels
under the command of Garçon, whom Prieto recognized immediately
as "uno de los huidos de la Plaza de Panzacola" ("one of the runaways
from the plaza of Pensacola"). The black troops refused the travelers'
request to approach the fort, and the situation grew tense until Prieto
recognized the "Sargento de la Guardia" ("Sergeant of the Guard") and
struck up a conversation. In Pensacola, Hilario was a domestic servant,

cooking meals for Jose Noriega, a lieutenant colonel in the third battalion of the Louisiana Infantry, but now he was in charge. He ordered the Spaniards to remain in their canoe, while allowing an Indian intermediary to pass through the guard and deliver the letters to the fort. Having accomplished their mission and fearing for their lives, the Spaniards fled quickly on the water.[73]

In other cases, the defenders of Negro Fort drew on their extensive maritime experience as sailors, stevedores, and shipwrights to eliminate potential threats to the colony. Before departing Pensacola, the British and their allies had relieved the city's slaveowners of a large number of watercraft, including "Uno Piragua grande de 45 pies de largo con cubierto, una vela grande, ancha, Cable remos y demas, hus costo tres cientos pesos" ("A large forty-five foot long canoe with a cover, a large sail, anchor, rowing and other cables, worth three hundred pesos").[74] Nicolls believed strongly in the ability of his black recruits to build and maintain a fleet of ships, writing that "with the assistance of Black men I can build as fine gun boats at the Bluff, as can be made."[75] Piloting these vessels was another thing, however, as Nicolls learned quickly. "If any little accident happens," Nicolls lamented after watching a few vessels run ashore, "they don't know how to extricate themselves."[76] Despite some setbacks, the fort's black residents navigated a number of vessels successfully, including a "schooner and several large boats" that at times took the offensive.[77] "They are now organized as Pirates," wrote a Pensacola slaveowner in the summer of 1815, and they "have several small Vessels well armed, & some Piracies that lately occurred in the Lakes are supposed to have been committed by them."[78] With fugitive slaves controlling the heavily armed fortress and adjacent waterways, trading company owners in Pensacola admitted the impossibility of business ever returning to normal until "the hornet's nest of negroes is broke up."[79]

In the end, the destruction of Negro Fort required more than the concerted effort of aggrieved businessmen in a remote Spanish outpost. To the contrary, the situation called for the intervention of an extraordinary force undaunted by the prospects of waging a frontier war against an army of determined and undaunted fugitive slaves. Andrew Jackson, as he had done before in Pensacola and New Orleans, seized the opportunity. Since the conclusion of the War of 1812, the major general had kept a watchful eye on Florida and especially Negro Fort. In the spring of 1816, Jackson warned the governor of West Florida that he would not allow a colony of fugitive slaves to survive so close to the United States, and he promised to act decisively should the Spanish government fail to remove the threat.[80] Indeed, two weeks earlier Jackson had already informed Major General Edmund Gaines that because Negro Fort was a refuge for fugitive slaves from the United States, its defenders "ought to be viewed as a band of outlaws, land pirates, and ought to be destroyed." Jackson ordered Gaines to move his troops into Florida, declaring, "I have very little doubt of the fact that this fort has been established by some villains for the purpose of murder, rapine, and plunder, and that it ought to be blown up regardless of the ground it stands on." Jackson then gave the general the authority to attack the fort, if only tacitly, stating, "If your mind should have formed the same conclusion, destroy it, and restore the stolen negroes and property to their rightful owners."[81]

The United States' assault on Negro Fort began in July 1816 when Gaines and more than one hundred U.S. troops, along with several hundred friendly Creek Indians under Chief William McIntosh, descended the Apalachicola River from their base on the Florida–Georgia border and began capturing black settlers along the water's edge. At the same time, two United States gunboats arrived at the mouth of Apalachicola Bay and headed upstream. When five sailors among this contingent spotted a black man on shore and exchanged words, as many as forty black and Indian soldiers under the command of Garçon and an unnamed Choctaw chief emerged from woods and opened fire on the Americans, killing three instantly and wounding a fourth who managed to swim to safety. The attackers then seized the boat, took the fifth American, Edward Daniels, captive, and returned to the fort. As an exhibition of their power, they then tortured and burned Daniels alive and put his scalp in the hands of a black messenger, with the instructions to deliver the bloody souvenir to their Seminole allies in the vicinity.[82] The strategy backfired, however, for American soldiers intercepted the messenger and after viewing the scalp prepared not only for war but revenge.

When the combined American and Indian force approached the fort and demanded the surrender of its residents, Garçon refused. Declaring that the British had left him in control of the fort, he vowed to destroy any American vessel that threatened it. He moreover avowed that "he would himself blow up the fort" if he could not protect it. The fugitive slave from Pensacola kept his word, and at dawn on July 27, after raising a red, or bloody, flag alongside the Union Jack, ordered his men to open fire with a large thirty-two-pound cannon on the American gunboats that approached from the south. A terrible firefight ensued, but in the words of Lieutenant Colonel Duncan L. Clinch, "the contest was but momentary." On their fifth attempt, sailors on one of the gunboats launched a red-hot cannonball, which landed directly on the fort's magazine. The incredible explosion, which some reported hearing in Pensacola more than one hundred miles away, obliterated the fort and killed nearly all of its inhabitants instantly.[83]

Witnesses struggled to describe what became of Negro Fort and its residents. According to Clinch, "The explosion was awful, and the scene horrible beyond description." Though it was a glorious day for the American republic, "the war yells of the Indians, the cries and lamentations of the wounded, compelled the soldier to pause in the midst of victory, to drop a tear for the sufferings of his fellow beings, and to acknowledge that the great Ruler of the Universe must have used us as his instruments in chastising the blood-thirsty and murderous wretches that defended the Fort."[84] Marcus Buck was equally moved by what he witnessed. "You cannot conceive, nor I describe the horrors of the scene," wrote the young army surgeon who served under Clinch's command. "In an instant, hundreds of lifeless bodies were stretched upon the plain, buried in sand and rubbish, or suspended from the tops of the surrounding pines. Here lay an innocent babe, there a helpless mother; on the one side a sturdy warrior, on the other a bleeding squaw." All that remained were "piles of bodies, large heaps of sand, broken guns, accoutrements, &c.," which covered the site of the once impregnable fortress.[85]

The graphic descriptions help explain the great disparity in the estimates of the number of casualties. Sailing master Jarius Loomis, who piloted the gunboat responsible for the hot shot that annihilated the fort, reported before the explosion the presence of three hundred black men, women, and children, along with twenty Choctaws. Of these, he estimated 270 died "and the greater part of the rest mortally wounded."[86] Clinch testified similarly, believing "the fort contained about one hundred effective men (including twenty-five Choctaws), and about two hundred women and children, not more than one-sixth part of which number were saved."[87] According to Buck's account, only three of the fort's inhabitants survived the explosion, Garçon and an unnamed

Choctaw chief among them. Buck related further that in retaliation for the execution of the sailor Edward Daniels, "The Indian chief was scalped alive, and stabbed, the Negro Chief was shot."[88] Only one person claimed to know the identity of the third survivor. Edward Nicolls asserted several years later that Garçon's wife "was the only person alive when the Americans entered the Fort, and the cowardly miscreants hewed her head with their Swords until they killed her."[89]

Despite the various accounts to the contrary, there were more than three survivors of the explosion. This included at least a dozen black men, women, and children whom the Americans captured and re-enslaved.[90] Several weeks after the destruction of the fort, Clinch reported from nearby Camp Crawford the confinement of nine "American negroes," who hailed from Virginia, Georgia, and Louisiana. One belonged to the Indian agent Benjamin Hawkins.[91] Clinch transferred the surviving "Spanish negroes" to trading store employee William Hambly, who delivered them immediately to Pensacola.[92] Among them was Castalio, who had fled to Negro Fort with his wife, Harrieta and their two children during the British occupation of the city. As punishment for running away and encouraging others to join him, company owners put Castalio to work on "the Public Works with a chain about his leg."[93] Also among the captives were the house servant Tom, a bondswoman named Dolly, and her five children, all of whom had lived and worked at the company's small store on the Apalachicola River not far from the site of Negro Fort. The group refused to go west with Hambly, however, and insisted they remain at the store. Edmund Doyle explained to their owners, "The negroes do not wish to go to Pensacola, & if they got the least hint of it might run away."[94]

In the face of incredible odds, many of the fugitive slaves at Negro Fort escaped death and re-enslavement by fleeing into the forest before the American invasion.[95] Indeed, some reports indicate that the vast majority of the fort's inhabitants and even many of the villagers who settled on nearby farms had deserted Prospect Bluff prior to the assault. The defectors dispersed throughout various parts of East Florida, some going as far South as Tampa Bay to avoid further conflict with the United States.[96] Others found refuge with the Seminoles. This included Prince, one of the three commanders of Negro Fort, who joined the Seminole several months before the fort's destruction.[97]

In the aftermath of the destruction of Negro Fort, many of the fortress's former defenders joined the Seminoles in igniting the first of three bloody clashes between the Seminoles and the United States in the antebellum period that became known as the Seminole Wars. The British also contributed to the eruption of the First Seminole War, when, in the winter of 1817, George Woodbine appeared at the mouth of the Apalachicola River at the front of a band of black and Indian warriors, who stole horses and cattle and threatened to kill any white settlers who stood in their path. Nearby, six hundred black and Indian militants under the leadership of the Seminole chief Bowlegs spoke "in the most contemptuous manner of the Americans" and vowed to avenge "the destruction of the negro fort."[98] Besides Woodbine and Bowlegs, Second Lieutenant Robert Ambrister, who served under Nicolls at Pensacola and the British post, also endeavored to "see the negroes righted." From his base on the St. Mark's River, Ambrister distributed gunpowder, war paint, and other provisions to the Seminole and their three hundred black allies, including those "of the negro fort, collected by Nicholls and Woodbine's proclamations during the American and English war."[99] By the end of 1817, as the number of Seminole and fugitive slaves grew to more than two thousand, Andrew Jackson returned to Florida yet again, bound and determined to end any threat to the United States emanating from beneath its southern border.[100] With several thousand men at his disposal, Jackson wreaked havoc on Seminole towns and fugitive slave settlements throughout East Florida. Eventually, Woodbine fled the country and Ambrister faced a U.S. firing squad; nevertheless, resistance continued. Bowlegs retreated into the Florida wilderness, where he and a desperate army of black and Indian fighters continued to resist American aggression for decades.[101]

Among the leaders of the resistance were two refugees from Negro Fort who years earlier worked for John Forbes & Company on the Pensacola waterfront building and repairing ships. Prior to the War of 1812, Harry and Abraham were among the most skilled and highly valued commodities in West Florida. Harry "los calafate" ("the caulker") was a literate sailor and "carpintero constructor" ("shipwright") valued at an extraordinary seventy pesos per month or two thousand pesos outright. Abraham was a multilingual "carpintero de ribera" (shipwright) worth thirty-seven pesos per month or one thousand pesos outright. Both bondsmen fled Pensacola with the British in 1814 and resided at Negro Fort before heading deep into Indian country. Years later, they reemerged as powerful leaders among Florida's indigenous people.[102]

Negro Abraham.

Engraving of the famous
Black Seminole Abraham.
From Joshua R. Giddings,
The Exiles of Florida (1858).
Courtesy of Special
Collections, University of
Houston Libraries.

For these former slaves, it was the Seminole rather than the British who provided the best opportunity to maintain their freedom. Harry commanded a group of one hundred warriors known as the Pea Creek Band of the Seminole some forty miles southeast of Tampa Bay. The group was responsible for "most of the mischief" between Indians and Americans in central Florida and perpetrated what became known as the Dade Massacre—the annihilation of nearly an entire U.S. Army regiment in December 1835 that sparked the Second Seminole War. Abraham may also have participated in the historic American defeat, for he remained an "intimate" of Harry in the days just prior to the massacre.[103] Two decades after abandoning Negro Fort, Abraham's reputation as a leading Black Seminole was unrivaled. He worked as a translator and adviser for Chief Micanopy, and, while nominally a slave, lived as a freeman, marrying the daughter of an Indian chief and integrating fully into Seminole culture. By the 1830s, Abraham commanded an army of "about five hundred negroes" that assisted the Seminole in resisting American expansion into Florida.[104] "The principal negro chief," is how Major General Thomas Jesup described Abraham's position among the Seminole. He was "a good soldier, and an intrepid leader," who the U.S.

Army considered "the most cunning and intelligent negro" among the Indians.[105] Abraham played a pivotal role in the peace negotiations that brought the Second Seminole War to a conclusion; therefore, the U.S. government granted the fugitive slave from Pensacola his freedom and that of his family permanently.[106]

Though extraordinary, Abraham's ability to die a freeman symbolizes the indomitability of fugitive slaves from Pensacola during both the final years of Spanish colonial rule and the first decades of American governance. From the American Revolution through the War of 1812 and its aftermath, the city's slaveowners struggled to control the men and women they considered their possessions. Nevertheless, the expansion of the United States' slave society across the Atlantic frontier, which Andrew Jackson accelerated with his separate invasions of the West Florida capital, promised great changes, most significantly that Pensacola would become a part of the South. The United States' formal acquisition of Florida in 1821 ended Spanish rule permanently, but it also marked a historic counterrevolutionary moment by eliminating the possibility of any further large-scale frontier alliance between African Americans, Native Americans, and European Americans. Still, despite the incredible changes brought by American rule, bondspeople and an assortment of their free friends, neighbors, and coworkers continued to challenge the new racial and social order and thus kept the city both a launch and landing for fugitive slaves.

INTERRACIALISM AND RESISTANCE

SHORTLY AFTER the destruction of Negro Fort, an African-born sailor named Joe Cook, who enlisted in the British marines during their occupation of Pensacola in 1814, returned to the city where he remained during the last years of Spanish rule. After the United States took possession of the former Spanish capital, the former bondsman settled in a small Indian village just outside town until Theofield Philibert chanced upon him and, "supposing him to be a runaway slave," apprehended the former sentry and delivered him to the Pensacola jail. Philibert returned to the jail two weeks later hoping to collect a reward but instead learned that the constable had liberated the prisoner, who he considered "a free man." Cook found himself the target of slave catchers again nearly a decade later, when Levi James, an "old acquaintance" and shipmate, attempted to sell him to Eulalie Garcon, the wife of a former Spanish official. Whereas the British Colonial Marines first conducted Cook to freedom, and then Pensacola's constable, this time Dr. Christopher Yates Fonda, a recent migrant to Pensacola from upstate New York, flew to his defense. The doctor implored Judge John Jerrison of the Escambia County Court to grant Cook a writ of *habeas corpus,* which the judge did immediately.[1]

In October 1829, the Escambia County Court for the Territory of West Florida took up the case of *Joe Cook v. Eulalie Garcon.* As territorial laws required persons "whose colour is presumptive evidence of slavery to establish his freedom," seven men appeared and testified on Cook's behalf. The group consisted of four white men, two free men of color, and two bondsmen. Providing the most convincing testimony was Peter Alba, the former mayor who swore Cook was, during the late war, "a Soldier in the British Army in British uniform and under arms." The evidence from Alba and the other witnesses convinced Jerrison that Cook was a veteran of His Majesty's service and thus a freeman; consequently, the judge ordered Cook's release. The ruling must have convinced Cook of the prospects of remaining in Pensacola, for he made the city his home for the rest of his life. Cook appears in the Escambia County Census of 1860 a freeman. His listed age of 106 is apocryphal—the fact that he remained a freeman is not.[2]

Joe Cook's decision to remain in Pensacola is worth considering given the city's transformation following the United States' acquisition of Florida. In the four decades before the Civil War, Pensacola became a typical Southern city in many respects. A small group of wealthy and connected white men held a disproportionate amount of economic and political power over the town's less fortunate European American majority. Ships sailed in and out of the harbor, importing and exporting products such as cotton, bricks, timber, and all variety of manufactured goods, along with information and ideas from ports both near and far. Weekly newspapers kept readers informed of important local news while providing a cursory review of the most salient national and international events. All the while, the lives of African Americans reached a nadir. Laws copied from Florida's neighbors stripped away every right and liberty once available to bondspeople during the days of Spanish rule, and the color line separating free and enslaved people grew larger and more menacing daily.

Even so, Pensacola remained on the South's margins for several reasons. First, unlike other Gulf Coast seaports, the ground beneath the city lacked the nutrient-rich soil necessary to cultivate cotton.[3] Second, both the shallowness and the shortness of the tributaries that fed into Pensacola Bay placed severe limitations on cotton exports from the Southern interior. The constant threat of destructive tropical storms and deadly tropical diseases was an additional concern. Collectively, all of these problems left Pensacola bereft of the ambitious and intrepid entrepreneurs that flooded areas of similar size throughout the region. Absent these upstarts, the port attracted men and women with limited aspirations and even more limited resources who contributed little to the city's growth and development. As a result, Pensacola remained a frontier outpost rather than the "the great emporium of the Gulf of Mexico" some had predicted.[4]

For African Americans like Joe Cook, Pensacola's marginality revealed itself in various ways. Freemen and freewomen of African descent owned land, small businesses, and their own homes; free black and white laborers who had little choice but to toil side by side during the day enjoyed each other's company freely late into the night. As for slaves, a great number lived and worked apart from their owners and rarely if ever performed the type of mindless soul-crushing labor required of field hands on plantations across the Deep South. While slaveowners and other white elites had the power to check the efforts of free and enslaved people to subvert the racial status quo, the frequency with which fugitive slaves passed through Pensacola—and, in the case of Joe Cook, remained—indicates the limits of those checks. Indeed, despite slavery's expansion across the Southern frontier, significant challenges to the institution remained in Pensacola throughout the antebellum era, which is why the city remained both a point of departure and destination for fugitive slaves.

On July 17, 1821, Andrew Jackson met Spanish governor José Callava in the Government House on the edge of the public square in downtown Pensacola while outside U.S. troops sent an American flag up a pole overlooking the city. Though anticipated for several months, the two events marked officially the end of four decades of Spanish rule over East and West Florida. Seeing the United States' acquisition of Florida as an anticlimax, Jackson, the new governor of the territory, left no account of the historic day; his wife, Rachel, however, in a letter to a close friend described the public ceremony that evoked great emotion in the largely Hispanic crowd. She then offered her first impressions of the town, its people, and their customs.

Florida's first First Lady was unimpressed. Jackson considered the beaches the most beautiful she had ever seen, but the city was different. "All the houses look in ruin, old as time. Many squares of the town appear grown over with the thickest shrubs, weeping willows, and the Pride of China; all look neglected." Besides the lack of modern conveniences like regular mail delivery and a post office, the diversity of the people stunned the Tennessee belle. "The inhabitants all speak Spanish and French. Some speak four and five languages," she observed. "Such a mixed multitude, you, nor any of us, ever had an idea of." In Pensacola, "white people," who were the minority, "mixed with all nations under the canopy of heaven." Having spent several Sundays in Pensacola, Jackson censured the local population for its sacrilege. "The Sabbath profanely kept," she complained, "a great deal of noise and swearing in

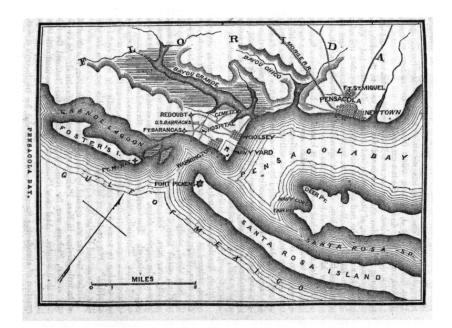

Appearing in a popular Civil War history published during the war, this map shows how Pensacola and the surrounding areas appeared throughout much of the ante-bellum era. From John S. C. Abbott, *The History of the Civil War in America*, vol. 1 (1863–1866). Courtesy of Special Collections, University of Houston Libraries.

the streets; shops kept open; trade going on, I think, more than on any other day." The violators of the most basic rules of public conduct were numerous; yet, Jackson concluded, "the worst people here are the cast-out Americans and negroes." Jackson saw great improvements in the future now that Pensacola had joined the South, but she was mistaken.[5]

Pensacola would prove resistant to change in many respects especially regarding demographics. While the populations of neighboring cities exploded in the four decades before the Civil War, Pensacola's experienced a net loss. From a high of four thousand residents during the short-lived governorship of Andrew Jackson to a low of several hundred several months later, the city's population never again surpassed three thousand. By contrast, the population of Mobile, Alabama, which paralleled Pensacola's closely in 1822 when twenty-eight hundred residents called the city home, skyrocketed to nearly thirty thousand in 1860. New Orleans was a different story altogether. With a robust population of 27,176 in 1820 the city grew to an astounding 168,675 on the eve of the Civil War, making it the sixth-largest city in the United States and the largest below the Chesapeake Bay.[6]

Unable to attract a significant number of migrants from the United States, Pensacola's population remained multiracial and multinational, consisting largely of native-born people known as Creoles. Often the source of confusion today, the term *Creole* carried a variety of meanings along the Gulf Coast, often referring to Spanish-speaking Catholics with a combination of European ancestry; in many cases it was a reference to people of mixed European and African descent or free people of color more generally. In either case, Creoles inhabited the seaports along the Gulf Coast from Florida to Texas and were highly regarded citizens of property and standing, though, according to Virginia Gould, "during the nineteenth century *creole* began to imply a cultural identity that transcended race and class."[7]

U.S. census takers failed to account for Pensacola's Creoles fully by categorizing residents along strict racial lines without taking any account of nationality or ethnicity; nevertheless, short-term visitors and long-term residents agreed the group constituted a significant presence. The renowned painter George Catlin visited Pensacola in the winter of 1834 and estimated the city "contains at present about fifteen hundred inhabitants, most of them Creoles."[8] Nearly a decade later, a rector at Pensacola's first Episcopalian church was more direct, affirming, "The town contains only about 22 or 2400 inhabitants—a majority of them Spanish, Creoles and Negroes."[9] When an agent for the American Tract Society came to Pensacola shortly after Florida achieved statehood in 1845, he expected to find a ready market for the society's books. He was disappointed, however, explaining, "I supposed at least half of the entire population are Spaniard and French and a mixture of these with the coloured race. These are nearly all Roman Catholics or nothing."[10]

By all accounts, Pensacola's Anglo-American inhabitants respected and admired their Creole neighbors, whom they considered "among our best citizens, industrious, orderly and well behaved."[11] Visitors to the city expecting to see a strict ordering of society along racial lines were surprised by "the happy union of the American and Spanish population";[12] nevertheless, relations between the two groups changed as the South's system of racial apartheid spread across Florida. Territorial statutes restricted the suffrage to free white men, outlawed interracial marriage, and banned the immigration of free people of color.[13] The territorial legislature also barred people of color from owning guns or any firearms—though it is worth noting that exceptions were made for residents of Pensacola and Saint Augustine.[14] Most extreme of the racially motivated laws were those requiring free people of color to procure the consent of a white man to remain in the state legally. These volunteer guardians, the laws declared, "shall have the same privilege over each and every of such free negroes of free mulattoes as masters, except the right of property in every other respect."[15] Pensacola's residents largely ignored the laws promulgated in Tallahassee, considering them "arbitrary and unjust," a consequence "of the utmost negligence."[16]

But as the targets of these new laws, some Creoles decided to emigrate to Tampico on Mexico's Gulf Coast in the winter of 1857.[17] The *West Florida Times* was outraged. It lambasted the state legislature for targeting "the most sober, industrious and law abiding of our citizens," who had no recourse in the courts. "A consequence of such stringent enactments is the expatriating of a large number of colored persons, mechanics, etc., whom the town can ill afford to lose." The paper asked the Creoles to reconsider their decision and hoped that "the next Assembly will so modify existing statues as to render the position of the free colored people more bearable."[18] Before the legislature could act, however, the Creoles began disposing of all of their furniture, houses, and property in preparation of their departure.[19] In April, the *Pensacola Gazette* lamented, "On Tuesday last thirty five free colored persons took their departure from this city for Tampico, and in a few days the balance who are still remaining will also leave for the same place. It was a painful sight to see them parting from their friends and their native country to seek homes in a foreign land." The Creoles left Pensacola with little besides "the sympathy of all our citizens on account of the causes which have led them to leave us, and also their best wishes for their future happiness and prosperity in their new home."[20] Despite the prediction, nearly half of Pensacola's Creole population remained in the city where they and their descendants remained a strong presence through the early twentieth century; nevertheless, the "exodus" marked the triumph—albeit belated—of the black-and-white racial binary that prevailed throughout the rest of the South.[21]

Like Creoles, bondspeople subverted the South's racial hierarchy simply by inhabiting a dynamic urban environment. "A city slave is almost a freeman, compared with a slave on a plantation," Frederick Douglass wrote in his seminal autobiography.[22] The hyperbole of the iconic abolitionist notwithstanding, urban spaces where maritime and industrial labor prevailed provided unique opportunities for bondspeople. In antebellum Pensacola, domestic servants worked and often lived in the homes of prominent business and political leaders. In addition to providing child care, female domestics worked as seamstresses, cooks, and cleaners, while male servants prepared meals, waited tables, tended horses, and steered a variety of carts and wagons along the city's streets. Increasingly, however, industrialization and a dearth of free labor resulted in a growing number of bondspeople spending their days in lumber mills, brickyards, and railroad depots beyond the prying eyes and searching ears of their masters and mistresses. Bondsmen in particular possessed the skills required of early American manufacturing, but bondswomen also worked in the dozens of factories that sprang up along Pensacola Bay and adjacent waterways.[23]

In antebellum Pensacola there were three types of enslaved industrial workers. The first type belonged to corporations like the successful brick-making firm Bacon and Abercrombie, which owned more than a hundred bondspeople. Though it is impossible to determine precisely the number employed in their brickyard or their ratio to free workers, one historian concluded the company's proprietors "owned most, if not all, of their labor force."[24] The second type belonged to individual slaveowners, who leased their bondspeople to local businesses on a daily, monthly, or yearly basis. Highly skilled craftsmen primarily, these carpenters, blacksmiths, and bricklayers earned their owners as much as several dollars per day.[25] Bondspeople who hired themselves out to employers were the third type. Granted a degree of personal and professional liberty that was unthinkable on rural farms and plantations, self-hired slaves selected their employers and secured room and board independent of their masters to whom they handed over a percentage of their earnings. Charles Lewis for example, was a skilled shipbuilder who, in addition to hiring himself out "to those needing his services," also hired out "those children belonging to him who were old enough to work." In return for his independence, Charles paid his owner a percentage of his family's total earnings and kept the remainder.[26] In a similar case, Frederick worked "about the city of Pensacola, on contracts of his own, paying his owner a particular sum a day for his time." Provided the opportunity to purchase his freedom for one thousand dollars, the ambitious middle-aged bondsman twice earned the necessary amount. He remained enslaved, however, for on both occasions he "deposited his money with white men, and they defrauded him and left him in slavery."[27]

Frederick's failure to obtain his freedom underscores the exploitation of all enslaved people regardless of skill or trade; still, his ability to earn a substantial income made him and others like him a threat to the notion of black inferiority and thus the institution of slavery itself. Consequently, throughout Florida, city, territorial, and state lawmakers tried to eradicate self-hiring by passing a series of laws forbidding the practice. The codes went largely unenforced in Pensacola, which led a grand jury to warn citizens "of the evil which must arise from this practice" and beg authorities to enact "a rigid enforcement of the law e'er it be too late."[28] Court records indicate the public ignored the grand jury's wishes. Self-hiring continued unabated even after a concerted effort in the 1850s to prosecute some of the city's most prominent residents who took part in the nefarious tradition. Clearly, bondspeople who hired their own time benefited from the arrangement, but the practice continued only because white elites profited from it. As was the case throughout the industrial South, slaveowners were willing to experiment with various forms of enslavement in an effort to reap significant economic rewards.

In 1845, for example, six of Pensacola's most "wealthy and enterprising citizens" formed the Arcadia Manufacturing Company and built a water-powered cotton mill on the site of a former sawmill and bucket factory at Pond Creek several miles north of Pensacola Bay. The two-story rectangular mill, which cost roughly sixty thousand dollars to construct, measured ninety-four-by-thirty feet. Inside were twenty-four water-powered looms with 960 spindles that within a year produced four thousand yards of twilled and cotton cloth weekly and nearly one thousand yards per day, just short of the company's goal of producing six thousand yards per week or "three millions per year."[29] Company owners early decided to use slave labor "to avoid the possible inconvenience of white operatives becoming dissatisfied and leaving their work."[30] The result was that with the exception of several "white overseers," the entire workforce consisted of approximately one hundred young bondswomen brought to Pensacola from as far away as Virginia.[31] The female manufacturers were, according to one observer,

"Well clad, well fed, moderately worked, and in every way humanely treated, they are very happy and contented, and they vie with each other in learning, as much as would do the young misses of a school room."[32] By all accounts, the experiment in enslaved industrial labor was a marked success. Arcadia Mill was "the largest and most success-ful of the cotton factories operated in ante-bellum Florida" until a fire brought the enterprise to an end in 1855.[33]

Prior to its demise, Arcadia Mill's success spurred local promoters to make a strong case for industrial slavery. Even before the first spindle at the mill rotated, the editor of the *Pensacola Gazette* asserted, "The silliest of all fallacies is that of supposing that negroes cannot do the work of a factory, it has no more foundation than would have the assertion that they cannot see as well or hear as distinctly as the whites." The myth of the inferiority of black labor was the result of "ultra southern politicians of the South Carolina school" who insisted "that slaves cannot work as cheap as they get labor at the north." To the contrary, "slave labor would be much cheaper than the white labor at the north." If Southern statesmen focused on industrialization instead of sectional politics, "the south would now be independent of northern capital."[34] Almost two years later the mill's success pushed the paper to reiterate its bold asser-tion regarding young black female workers. "To suppose as many have pretended to do, that they are not equal to white girls in a factory, is ridiculous nonsense. It is to suppose that the power of manipulation, depends on the colour of the fingers."[35] The success of the experiment in industrial slavery at Arcadia Mill reached a national audience when *De Bow's Review,* in a short piece on cotton manufacturing in Pensacola and throughout the South, concluded matter-of-factly, "The blacks do their work in every respect as well as the whites."[36]

The employment of young bondswomen at Arcadia Mill was only one of several attempts of Pensacola's entrepreneurs to experiment with some of the varieties of cheap labor available in the new republic. The employment of African American bondsmen alongside European immigrants in the construction of the Pensacola branch of the Alabama, Florida & Georgia Railroad provides another notable example. The two-million-dollar project, which intended to put cotton plantations in Alabama and Georgia within Pensacola's reach, began in August 1836 when calls went out for bondsmen available for hire. To capitalize on a thriving domestic slave trade that brought hundreds of thousands of slaves from the Upper South to the Deep South, the company placed advertisements in newspapers in Washington, DC, Maryland, Virginia, and North Carolina seeking "400 or 500 able-bodied negro men, from 18 to 40 or 45 years of age, to be employed in felling, cutting, and hewing timber, and in forming the excavations and embankments upon the route of said railroad." The company offered slaveowners two hundred dollars per bondsman per year, plus "ample food and clothing, as well as medical attendance and medicines, in case of sickness, at the company's expense, and free of charge to the owners." To facilitate the long-distance arrangement, the company invited slaveowners "to ship or send their hands direct to Pensacola, under the charge of their own agents or overseers, and they will be received into the company's service as soon as they arrive." The company offered one final incentive, an additional "$5. a head" to the owners of the first one hundred bondsmen to arrive, provided the bondsmen remained on the job an entire year.[37] Soon, a sizable number of enslaved men and women converged on Pensacola and went to work. The group consisted of "Engineers, Blacksmiths, Pilots, Wagoners, Stewards, Cooks, Washerwomen and children."[38]

Joining them were hundreds of European immigrants brought to the Gulf Coast from New York and other distant ports. In September, Colonel Joseph Pickens reported the arrival of one hundred Irish workers, adding "more are expected shortly."[39] The men "worked like beavers," but since they also "fought like devils" four shiploads of Dutchmen soon arrived to take their place. Workers on two of the vessels refused to disembark at Pensacola and continued onto New Orleans "as they did not like the looks of the town." Those who came ashore clashed with their employers immediately. Demanding steins of beer twice a day, they threw down their picks and spades and refused to work. Exasperated, the engineer entreated the captain responsible for their immigration to "take his d— Dutchmen and drown them."[40] Only the arrival of German immigrants portended a positive change in the railroad's future. "It will be gratifying to our friends, at home and abroad," a local writer informed in October, that a railroad agent "has just returned from New York after having made the necessary arrangements for bringing out six hundred German laborers." These men "added to the number of white laborers, already brought from the North to labor upon this work, will make little short of nine hundred, beside the slaves."[41] Despite the optimistic report, the search for additional employees continued the following year as company officials continued advertising for two hundred "white Labourers" and four hundred "BLACK LABOURERS" to assist in the construction of the first fifteen miles of track.[42]

Like other efforts to improve Pensacola, the Alabama, Florida & Georgia Railroad faltered. The Panic of 1837 forced the closing of the Bank of Pensacola, which brought the capitalist venture to an abrupt end, robbing investors of at least five hundred thousand dollars, an astronomical sum for the time.[43] Extant records shed little light on the fate of the bondspeople employed on the railroad, though some remained in Pensacola and continued to earn their owners and agents considerable wages by working in homes, factories, mills, yards, and on a variety of public works projects. Immigrant laborers who remained in the area struggled to find new employment and became desperate for food and shelter. The wife of a local politician recalled, "a poorhouse was altogether unnecessary, for a beggar was a thing unheard of in Pensacola, until the importation of some hundreds of paupers, sent out from this goodly city of Gotham, to assist in blowing a mighty bubble, which for the time, was dignified with the name of the 'Florida, Alabama, and Georgia rail road.'" Referring to these workers as a "rabble rout," she explained they were "exported by conscientious *men*, warranting the invoice to be strong and able bodied *men*, though from some cause to us unknown, upon reaching their destination, one half had assumed the garb and appearance of women and children."[44]

Even more mysterious than the fate of the free and enslaved workers of the short-lived Alabama, Florida & Georgia Railroad was their experience at the railroad's multicultural worksites. Scholarship on industrial labor in the antebellum South suggests the enslaved African Americans and free Irish, Dutch, and German laborers may have coexisted peacefully in their short time together. In his study of interracial industrial worksites, for example, Robert Starobin concluded that "racial hostilities occurred, of course, but they were much less significant than the striking extent of interracial co-operation among workers at most integrated industries."[45] Interracial relationships forged in the fire of early American industry often continued beyond the worksite, where workers ate, drank, and danced together late into the night and made a mockery of prescribed racial boundaries. Urban areas in particular offered numerous places for men and women of different races and ethnicities to revolt against many of the forces meant to restrain them. The result in Pensacola was a volatile urban crucible that frequently spilled over.

Among the sites for interracial gatherings after a long workday were boardinghouses and grogshops that offered female companionship and copious amounts of alcohol to paying customers regardless of race or rank. While prostitution tended to blur the lines between race, class, and ethnicity, cheap alcohol was an even greater leveler.[46] Joseph Alton's establishment along the shore of Pensacola Bay offered female companionship for patrons—and much more. According to one complaint, Alton's public room was "a disorderly tippling house" where "black and white, men and women, of evil name and fame" came together and engaged in "drinking, tippling, whoring and misbehaving themselves" both day and night.[47] The boardinghouse run by Andrew and Barbary Hosler invited the scrutiny of the city's more discerning residents because of the owners' reputation for having operated "a whore house in New York." According to one "cocksman" who visited the establishment and availed himself of its services, Barbary Hosler "hired out" bondswomen to guests for two dollars a night and for wealthier patrons offered herself for five dollars.[48]

Though hardly the epitome of interracialism, sexual intercourse and binge drinking across racial lines challenged the rigid racial system slaveowners and their collaborators imposed on antebellum Pensacola.[49] Consequently, lawmakers outlawed "negro gambling houses and tippling shops" and made it illegal for "white persons" to gamble with or sell "any spirituous liquors" to any bondsperson or person of color.[50] As shop owners ignored the decree, Jesse Pritchett, one of Pensacola's leading industrialists, placed a stern warning in the *Pensacola Gazette*. "Look out Grogshop Keepers," the announcement began, "I AM determined to enforce the law against any one who trades with or sells Liquor to any of my Negroes or those in my employ."[51] Pritchett's seriousness was evident several months later when a jury convicted the "Scotsman" Joseph Rosique for the crime of selling "spirituous liquor" to one of Pritchett's enslaved laborers.[52] Despite the successful prosecution, slaveowners and public officials failed to stop the proliferation of private businesses that catered to a rough and rowdy interracial clientele. The success of these inns and taverns stained Pensacola's reputation and for some called to mind a famous New York City slum infamous for ignominious interracial relationships. After an arsonist destroyed several structures on a popular thoroughfare in downtown Pensacola, one writer was hopeful "that this part of the town will never again be filled up with 'rookeries' and 'grogeries' which has made it heretofore the 'five points' of our city."[53]

When black and white workers failed to quench their thirst at public houses and grogshops, they at times prowled the streets together seeking stolen treasure in liquid form. The *Pensacola Gazette* made light of a bungled heist that brought an end to a series of "petty robberies" one group of thieves had "carried on with impunity." The crime began one night when the burglars broke into Francis Bobe's store and "deliberately rolled away a *barrel* of whiskey." A police officer who happened on the crime scene stopped one of the criminals in the street and retrieved the barrel, but the "roller" fled into the darkness. When the officer entered the store to investigate further "another of the gang jumped over a fence and coolly shouldered a demijohn of whiskey, with which he escaped, thereby showing a predetermination not to be entirely deprived of his liquor." Several days later, a local bondsman "implicated a white man, named Viccar, and an old black, named Lucar." As a result, "the parties were arrested, examined before a magistrate on Friday, and committed to jail, for trial." With the pair safely behind bars, the paper joked that "in the attempt to roll off the barrel of whiskey they have all got themselves in the jug."[54]

Not all of the encounters between free and enslaved people involving alcohol ended so peacefully. A party at the home of a respected Spanish couple ended in murder when U.S. Army lieutenant William Baker, who was "in the habit of playing roughly with his pistols," sat down beside the bondswoman Maria. At first the two "were in good humour playing together," but the horseplay escalated into something more serious when a scuffle ensued and Maria slapped Baker in the face. Baker cursed at Maria and pointed his pistol at her chest at which point she grabbed a piece of firewood and threatened to use it in self-defense. Suddenly, Baker's pistol fired and Maria dropped dead to the floor as blood poured out of a hole in the left side of her head.[55] In another instance a free woman of color who lived with Antonia Gonzalez along the northern edge of Pensacola Bay "was drunk and making a great noise." The racket drew the attention of three men who disembarked from a small boat and approached the intoxicated woman. William Davis, a large white man, "commenced whipping the woman with switches which he brought with him with great severity." A fisherman known as Dutch John who lived with Gonzalez and the black woman interrupted the beating, exclaiming, "I would not whip her but law it out." Enraged, Davis grabbed an oar and struck the recent immigrant from Pennsylvania on the side of his head, causing injuries that resulted in John's death several days later. An autopsy revealed "two blows had been struck on the opposite sides of the head, and the skull broke in both places." Further investigation revealed the type of white man it was who lost his life defending the civil rights of a black woman on the Southern frontier: "No money, property or effects was found about him or known to belong to him."[56]

As each of these violent outbursts make clear, when Pensacola's denizens sought a respite from the docks, yards, and mills where they spent the majority of their lives, racial boundaries blurred and sometimes even faded away, often in direct relation to the amount of sunlight visible and alcohol consumed. But even daylight and sobriety produced interracialism. This was particularly the case on Sundays, when downtown streets became a popular gathering spot for black and white workers unrestrained by owners or employers. Visitors decried "the most awful profanation of the Lord's day," assuming it was the result of the influence of the city's Roman Catholics, who attended mass in the morning and spent "the rest of the day in tippling and gambling shops, sporting, hunting, dancing, &c."[57] To make matters worse, "some of the negroes of the town" were in the habit of assembling together each Sunday evening "for the purpose of amusing themselves in the way of 'Congo' dancing." The immoral tradition, "which would much better suit the coast of Africa than a civilized community," was "an insult to those holding views favorable to a proper regard to the christian Sabbath." Worst of all, "some of the white boys of the town are to be seen at these places."[58]

Determining the makeup of the interracial crowds that gathered on Pensacola's streets is impossible given the city's transient population; indeed, despite its reputation as a stereotypical sleepy Southern town, antebellum Pensacola was an international crossroads of people and cultures. Immediately after the United States acquired Florida, a correspondent of the *Western Carolinian* who visited Pensacola claimed there was "a greater diversity of character, color, and physiognomy, and withal a greater variety and confusion of tongues, than any one place, of the same magnitude, could boast of since ancient days of Babylon."[59] Two decades later little had changed. A writer described the city's waterfront population similarly: "There may be seen the Dignitary, the Lawyer—the Doctor, the Merchant—the Grocer, the Printer—the Mechanic—French—Spaniards—Americans, English, German, Dutch—the schoolboy—negroes, mulattoes, of all hue—tongues and garb."[60] Native-born Creoles and globe-trotting mariners who arrived continually from distant ports ensured Pensacola's continued diversity through the antebellum era.

But they also contributed to the city's reputation as an interracial bacchanalia, as one memorable evening at a popular waterfront theater demonstrates. U.S. Army officer George McCall arrived at the Tivoli Theatre expecting to enjoy a French play.[61] What he saw instead was a riot. The building consisted of loosely attached wood walls, "while the sails of several foreign as well as American vessels contributed to the formation of the canvas dome, which reared its white crest above." The city's most respected residents occupied the rows closest to the stage, while those "of more humble station" sat behind them. Last were "the retiring and inoffensive quadroon women, who, quietly seated in the rear, thought not of making themselves conspicuous." Among them was a heavy-set woman in a brightly colored dress, and next to her sat an Irish waiter known as O'Donnelly, who scanned "the portentous proportions of his neighbor with wondering eyes." The Francophonic performance proceeded without interruption until a drunk and "brawling British tar" manifested his contempt for "Mounsheers" in a loud and "very audible soliloquy." Unable to understand "a single word" of the performance, he stood on his seat, shouted "Stage ahoy!" and then "with the agility and *aplomb* of a foretopman, bounded over the heads of the intervening spectators, and alighted in full force on the hindmost bench between" the corpulent Creole and her adoring Irishman. Wood shards flew in the air while men and women tumbled to the floor. "Some of the unfortunate victims were dragged forth, while others crawled out of the ruins, and the hubbub of the instant was subsiding into wailing and lamentations." The play resumed eventually, "but the ill-starred tar who had caused all the mischief, having taken advantage of the momentary confusion, had made his escape, and was nowhere to be found."[62]

In most cases, disagreements among sailors that spilled onto the city's streets and alleyways were no laughing matter. Frequently pitting locals against foreigners, with bondspeople caught in the cross fire, they often led to bloodshed and even death. One Sunday afternoon, a group of drunken sailors confronted several Pensacola families that were en route to the Catholic Church. Some of the ladies "turned back in fear," though the men stood their ground. One of the sailors carrying a broom shouted for everyone to "sweep away" before striking a bondsman who accompanied the churchgoers. The sailor then turned his weapon on Sebastian Caro and Joseph Vidal, two well-respected Spanish residents, who fought back. The "American sailor" bested Vidal until a bystander pulled him off the Spaniard's collar by "beating him with a club." Soon a battle erupted on the public square between the sailors and citizens, including several women who proved their mettle by tackling one of the tars and holding him forcefully on the ground. The situation escalated when one of the sailors fell to the ground with a gash in his stomach roughly the size of a half-dollar. The victim of a knife wound, he survived the attempt on his life; yet, like so many crimes committed on the city's streets, neither the perpetrator of the stabbing nor any other individual who participated in the brawl ever received punishment.[63]

Though seamen sometimes abused bondspeople, they also demonstrated solidarity with those held in bondage. Life on the water was harsh and, like Southern slaves, nearly all sailors felt the sting of the lash. The empathy for enslaved people that resulted from corporal punishment and other mistreatment contrasted sharply with the growing antagonism most European Americans demonstrated toward African Americans in the antebellum era; nevertheless, it endured wherever the two groups interacted. U.S. Navy chaplain Reverend Charles Rockwell recounted the story of an aged quartermaster who had been at sea since childhood. "On one occasion he was paid off at Pensacola, and finding it difficult to get rid of his money, he hired a house for a month, with a man-servant, and a yellow girl for a house-keeper." After staying for several days and paying all of his bills, "he had sixty-five dollars left, and not knowing how else to get rid of it, he had it all changed into silver half dollars, when, going to a plantation near, he gave each negro one of these coins, and then went and shipped for another cruise." Rather than interpreting such interracial altruism as a virtue, Rockwell considered it "conclusive evidence of" the "utter recklessness, profligacy, and vice" of seafaring men.[64]

Evidence of the analogousness of the lives of sailors and enslaved people appeared in weekly advertisements offering rewards for military deserters, which officials published in Pensacola's newspapers alongside those seeking the return of fugitive slaves. Major J. M. Glassel of the U.S. Army offered $120 for the capture of four privates who fled from Cantonment Clinch "near Pensacola" and another twenty dollars for the apprehension of another "lad" who absconded from the Pensacola Navy Yard before stealing the major's boat and taking off across Pensacola Bay. The five fugitives were Toussaint Felieu, a seaman from Sète in southern France; Hugh Donagy, a weaver from Tyrone, Ireland; James McIntire, a laborer from Donegal, Ireland; William Housholder, a laborer from Hagerstown, Maryland, whose "face resembles that of a pug dog"; and William Woodruff, who wore "blue pantaloons, white vest and blue roundabout with covered buttons."[65] Another band of deserters swam into Pensacola after leaping over the edge of a U.S. Navy ship from New York. Ordinary Seaman Henry Torbitt was a shoemaker from Baltimore, Maryland; Landsman Robert McClain was a blacksmith from Philadelphia, Pennsylvania; and Landsman Bryan Whetmore was a farmer from Bordenham, New Jersey. In this case, the reward for the "apprehension and delivery" of the three sailors to their superiors was twenty dollars per person. Appearing alongside an advertisement offering twenty-five dollars for the capture of a fugitive slave, the announcements demonstrate the relative equality of free and enslaved labor on the Southern frontier along with its complexity regarding race.[66]

So do the black seamen who sailed in and out Pensacola regularly. Peter Porter was a case in point. The steamship pilot kept half of the $150 his talents earned his master monthly. According to one of his passengers, the English travel writer Charles Lanman, it was an advantageous arrangement for Porter, who as a result "frequently refused his freedom." After sailing with Porter from New Orleans to Pensacola and then east to the Chattahoochee River, Lanman wrote admiringly, "Besides being the best pilot on the river, and scorning the idea of being a free man, he was the best swimmer in the country." Having the misfortune of being on several sinking cotton boats, Porter "had saved the lives, of no less than seven persons—one colored girl, two ladies, two boys, and two young children." If, as Lanman suggests, Porter preferred slavery over freedom, it is evidence of the elite status skilled black sailors enjoyed on the Southern frontier—though, to be sure, unskilled black sailors also benefited from life on the water. Lanman noted that "all the subordinates" on the vessel Porter piloted were enslaved. These twenty boatmen "were hired from their owners, and our captain informed me that it was customary everywhere in the South for the steamboat men to pay their hands from five to eight dollars per month more than their regular wages." This additional sum, which the captain referred to as "'Sunday wages'," was "for the exclusive use of the slave."[67]

High demand for experienced laborers created a brisk market in black watermen as local classified pages demonstrated. Pensacola merchant C. P. Knapp sought twelve "able bodied Negroes, for Firemen and Deck Hands" aboard the steamship *James L. Day*. For the employment of their bondsmen along the entire coastline from Galveston, Texas, to Boston, Massachusetts, Knapp offered slaveowners twenty dollars per month per laborer "and Insurance."[68] The prominent shipping firm of Pattison & Avery promised "high wages" to any owner willing to hire out "Eight good BOAT HANDS" to ply the waters in and around Pensacola.[69] As part of an estate sale, the auction house of Francisco de la Rua announced the availability of a "quantity of Household and Kitchen Furniture, consisting in part of Beds and Bedding." Also available for purchase was a "negro man named ROBERT, about 36 years of age, accustomed to a sea-faring life."[70]

Like other harbors, Pensacola was a port of call for men who dwelled in a maritime world where racial barriers could dissolve rapidly in the face of tremendous adversity. An example is the crew of the bark *Emperor*, which sailed east from Pensacola to the Apalachicola River, consisting of "four white men, two negroes, and a black woman," in addition to the captain Henry Nunes. The vessel wrecked along the Florida coast, forcing the group to head inland, where they encountered what they thought were friendly Indians. However, "taking advantage of the separation of the party one day, the Indians fell on the black woman and two of the men, killing the woman and one of the men and firing three shots into the third, leaving him for dead." Finding security in numbers, Nunes and the other survivors stayed together and fled further inland until finding safety in a house some fourteen miles from the shore.[71]

Men who spent much of their lives on the water as members of racially integrated crews developed a transcendent collective identity that revealed itself on land in a distinctive style of speech, clothing, and camaraderie that contrasted markedly with the dominant racially divisive terrestrial culture. Sailors resented many of the constraints land-locked societies placed on their unfettered lifestyle and thus resisted attempts to restrain them. An incident involving several deserters of the U.S. schooner *Flint* demonstrates this. When Pensacola city marshal James McCaskell approached a busy intersection and spotted an inter-racial gathering of sailors fitting the description of several deserters, he quickly sprang into action. McCaskell ordered the men to surrender, but William Mercer, "a free negro," refused. Taking several steps back, Mercer warned the officer, "Don't advance on me"; McCaskell moved forward, nonetheless, prompting Mercer to fire his pistol at the mar-shal and then flee with his associates. McCaskell captured Mercer with the help of his dog, but not before the suspected deserter fired off two more shots. In the coming days, Mercer received a punishment familiar to many recalcitrant African Americans throughout the South—"one hundred stripes."[72]

There is a tendency to romanticize the experiences of slaves, ser-vants, and other subalterns who spent their lives at sea in the first part of the nineteenth century; the impulse fades, however, when studying sea-men of color like Mercer who found themselves in Pensacola's jail after being charged with committing various violent crimes. The sloop *Lalla Rookh* arrived at Pensacola with an "East Indian coloured man com-monly called Lascar" tied to the mast. For having committed a number of shipboard "misdeeds," Lascar remained in this position an entire day until the shipmaster heard a scream. After rushing on deck, he found the sailor who had tied Lascar to the mast coughing up copious amounts of blood as a result of "the stroke of an axe on his head." The Escambia County Circuit Court indicted Lascar on the charge of attempted murder as there was no other "living being within a short distance" of the victim when the crime occurred. Under oath, the defendant testified that his real name was Vincente Gomes, and though a native of the East Indies, he was now the bondsman of Levi Jones of Mobile, Alabama. Gomes denied the charge against him, claiming that he saw two men strike the victim on the head twice with an axe. He also testified that while he could not identify these individuals or "distinguish whether they were black or white," he did see them run from the boat shortly after the assault. The judge set a trial date and released Gomes to the custody of his master.[73]

The same court also charged the black cook John Munroe with mur-der, even though the crime he stood accused of committing occurred in Mexican waters. While off the coast of Vera Cruz, a fight broke out between Munroe and a white cook named John Dunmore after the two men exchanged words below deck. Dunmore, who one witness described as "a large, powerful man," threatened Munroe, promising, "If you call me a son of a bitch I would knock your head off." Munroe responded in kind, daring the larger sailor to "come and knock it off." The two men wrestled and traded punches until a master-at-arms stepped between them. At this point, Munroe reached around the peacekeeper and struck at Dunmore with a foot-long sheath knife, which found its mark three separate times. Dunmore escaped by climbing a ladder to the deck, though the four-inch gashes in his breast led to his demise several minutes later. A witness to the murder testified that sailors on board the *Erie* "were in the habit of plaguing [the] Prisoner & it was generally known to try him." It was for this reason perhaps the all-white Pensacola jury found the black defendant "not guilty."[74]

Of all the African Americans who sailed in and out of antebellum Pensacola, none proved the capacity of black seafarers to subvert the racial order more than Thomas Henry, whose actions sent shock waves across the Southern frontier. At the age of twenty-four, the Pensacola native enlisted in the U.S. Navy in 1833 at the rank of ordinary seamen and for two years served on the USS *Grampus*, a one-hundred-foot-long schooner that as part of the navy's West Indian Squadron patrolled the West Indies for pirates and illegal slave ships.[75] Months in the heat and humidity of the Gulf of Mexico exposed the crew of the *Grampus* to a variety of dangerous tropical illnesses, and in August 1834 Henry was among thirty-nine other sailors who arrived at the naval hospital just west of the Pensacola Navy Yard after contracting yellow fever. While several of the patients succumbed to the deadly disease, Henry slipped out of the sight of doctors, scaled the brick wall surrounding the hospital complex, and raced toward Pensacola. Two days later, Isaac Hulse, the hospital's chief surgeon, published the following advertisement in the local paper: "Twenty Dollars Reward. DESERTED on the morning of the 6th instant, from the U.S. Naval Hospital, near Barrancas, THOMAS HENRY, a seaman, belonging to the Schr. *Grampus*. He is a bright Mulatto, and had on sailor's clothes when he left. The above reward will be given to any person who will deliver said deserter at this Hospital."[76]

Henry remained out of the public eye for more than a decade. In 1845, however, he reappeared, following the double murder of Joshua and James Hawthorne, two brothers in Belleville, Alabama. Early reports indicated that the suspected killer, who was the husband of a bondswoman owned by the Hawthorne family, was "a free mulatto fellow named THOMAS HENRY." Nothing suggested "what induced the man to commit the murder," though the type of act that sent the bondswoman's husband, Henry, into a murderous rage is easy to imagine. Soon newspapers across the Deep South beseeched concerned citizens to assist in the manhunt. For his part, the Hawthorne boys' father urged them to look southward, writing, "This fellow formerly lived in Florida and is acquainted about Pensacola." It was here or adjacent points along the Gulf Coast where "he will probably make his way in order to get on some vessel so as to escape." With a "heavy beard, and black bushy head," Henry fit the description of many black men in the area, though a knife wound in the head and shoulder, which Henry acquired in the "affray," distinguished him from other possible suspects.[77]

Something else on Henry's body set him apart. "He is marked on one arm with letters and on the other with figures or characters," the notice for his capture informed additionally.[78] No ordinary artwork, the tattoos carried great symbolism. According to Simon Newman, "sailors were virtually the only Americans of that time to wear tattoos," and those that did were ordinarily professional seafarers who wore their ink "a little like artisans' leather aprons, as distinctive albeit more permanent emblems of trade, experience, and proficiency"; this was opposed to part-time watermen who claimed no craft identification and thus left their bodies unmodified. In this case, the tattoo's function as an emblem of occupational pride backfired, as it may have aided in the seaman's capture.[79] Officials spotted Henry in southern Alabama two months after the Hawthorne brothers' murders, and, subsequently, "the freedman was arrested, lodged in jail, at Sparta, at the approaching term of court convicted of murder, and was publicly executed by hanging, in October of the same year."[80]

Blatant disregard of the antebellum South's racial order by an enlisted man like Henry is worthy of consideration, for it confounds the standard narrative of the federal government's role in the expansion of slavery. "In Pensacola and perhaps some other Gulf Coast towns," concludes one historian of the region, "the American military inspired the extension of slavery as much, if not more, than any other influence."[81] The argument is irrefutable. In antebellum Pensacola, the navy and army employed thousands of bondspeople on various public works projects, while individual soldiers—from high-ranking officers to ordinary enlisted man—owned slaves. Nevertheless, as is often the case with the history of slavery, the reality is far more complex than it first appears. For while encouraging slavery's growth along the Gulf Coast, the U.S. military also imposed institutional traditions on Southern society that undermined the prevailing regional culture regarding race. Understanding how this happened requires some explanation.

During the days of Spanish rule, a visitor to Pensacola predicted, "Should the Floridas be ceded to the United States, Pensacola can only be important as a military and naval station for the southern country."[82] He was correct. Within five years of Florida's annexation construction began on a naval station that proved a substantial boon for the local economy for decades. Located on the northern shore of Pensacola Bay about six miles south of the city, the Pensacola Navy Yard comprised a one-mile square tract of land surrounded by a seawall on the eastern and southern edge and a twelve-foot high brick wall on the northern and western perimeter. With paved walkways meandering between sturdy oak trees, bright green grass, colorful gardens, and a variety of elegant homes for officers and the Commandant, some considered it "the largest and most beautiful yard in the country." Upon its completion in the 1850s, the yard contained a four-hundred-foot-long floating dry dock, a three-hundred-foot-long granite permanent wharf and basin, as well as blacksmith, carpenter, and joiner shops along with several massive brick warehouses for the storage of masts, sails, rigging, and ship stores. Sailors' barracks were at the northeast corner of the site, while at the center of the yard stood two circular brick buildings that served as the officers' headquarters and a chapel. The navy hospital rested on a bluff overlooking the bay several hundred feet to the west. The Pensacola Navy Yard served multiple functions for more than three decades, making it one of the young republic's significant Southern internal improvements.[83]

Pensacola lacked the manpower the navy required to lay bricks, bend iron, and hew and haul lumber at the Navy Yard; therefore, government officials hired Northerners and immigrants and employed them alongside hundreds of bondspeople whom they leased from local slaveowners.[84] The result was a bustling waterfront district that, like Pensacola nearby, reflected the diversity of the Atlantic world. The variety of workers at the Navy Yard and several adjacent villages surprised some visitors, including a traveling missionary who described the multinational, multiethnic, and multiracial lot with the following: "These operatives are from almost every part of the known world. Philadelphians, New Yorkers, Baltimoreans, Scotch, Irish, Dutch, Swedes, Danes, Norwegians, Spaniards, French, Italians, Portuguese, English, Creoles, and Africans, mingle here promiscuously together." The missionary expressed optimism about the prospects of converting "this mixed population," but, he admitted, "we are liable to make mistakes."[85]

Despite the diverse labor pool, bondsmen constituted a majority of the employees at the Navy Yard. They performed nearly every task required, including ship construction and repair, carpentry, blacksmithing, bricklaying, and general labor. Bondsmen also worked alongside bondswomen in the homes of officers as servants and in the naval hospital as nurses.[86] To secure the bulk of the Navy Yard's unfree labor force, agents advertised for "NEGRO MEN" in newspapers along the Gulf Coast and in the process left a detailed account of public slavery.[87] With little variation, owners received between twelve and fifteen dollars per month for each bondsman they rented to the navy, depending on the skill level of each employee. Slaveowners took a great risk by transferring their property to another party, though most considered consistent federal income well worth the risk.[88]

Bondspeople benefited from the arrangement undoubtedly. For the common laborer at the yard, work began at sunup and lasted until sundown with one hour for breakfast and one hour for dinner during the winter and two hours for dinner during the summer. For sustenance, each worker received one navy ration daily that was worth twenty cents and consisted alternately of fresh or salted beef, pork, vegetables, flour, bread, beans, rice, molasses, and vinegar "all of which is the best quality." This was the same ration provided enlisted men with one exception. According to the Commandant of the yard, "The whiskey part of the ration is not drawn in kind, but the value thereof (90 cents per month) is paid the slaves in money." In addition to nutritional diversity and cash, bondsmen at the Navy Yard received medical attention from the navy hospital, which allowed them to miss up to a week for any given illness before subtracting from their owner's income.[89] The navy assumed complete control over all bondspeople they leased and supervised the amount and quality of work performed closely; nevertheless, their reputation for lax enforcement of the guidelines regarding worker discipline was widespread. Long after the end of slavery, a Pensacola native recalled of the treatment of bondspeople, "At the Navy Yard in Pensacola they treated them well. You couldn't whip a slave here." This was in stark contrast to "some places" nearby, where "they was mean as dogs."[90]

Though still in bondage, enslaved Navy Yard workers enjoyed a standard of living that few observers failed to notice. Indeed, when a writer calling himself Pro Tempore warned of a slave insurrection emanating from the Navy Yard because of the large number of unsupervised bondsmen who lived and worked in close proximity to large caches of weapons and ammunition, Veritas disagreed. In a brief editorial, Veritas countered that no military power could suppress an actual revolt once it commenced; therefore, the avoidance of such a catastrophe depended on restricting the movement of enslaved laborers, ensuring they "do not collect in too great bodies and thereby concert measures for mischief." There was, moreover, reason to believe the slaves at the Navy Yard would never revolt because of the "many advantages" afforded them by their federal employers. In fact, in the case of a slave insurrection in Pensacola, the enslaved mechanics and laborers at the Navy Yard were likely to ally "themselves with the citizens and assist in preserving the occasion for their services."[91]

Veritas's column downplayed real concerns over the possibility of a slave revolt; nevertheless, it illuminated one of the freedoms bondspeople at the Navy Yard enjoyed that most differentiated them from other enslaved people—mobility. While many bondsmen lived in quarters near the entrance to the yard "under the eye of the marine guard there stationed," others lived beyond the yard's walls in privately owned boardinghouses and hotels.[92] With little or no supervision from owners or employers, they moved freely about the two neighborhoods around the Navy Yard, Warrington and Woolsey, as well as Pensacola and the adjacent areas. To the dismay of concerned citizens, they frequently joined free people of color in large groups, which prompted a Pensacola grand jury to issue a formal presentment to the owners and employers of bondspeople. The jurors "found the law in relation to the unlawful gathering of slaves, free negroes and mulatoes" ignored entirely throughout Escambia County and in particular "in the city of Pensacola and in the vicinity of the Navy Yard." The illegal meetings "were a public nuisance and calculated to produce an injurious affect"; consequently,

the jury requested slaveowners, employers, and law enforcement officials uphold the law. It moreover solicited respectfully "that the law in
relation to Patrols also be enforced."[93] In another instance, the editors of
the *Pensacola Gazette* used a fatal drowning accident as an opportunity to
censure those who granted bondspeople free access to the water. After
a vessel carrying three bondsmen employed at the Navy Yard capsized
in a terrible storm, killing all three passengers, the editors admonished,
"We trust that this will be a lesson to all owners of negroes [to] not allow
them to come [and] go by [the] water at their pleasure."[94]

Efforts to stop the free movement of bondspeople on land and water
indicate how public slaves in Pensacola and at the Navy Yard sometimes
occupied the middle ground between freedom and slavery. Indeed,
the case of a bondsman named Robert reveals how even determining
whether an individual was free or enslaved could prove difficult. After a
break-in at a Pensacola dry goods store that resulted in the theft of more
than one hundred dollars in cash and valuables, suspicion fell immediately on Robert, a well-known bondsman who owned a two-and-a-half-
inch augur that officials suspected he used to pry open the store's front
door. Robert belonged to Dr. John Brosnaham, one of the city's most
respected residents, but he lived alone in a "shanty" several miles south
of the city, where he worked transporting rafts of wood on the water
between local lumber mills and the Navy Yard. For the most part, Robert
lived as a freeman. He owned his own boat, negotiated and traded freely
with local businesses and the navy, and "was generally capable of buying anything a person would trust him to." As a further indication of
his autonomy, Robert employed several bondsmen on the water himself. It is unknown what led this enslaved man to risk his extraordinary
lifestyle and resort to theft, though alcohol was likely a contributing
factor. Shortly after the break-in, Robert appeared in Pensacola intoxicated and, upon questioning by the sheriff, handed over banknotes, silver coins, and a watch, all of which matched the description of the items
stolen from the popular store.[95]

That a bondsman who frequented the Pensacola Navy Yard developed a drinking problem is anticipated given the navy's lax enforcement of its own regulations. In one popular watering hole just beyond
the Navy Yard's western wall, A. J. Lamberton, who also served as the
navy's postmaster, offered paying customers a cornucopia of intoxicating beverages, such as brandy, whiskey, gin, rum, and wine, as well as

several types of beer and cider.[96] The navy barred store owners from selling their products to both slaves and enlisted men but enforced the regulations only rarely. One investigator explained, "The liquor dealers of Pensacola are not permitted to sell drink to sailors, marines or negroes, it being a military reserve. A flag-officer, however, makes a nice little income by allowing flavored rum-sellers to be patronized by the men, for which privilege $10 wholesale and $15 retail are paid."[97] In one notorious case that resulted in a court-martial, Navy Commandant John H. Clack complained about the sale of liquor to bondsmen at the Navy Yard after "a negro laborer was detected with a bottle of whiskey." Clack blamed the egregious violation on Captain Melancthon Woolsey, who allowed the navy's purser "to keep a 'Grog Shop' in the Navy Yard to retail spirits to the Mechanics & Laborers of said yard <u>in working hours</u> much to the prejudice of the public service."[98]

Bondsmen at the Navy Yard not only consumed alcohol but earned income as retailers. An episode described by a soldier stationed at Fort Pickens on the opposite side of Pensacola Bay confirms this. George Ballentine immigrated to New York City from England in the search of employment as a weaver, but the promise of food, clothing, and a steady income led him to enlist in the U.S. Army. Shortly after his arrival on Santa Rosa Island on the southern shore of Pensacola Bay, Ballentine and the rest of his regiment turned their attention to acquiring strong drink. "The illicit traffic was carried on by the blacks, at the time employed in the repairs of the fort," Ballentine recorded. "They had an abundant supply of the corn whiskey used in the States, a coarse liquor, unpleasant in taste, and intoxicating in the proportion of about two bottles to one of the low priced Irish or Scotch Whiskey." The enslaved proprietors purchased whiskey across the bay near Fort Barrancas and the Navy Yard at fifty cents a gallon; however, after bringing it across the bay to the island they "retailed it at a dollar a bottle, or five dollars a gallon, clearing the very moderate profit of nine hundred percent, on their business." The lucrative trade was risky as the enslaved salesmen "incurred the risk of a severe flogging if detected selling liquor to the soldiers." Nevertheless, because of the large number of soldiers who were untroubled by slaveowners' aversion to black entrepreneurship, the trade flourished."[99]

As Ballentine's story indicates, the army also relied heavily on enslaved labor. Beginning in 1829, the Army Corps of Engineers began the construction of three brick forts on the beaches that bounded the

entrance to Pensacola Bay.[100] Like the Navy Yard, the majority of workers who built Fort Barrancas, Fort McRee, and the mammoth pentago-
nal fortress Fort Pickens were bondsmen. But where various local elites
leased the men and women who worked at the Navy Yard, only Captain
William Chase and his associates, including Jasper Strong and Frederick
Underhill, rented bondspeople to the army. Ballentine described the
workers at Fort Pickens thusly, "These blacks were slaves, and hired out
by their owners to the government; some of them had been taught the
trade of bricklaying, and their owners received upwards of twenty dollars a month for their labor, after deducting the cost of a slave's living."
Offering an indication of the great wealth bondsmen brought Chase and
the other contractors, Ballentine continued, "one of these slaves could
not have been purchased under a thousand dollars."[101]

Despite its ubiquity at the Pensacola forts, the practice of leasing
bondspeople to the army violated official policy. Therefore, Chase and
his associates reached a series of "gentlemen's agreements" with the
army that stipulated the terms of all contracts related to slave labor.[102]
Years after the need for secrecy dissipated, however, Chase admitted in
a private letter, "Forts Pickens, McRae, Barrancas, and the barracks and
redoubt of the Barrancas, were for the most part built by slave mechanics
and laborers." He also described the living arrangements of these workers, adding, "owners were permitted to construct barracks, or houses for
their accommodation, by which the United States were saved the considerable expense of erecting similar structures." Chase recalled proudly
that the slave barracks "were exclusively used as quarters for the work-
men" and that "quiet and order have always been maintained in and
about the premises."[103] The claim was specious. Frequently after the sun
retreated and sometimes before, the fort's workers joined those from
Pensacola and the Navy Yard for an evening of carousing at homes, taverns, and saloons far beyond the view of their owners and employers.[104]

While both the army and navy embraced slave labor, one important practice distinguished the two services in the eyes of Pensacola's
slaveowners. In the antebellum era, the navy was the only branch of
the U.S. military that sanctioned the enlistment of African Americans.[105]
The practice took root during the War of 1812, when the demand for
seamen forced a color-blind recruiting strategy that free and enslaved
black men took full advantage of, but it continued for decades after the
war as the navy continued to struggle to find white volunteers. The

ubiquitousness of African Americans in navy uniforms and at Navy Yards spurred a Pensacola writer to propose a radical scheme for ending the navy's recruiting problem—while abolishing slavery in the process. Conceding the sin of slavery, the outspoken editorialist reasoned, "We differ with our northern friends therefore, not as to the existence of the evil, but as to the remedy." He then suggested the navy purchase several hundred bondsmen from their owners for six hundred dollars and enlist them in the service as landsmen. The black sailors would receive ten dollars per month for their service, and after five years "they shall be free, on condition that they be sent to Liberia by the government."[106]

Nothing ever came of the bizarre proposal to end slavery by conscripting bondspeople into the navy; nevertheless, black sailors remained a ubiquitous presence on naval ships, where their faithful service often endeared them to their white shipmates. One naval surgeon who spent several years at sea boasted of his time spent aboard racially integrated naval vessels. "The white and colored seamen messed together," he recalled some years later, and "there seemed to be an entire absence of prejudice against the blacks as messmates among the crew."[107] It is important to resist the urge to romanticize the relationships forged between men of varying races aboard navy ships during the era of American slavery; nevertheless, even after Southern politicians forced the navy to institute a quota system, limiting the number of black sailors to less than 5 percent of every crew, there was likely "less racial prejudice and tension on naval craft than anywhere else."[108]

The trial of Lieutenant George Mason Hooe illustrates how the rights enlisted black men enjoyed in the U.S. Navy undermined the racial ideology of slavery in Pensacola as well as the rest of the antebellum South. While on board the USS *Vandalia* in January 1839, Hooe ordered the whipping of several black and white sailors without the authority of the ship's Jewish commander, Uriah Levy. When Levy confronted Hooe about the unsanctioned punishment, the lieutenant roared defiantly, "I'll be damned if this old Jew shall come here to order me about."[109] In a resulting court-martial that took place on a frigate lying off the Pensacola coast, nine witnesses testified to Hooe's illegal actions. Among the witnesses were two black enlisted men, Daniel Waters and James Mitchell, the captain's cook and steward. The court dismissed Hooe's request to disregard the testimony of Waters and Mitchell "on the ground that they were negroes" and found him guilty of several acts of insubordination and dismissed him from the West Indian Squadron promptly.[110] When word of the controversial decision reached the desk of President Martin Van Buren, the response from the White House reverberated among slaveowners throughout the South: "The President finds nothing in the proceedings in the case of Lieut. Hooe which requires his interference."[111]

Van Buren's comments prompted secessionist rhetoric from pro-slavery forces who vilified the president and navy for advancing a radical policy that flew in the face of Southern rights and traditions. The *Richmond Whig* fumed, "The Commander-in-Chief has given his deliberate sanction to the principle, that a negro is a competent witness in Naval Courts martial against the gallant officers of our Navy." Worst of all, the ruling extended beyond the republic's borders and out "to every sea where floats an American ship. Every where, where Federal rule obtains, a negro, in the eye of the President and the law, which he makes, is the equal of the most gallant Captain in the Navy or Army."[112] E. S. Davis, a prominent South Carolina doctor and legislator, pointed out in a widely-read public address that every court forbade the testimony of black people in the trial of white men: "Yet, in the face of these facts, and within a Southern Territory, negroes are permitted to give testimony, and the proceedings of the court approved by the President of the United States." The episode demonstrated the necessity of placing a Southerner in the White House, for only an individual "whose early associations, habits, and education would make him act with caution, if not, with propriety, however much he might in the abstract be opposed to slavery."[113]

In Pensacola, where economic survival depended on federal largess, reaction to the court-martial was measured. The editors of the *Pensacola Gazette* sympathized with those who thought Van Buren held "southern rights and southern institutions" in contempt; yet they affirmed the supremacy of the U.S. government and defended the president's actions. "The laws which did govern, and which must always govern naval courts martial, are the laws of the United States," the rejoinder began, "and it is scarcely necessary to remind the intelligent reader that, as universality and uniformity are indispensable attributes of the law, a rule which would, on the same state of facts, convict a man at New-York and acquit him at Pensacola, would not deserve the name of a law." In an effort to remind readers of Pensacola's exceptionality regarding the tradition of allowing black testimony, the editors boasted, "It is a fact not unworthy of remark, that there have, within the last ten years, been more Naval Courts Martial in this harbor than in all the other ports of the United States, and although in many of these courts, coloured witnesses have been called to testify, no question has ever been made as to their competency."[114]

Testimony in one of these cases—a murder trial in the Superior Court of the District of West Florida—confirmed the fears of many of Pensacola's slaveowners by establishing the open interaction of slaves with armed and inebriated free black men. The incident involved Major Trusty and Sam Jones, two mulatto sailors stationed at the Pensacola Navy Yard. Late one Saturday evening, the two enlisted men, along with a white sailor named Rulon, scaled the Navy Yard wall and walked to a grogshop where they obtained three bottles of whiskey. After downing the liquor, Trusty and Rulon returned to the yard, while Jones met up with several bondsmen at a local boardinghouse. Several hours later, Trusty joined Jones at the residence, where, after a brief argument, the two men drank, sang, and toasted each other beside their enslaved friends late into the night. At the party's conclusion, Jones tried to convince Trusty to accompany him to Fort Barrancas, a short walk away, but Trusty refused. Moments later, after the two sailors exited the boardinghouse, the cry rang out: "Lord and murder!" Witnesses who arrived on the scene found Trusty lying on his back, crying out, "I am killed, help me for God's sake, Sam Jones has stabbed me." The bondsmen from the boardinghouse and several sailors carried Trusty's bloody body to the Navy Yard hospital, where he died moments later. Upon questioning, Jones denied committing the murder, though a bloodstained sailor's knife found in his possession suggested otherwise.[115]

An interracial orgy of alcohol and violence involving free and enslaved federal employees was not what most people envisioned of Pensacola following Florida's annexation in 1821. At that time, politicians, entrepreneurs, land speculators, and potential landowners from the United States expected the city to become a nexus of the South's rapidly expanding cotton kingdom. Among those with extraordinarily high expectations was Governor Andrew Jackson, who declared shortly before taking possession of the city from the departing Spanish, "I have no doubt but Pensacola will rise into notice as a commercial city faster than any other place in the United States."[116] Unfortunately, the anticipated transformation never took place, even after the federal government established the Navy Yard and funded the construction and maintenance of three army forts, thus providing much-needed economic stimulus.

After Jackson's passing, it was left to his biographer to summarize the disappointment many Americans felt toward Pensacola. On the eve of the Civil War, James Parton lamented, "Pensacola has not yet, after thirty years of American government, shaken off the spell of dullness which the Spanish governors left upon it."[117] Parton exaggerated to make a case about American exceptionalism. In reality, Pensacola experienced significant changes in the first four decades of American rule, including the adoption of an American slave system whose foundation was imbedded much more deeply in the bedrock of white supremacy than its Spanish predecessor. With the assistance of the courts, lawmakers, and law enforcement officials, antebellum slaveowners were able to withstand the numerous challenges to the new racial order they deemed necessary to secure slavery's expansion across the Southern frontier; nevertheless, Pensacola remained a portal of freedom for enslaved people, as an analysis of the hundreds of documented cases of fugitive slaves who passed through the city in the four decades before the Civil War reveals.

RUNNING AWAY

IN JUNE 1839, Pensacola sheriffs jailed two bondsmen who were the target of a massive interstate manhunt. Caesar was a one-eyed steamboat pilot known for steering vessels on the rivers that flowed south from Alabama and Georgia to the Gulf of Mexico. Hunter also worked on the rivers that sliced through the Florida panhandle, and, like his companion, enjoyed an unusual degree of liberty for an enslaved man, living and working hundreds of miles from his master and hiring his own time. In April, the two enslaved seamen abandoned their vessels and "with plenty of clothes and money" fled into the woods on the east side of the Apalachicola River, where they joined a "gang of runaway negroes" at a secluded settlement near the site of the former Negro Fort.[1] Caesar and Hunter remained at the camp for several days until a group of cattle hunters chanced upon Caesar and attempted to take him into custody. The muscular bondsman was "well armed with knives and pistols," and he resisted his attackers, who "gave him many severe stabs in the side and back" with a hunting knife.[2] The "deadly struggle" between Caesar, several other fugitive slaves, and their potential captors concluded when one of the cattle hunters, Robert Herron, "was killed being shockingly cut and mangled; another of the party had his arm broken with a bludgeon, and was otherwise severely injured."[3] Caesar survived his wounds and fled with Hunter to Pensacola.[4]

When authorities captured the two fugitives several weeks later some wondered how two enslaved murder suspects were able to remain out of the reach of the authorities for so long. One Floridian placed the blame on frontier dwellers who inhabited the wilderness in and around Pensacola and were sympathetic to the plight of fugitive slaves. Evidence suggested that Caesar and Hunter were "in regular communication with the band of Creek Indians" who had "ranged" the swamps and waters of East and West Florida for years, and they were aided by "free negroes in the towns, and unprincipled whites" who furnished "them powder, arms, and such information, as has enabled them to elude their pursuers."[5] In the aftermath of the arrests, a grand jury convicted Caesar of murder and officials carried out the execution promptly. Hunter avoided a similar fate by escaping from jail. Whether the two-hundred-dollar reward offered subsequently by Florida governor Richard Call resulted in Hunter's apprehension is unknown, though the physical description provided of the suspected murderer suggested he would not submit readily to authorities: "Said Hunter is about five feet ten inches high, very black, has an impediment in his speech, and has scars of three gun shots and wounds in his left shoulder."[6]

Caesar and Hunter received much greater notoriety than the fugitive slaves who aimed for antebellum Pensacola typically; nevertheless, they shared much in common with them. The two bondsmen worked on or near the water at great distances from their masters, considered Pensacola and the surrounding areas a refuge, and upon reaching their destination received assistance from anonymous people about whom little is known. Though Caesar paid the ultimate price for freedom and Hunter's fate is unknown, the flight of these two boatmen to Pensacola confirms the seaport's continued function as a gateway for fugitive slaves in the decades before the Civil War. Even with the United States claiming the city and all Florida as its own, bondspeople continued to resist their enslavement by stealing themselves and often their friends and family members with alarming regularity.

Any attempt to calculate the number of fugitive slaves in antebellum Pensacola—or anywhere else for that matter—is futile as those who left a paper trail denote only a fraction of all those who made the audacious attempt at freedom. In the words of Peter Wood, "This group must represent little more than the top of an ill-defined iceberg."[7] Despite a dearth of evidence, documentation exists proving that at least three hundred bondspeople ran to or from Pensacola and the vicinity between 1821 and 1861.[8] Evidence survives in court records as well as personal correspondence and reminiscences, though the most extensive primary sources are the thousands of runaway slave advertisements that slaveowners, employers, and law enforcement officials posted in local and regional newspapers. Hidden in plain sight, they provide biographical information on bondspeople that went unnoticed by census takers, bookkeepers, and general observers, including slaves' names, ages, and gender. They describe the height, weight, and dress of runaways and list distinguishing personality and physical traits, including scars, brandings, and amputations. Even more remarkable, they often reveal the professional aptitude of absconded slaves, such as the ability to read or write, speak multiple languages, cook, clean, lay brick, or fell trees. Though historians once ignored these ubiquitous sources, they now consider them crucial evidence of slave life. They are, writes David Waldstreicher, "the first slave narratives—the first published stories about slaves and their seizure of freedom."[9]

In the case of antebellum Pensacola, runaway slave advertisements are invaluable local histories that illuminate a great deal about slavery and slave resistance on the Southern frontier in at least three respects. First, they reveal the immense resources that were at the disposal of slaveowners and other white elites to both prevent bondspeople from running away and apprehend those who did nonetheless. Even on the South's periphery, slavery was big business; therefore, Southern leaders organized slave patrols, constructed and staffed jails, provided prize money for slave catchers, and enacted a wide variety of legislation, all in an effort to protect slaveowners' property. Second, they testify to the perpetuation of the long tradition of slave flight and marronage on the Southern frontier in spite of these restraints. Even with powerful forces aligned against them, bondspeople who resided on the margins of the South's expansive slave society continued courageously to exploit the region's liminality and dash toward freedom. Third, they prove the existence of a disparate population of freemen and freewomen of various races and ethnicities who aided and abetted fugitive slaves in their bid for freedom. Though missing from the standard treatments of the Underground Railroad, these Southern radicals proved just as vital in challenging slavery as the legendary agents and conductors of the famous abolitionist network.[10] An analysis of these advertisements and other evidence of fugitive slaves running to and from antebellum Pensacola demonstrates the persistence of interracial slave resistance on the Southern frontier. It moreover reveals a significant crack in the foundation of Southern slavery—one that was possible to widen but incapable of being repaired.

"Where any slave shall be committed to the jail of any county within this Territory as a runaway, it shall be the duty of the sheriff or jailor forthwith to cause an advertisement, with description of the person and wearing apparel of the runaway, to be inserted in some public newspaper of the Territory most convenient to the place where such slave shall be committed, for the space of six months."[11] Thus read the antebellum law requiring local officials in first the territory and then the state of Florida to publicize the incarceration of suspected runaways. In antebellum Pensacola, the measure resulted in the publication of hundreds of advertisements reprinted thousands of times over that, besides providing the age, height, and gender of incarcerated black fugitives, revealed the extent to which the city beckoned to bondspeople from nearly every corner of the Deep South.

Most runaways came to antebellum Pensacola from farms and plantations just opposite the Alabama–Florida border. Among them were Jordan and Sayler, two bondsmen from Mobile whom James Miles captured about thirty miles from Pensacola and brought to the city jail.[12] Also in this group was the short dark-skinned bondsman named Abraham who belonged to Francis Pettis of Clark County and stated "that he ranaway from the plantation of the said Pettis on the east side of the Alabama River, four miles from Claiborne."[13] Others came from the more distant districts of central Alabama. John, who stood out for his "round and handsome face," as well as his "smiling countenance," came to Pensacola from the farm of "Mr. Norvel residing in the state of Alabama, eight miles from Cahawba."[14] The forty-year-old prisoner Sam told Pensacola's jailor that he belonged to John Aldridge, "who resides near Allenton, in Wilcox County and State of Alabama."[15] Henry was a twenty-six-year-old light-skinned bondsmen claimed by "Amos Jones who resides in Montgomery County in the state of Alabama, about three miles from Carter's Hill Post Office, and from fifteen to seventeen miles from the Town of Montgomery."[16]

Alabama was only one fountainhead of fugitive slaves to Pensacola. Many bondspeople came from Louisiana's Gulf Coast. This included two bondsmen who made the roughly two-hundred-mile journey together before landing in Pensacola's crude wooden calaboose. William claimed he was a freeman from Virginia, but, according to the city constables, he answered "the description of a mulatto advertised by A. Hill of New Orleans."[17] William's companion Louis made no such assertion of freedom, confessing that he "ran away from the nephew of his mistress, who lives opposite New Orleans, 3 or 4 years ago."[18] Mississippi was another frequent point of origination. Josiah had "a bad look & a disposition to be very talkative," while Frank spoke seldom and "in a low voice." In spite of their distinct personalities, the two bondsmen shared a yearning for freedom; thus, they "ran away together" from Green County and were not heard from again before being apprehended in Pensacola six months later.[19] Georgia also provided a steady supply of runaways. William White belonged to the recently departed Sandy King of India Springs, Georgia, some four hundred miles from the Gulf of Mexico near the conjunction of the Georgia, Alabama, and Tennessee borders. According to Pensacola's jailer, Florencio Commyns, "said Negro ran away about a month since from the heirs of the deceased and made his way to the city."[20]

Advertisements placed by jail authorities reporting the capture of fugitive slaves proved that Pensacola—regardless of its reputation as a refuge—was, in fact, a dangerous place for fugitive slaves; nevertheless, the same notices also indicate why this reputation endured among bondspeople as the city's free population often seemed unable or unwilling to assist in the apprehension of black fugitives. Several months after bringing Susan to Pensacola from Mobile, D. A. Northrop reported the twenty-four-year-old mulatto's disappearance. For more than a week, Susan avoided recapture without ever leaving the downtown area. "She has been seen in the city within the last three days," Northrop complained, "and I have reason to believe is harboured by some person." Desperate to reclaim the valuable servant, Northrop offered ten dollars to anyone who put Susan back in his possession and twenty dollars for the arrest and conviction of her protector.[21] The "bowlegged griff" Nelson also hid out in Pensacola, though he came to the city after fleeing from the area near Fort Barrancas. After avoiding detection for more than a month, Nelson's owner, Samuel Clifford, asked the public for its assistance in tracking the bondsman down, remarking, "Said boy is well known and has been seen about Pensacola during the past week."[22]

Clifford and other slaveowners were providing valuable information to the public when they informed them that absconded slaves were well known locally and thus easily recognizable. Yet their repetitive use of the language suggests a level of frustration with their fellow citizens for failing to assist in the capture of so many fugitives with familiar faces. When a "likely negro man" ran away from Byrd C. Willis, the former city marshal and navy agent asked the city's inhabitants to assist him in locating the runaway who was "well known in town by the name of Robert Johnson."[23] When a dark-skinned twenty-five-year-old bondswoman ran away from the small industrial village of Bagdad, so called because of its location on Pensacola's own Fertile Crescent, a miniature peninsula just north of Pensacola Bay between the Escambia and Blackwater Rivers, George Dennison offered one hundred dollars for her return or fifty dollars for her "recovery and arrest." The valuable servant's name was Ann Green, and she was "well known about Bagdad, and has a husband in said county."[24]

One particular phrase appeared commonly in advertisements to inform slaveowners' neighbors that fugitive slaves were hiding among them for extended periods of time. Joseph Forsyth offered fifty dollars for the return of Henry, who ran away three months earlier and, according to the wealthy industrialist, "has been lurking about the vicinity of Pensacola not long since."[25] Shortly after James Gonzalez sold Bill Myers to the operators of a large lumber mill on the Escambia River several miles north of Pensacola, the dark-skinned twenty-six-year-old ran away. Lumber company officials suspected the bondsman had returned to the city, where he was "supposed to be lurking about in the vicinity of said Mr. Gonzalez's Brick Yard."[26] Territorial Judge Dillon Jordan offered five dollars for the apprehension of Charles inside the city limits but added, "if caught out of the city, I will give such additional reward as would be just as reasonable."[27] The paltry reward might explain why the following year Jordan continued to advertise Charles's absence, now with the additional comment that the runaway was "supposed to be lurking about 'Cantonment Clinch,'" a small army garrison just west of the city.[28]

Notwithstanding the public declarations of desperate slaveowners, fugitive slaves did not intend to lurk on Pensacola's margins permanently. For those hoping to remain near family and friends, the best option was to attempt to live and work in the city as free people. When Jack, an eighteen-year-old mulatto with straight light-colored hair and blue eyes fled from a farm on the Alabama–Florida border, Thompson Hemphill had no doubt of the fugitive's intentions, informing, "Jack is endeavoring to get to Pensacola and pass for a free man."[29] William Taylor of Conecuh County, Alabama, was likewise certain of the destination of Harry, "a very crafty fellow" who "will no doubt try to pass for a free man." According to Taylor, the dark-skinned fugitive was "well known in Pensacola and its vicinity, and has no doubt shaped his course for that place."[30]

For fugitive slaves, possessing documents asserting one's freedom was one way to avoid re-enslavement. In Pensacola, one source of free papers was highly literate bondspeople like those who belonged to Jackson Morton, a prominent Florida politician and wealthy government contractor. According to interviews of surviving slaves conducted more than a half century after the Civil War, Morton encouraged bondspeople to learn how to read and write, which gave him "the most advanced group of slaves generally in the whole section." But he regretted the decision later, for as knowledge of the "underground railroad" reached Pensacola, prospective runaways turned to Morton's slaves, who "became valuable aides with their ability to forge 'passes' from one part of the country to the other for escaping slaves." As a result, Morton made literacy a crime punishable by "the cutting off of the first joint of the index finger of any slave found putting pen or pencil to paper."[31]

Because of the power of free papers, officials frequently challenged the validity of any documents in the possession of black strangers. Pensacola mayor Peter Alba informed the public of the arrest of a suspicious light-skinned man "who calls himself George Wilson." The "coloured man" came to Pensacola a month earlier with free papers from Pike County, Alabama, but "from their execution are supposed to be forged."[32] When Pensacola jailer Henry Nunes apprehended the suspected runaway Wiet, who admitted belonging to Thomas Ware of Monroe County, Alabama, the twenty-five-year-old prisoner produced papers proving his liberty. Nunes suspected the documents were forgeries, however, as they granted Wiet freedom for an entire year.[33] Several weeks later, two other suspected runaways from Alabama arrived in Nunes's custody. Kit was "a mulatto man, about 40 years of age," who came east from Mobile with his wife, Nancy. Though the married couple failed to convince Nunes of their free status, the jailer admitted, "Both the above have passes to come to Pensacola and return."[34]

Unlike public officials, employers desperate for labor were unlikely to question free papers in the possession of qualified black job applicants. The case of Daniel, a talkative bondsman who preferred "the company of whites to that of slaves," demonstrates this. After fleeing from his home in southeastern Alabama, Daniel's owner, Thomas Gilpin, placed advertisements in two newspapers on Florida's Gulf Coast avowing of the runaway, "He will no doubt change his name and have a free pass, or pass to hire his time as he has done before." Suspecting employers would continue to hire Daniel despite his enslaved status, Gilpin added a stern warning: "all persons are forwarned against harbouring or employing him, on the penalty of the law."[35] Another case proved the futility of the pass system entirely. After an enslaved lumberjack named Lewis fled from the eastern shore of Pensacola Bay, his owner learned the bondsman was "lurking and secreting himself" nearby. Daniel remained at large until his employer discovered him six months later in Pensacola, "where the negro was hiring himself" without any sort of documentation proving his status.[36]

As bondspeople often possessed unique talents or experience with a particular trade, slaveowners commonly provided brief employment histories of runaways in an effort to increase the likelihood of their capture. The owner of a fugitive slave from Monticello, Alabama, suspected the multitalented, violin-playing mulatto he claimed ownership of would try to find work in Pensacola, noting, "He can work at the blacksmith trade some and can work some in wood."[37] Another mulatto from Alabama with "hair nearly straight" professed to be a barber. But according to his owner, he was likely headed for a lumberyard since he had "been working in and about a saw mill for the last ten or twelve years."[38] J. K. Whitman offered one hundred dollars to anyone who took Bill, also known as William Hooper, into custody. Whitman suspected the well-traveled thirty-one-year-old bondsman would "pass himself off as a Cook or Brick Mason" and then "change his name and disown his true master, as he has done in the past."[39] Robert James of Monroe County, Alabama, suspected the enslaved bricklayer Sam would "make for Pensacola," where with free papers he would seek employment along the water "in that kind of work."[40]

While some fugitive slaves came to Pensacola hoping to find a new start, others tried to escape from the city entirely by disappearing into the inhospitable swamps and forests that stretched for hundreds of miles in all directions beyond the city limits. When the "Negro Boy Joshua, between twelve and fourteen years of age" vanished from Charles Lavalette's brickyard along Pensacola Bay, Thomas Lawson of the U.S. Army offered ten dollars for the boy's capture in the city and twenty dollars beyond its limits. Lawson added, "This Boy is lately from Norfolk, VA, and having no knowledge of the country, may in attempting to make this place, have taken a road leading into the interior of the country."[41] When a detachment of U.S. troops from Fort Barrancas went in pursuit of Indians responsible for the murder of a white settler, they "returned without being able to fine any recent signs of Indians." What they did find in the "old haunts of the Indians" was a group of squatters "supposed to be runaway negroes."[42]

In a more serious incident, which must have conjured memories of Negro Fort in the minds of slaveowners across the Southern frontier, the *Pensacola Gazette* reported the destruction of a "nest of runaway negroes" across the Alabama–Florida border at the fork of the Alabama and Tombigbee Rivers, a former Creek retreat. According to the party of men who destroyed the settlement in a violent confrontation with the slaves, three bondsmen were shot and apprehended, while several others managed to escape. The residents of the small community had already erected two cabins on the site "and were about to build a Fort." By all accounts, "Some of these negroes have been runaway several years, and have committed many depredations on the neighboring plantations."[43]

That bondspeople continued to maroon themselves in remote areas near Pensacola once inhabited by Native Americans terrified antebellum slaveowners as some Indians continued to eke out an existence near the homes of their ancestors.[44] In the 1830s, for example, fears of a combined Native American–African American assault on Pensacola or the surrounding areas grew in response to the outbreak of the Second Seminole War in East Florida and the less familiar Second Creek War in southern Alabama, what Brian Rucker calls a "forgotten struggle" between Indians and settlers in which "there were atrocities on both sides."[45] Groups of Pensacola's bravest young men organized rapidly for the defense of the city and went on a series of raids throughout the region to eliminate any possible threat. In a panic, John Hunt, a successful brick manufacturer in Bagdad, informed Pensacola's residents that the murderous Indians were "all around him" and insisted "that some government agent should be employed in collecting them." Even more disturbing than the Indians' proximity to Pensacola, Hunt asserted, was that "his negroes see and converse with them frequently."[46]

While the hinterland beyond Pensacola provided fugitive slaves an easily accessible retreat, the city's harbor provided them an even greater opportunity to escape from the house of bondage permanently. John

Hunt's bad fortune continued when the enslaved laborer John Betton, who wore "at all times rather a guilty countenance," escaped from Hunt's brickyard. Hunt wrote in an advertisement regarding the runaway, "It is expected he will make for Pensacola, with a view of making his escape in some vessel."[47] J. S. I. Autrey was certain of the destination of the bondsman who fled from Belleville, Alabama, in a southerly direction: "It is thought that he is making his way to Pensacola for the purpose of escaping on some vessel," Autrey announced before continuing, "Captains are cautioned against employing said boy."[48] Joel Lee of Conecuh County, Alabama, also begged the men who sailed in and out of Pensacola for their assistance in apprehending an absconded slave. Caswell was a twenty-year-old bondsman who could "write a tolerable school-boy hand"; accordingly, he would "forge himself a pass and probably a free one, and change his name." After accomplishing this, Lee affirmed, "said boy will attempt to get on board some boat or vessel bound to some other port as soon as possible." The long notice concluded with an appeal to Pensacola's watermen: "I therefore wish to give notice to all masters of boats and other vessels if such application be made to arrest said boy and confine him in jail so that I get him."[49]

In addition to warning shipowners and captains of the anticipated arrival of owned people, slaveowners and employers speculated on the likely destination of fugitive slaves to increase the likelihood of the slaves' capture. Three months after the "mulatto boy" Ned Sewall fled from Arcadia Mill, company owner Joseph Forsyth offered fifty dollars for the capture of the teenage bondsman he suspected "may have gone Eastward."[50] When Peter Lewis and his bilingual wife, Mary, stole themselves and their two small children from Richard Dealy, they also relieved him of "$10 in Geo. notes, Plate to a considerable value, Clothing &c." To secure the return of all his prized possessions, material or otherwise, Dealy offered a fifty-dollar reward and pointed any potential slave catchers to the area just west of Pensacola, for it was "presumed said negroes are gone for the direction of Mobile, or are loitering about the South West Bayou or Dog River."[51]

Remarkable are the frequent assertions by Pensacola's slaveowners that bondspeople who had fled from the city by water were en route to parts of the Upper South thousands of miles away. According to Z. A. Edwards, of Benton, Alabama, the bondsman Bill "was born in VA, and will probably try to get back there by sea." Given Bill's light complexion, it was expected he would try "to pass for a white man, and will probably represent himself to be free."[52] When three bondsmen belonging to William Bell absconded, the Pensacola butcher offered a thirty-dollar reward for their capture. Jesse was a thirty-five-year-old "Virginia mulatto," while Tom and Dave were brothers from North Carolina. Bell believed that North Carolina was the most likely destination of the trio, noting, "It is probable they will attempt to return there, and that Jesse will accompany them."[53] Just one month after arriving in Florida from Fredericksburg, Virginia, Daniel and Henry absconded from their owner, John Sweeney, who believed, "It is possible they may endeavor to return there." The bondsmen may have embarked on their nearly impossible journey several days later when Sweeney learned "they were seen at Cotton's Ferry on Wednesday evening last, where they stole a flat and crossed over to the Alabama side."[54]

Fugitive slaves from Pensacola who embarked on the water in a desperate attempt to rejoin friends and family many miles away evoke the "Migratory Generation" described by Ira Berlin. As victims of the domestic slave trade, their journey to Pensacola was only one leg of a nightmarish voyage through the Old South. John S. Miller of New Orleans suspected his "mulatto man" Barney Shields fled east toward Florida, noting, "He was bought by me of Mr. Hatcher, last spring, agent of Mr. Spencer Drummond, of Norfolk, Virginia, who sent him."[55] John Booth of Brookline, Alabama, offered a "liberal reward" for the capture of Primus, whom he suspected came from South Carolina or Georgia as the bondsman spoke in "the manner peculiar to most negroes raised in low country."[56] H. Warren of Sparta, Alabama, likewise offered a "liberal reward" for the confinement of Moses "in any safe jail so that I can get him." The six-foot thirty-year-old bondsman "was purchased in Richmond about two years ago by me; he was raised in Augusta Co. (Va.) and was formerly owned by Mr. Crawford" for whom he worked as a cook. "He left my plantation in Dallas county about the 10th of March last." Warren warned of the well-traveled serial runaway, "Moses, no doubt will change his name as he has done heretofore."[57]

Jailhouse interviews with black prisoners exposed some of the incredible distances fugitive slaves traveled across the Southern frontier prior to absconding. Billy, a thirty-two-year-old bondsman wearing a fur hat, blue coat, and Scotch plaid pants, "was purchased from the estate of Baptist Barber, dec'd. Maryland, Saint Mary's Co., some

time in November last, by one Mr. Garner, and runaway from him
between Oakmulgy and Flint Rivers, some time about the last of Jan.
last."[58] The light-skinned thirty-five-year-old bondsman John belonged
to "Mr. Cocherane who purchased him of Gen. William Williams of
Martin county, North Carolina, and that said Cocherane was taking him
to Mississippi or Louisiana." John claimed "he escaped from his master near Greensborough, Alabama, three weeks since."[59] On the eastern
side of Pensacola Bay, Santa Rosa County sheriff James Mims apprehended Tom near the Florida–Alabama border. The "not very dark"
forty-year-old bondsman came from North Carolina originally. But he
later belonged to "Jack Grady, speculator, who obtained him from John
Durgan, near Augusta, Georgia, and was on his way to New Orleans,
and while passing through Monroe County, Alabama, he ranaway from
his master."[60]

Professional slave traders bear much of the responsibility for the
forced migration of hundreds of thousands of bondspeople to the Deep
South in the first half of the nineteenth century; however, as Steven
Deyle has demonstrated in his chronicle of the domestic slave trade,
individual slaveowners bear much of the responsibility for human traf-
ficking in the antebellum era.[61] This was true in Pensacola, where individual and corporate slaveowners along with auctioneers and other
local businessmen profited from the buying and selling of black people
whom they employed in various occupations. But while bondspeople
in the neighboring ports of Mobile and New Orleans worked for slaveowners primarily, a large percentage of Pensacola's enslaved population
worked for the U.S. government. Consequently, public slaves appeared
often in runaway slave advertisements circulated in Pensacola. Shortly
after Charles Gambrile, "a black, stout, good-looking fellow, about 28
years of age, 5 feet 10 or 11 inches high," ran away from the Pensacola
Navy Yard, J. M. Stanard, a government contractor who in addition to
labor provided lime, cement, and nails to the U.S. Navy, offered twenty-
five dollars for his capture and return.[62] Thomas Wright offered twice
the amount for the apprehension of George, who "RANAWAY from
the United States Navy Yard, near Pensacola." The Pensacola entre-
preneur thought the broad-shouldered twenty-seven-year-old was
"secreted either in this City or in the neighborhood."[63] Following the
death of her husband, Celestino, a superintendent at Fort Barrancas,
Pauline Gonzalez continued to lease the family's bondspeople to the

navy. When the bondsman Lewis Archer absconded from Gonzalez, she demonstrated great tenacity in attempting to recover the family's property, offering up to twenty dollars for the apprehension of Archer, "who ranaway from his employment at the Navy Yard." Gonzalez alerted her Pensacola neighbors: "the above negro is well known in this vicinity."[64]

One fugitive slave from the Navy Yard attracted an unprecedented amount of attention, following a raucous celebration that culminated in murder. The incident began when, after several hours of drinking, gambling, and playing cards "in the neighborhood of the Navy Yard," an argument ensued among two bondsmen, Henry Prior and Adam. Moments earlier, the two partygoers were "like brothers," but following an accusation of cheating, Prior struck Adam on the side of his head with a wooden stick, "killing him instantly." Prior fled immediately from the Navy Yard, becoming a fugitive both from justice and slavery. Several weeks later, after Florida's governor Thomas Brown issued a proclamation offering one hundred dollars for Prior's arrest, authorities apprehended the bondsman and brought him back to Pensacola, where a jury convicted him of manslaughter. No doubt to limit the damage to the person who claimed ownership of the murderer, the court spared Prior's life and ordered him instead "to be whipped and to stand in the pillory."[65]

Given the number of bondspeople employed by the navy often numbered in the hundreds, it is anticipated that the Navy Yard was a frequent destination for fugitive slaves trying to reconnect with friends and loved ones or hoping to find employment as free laborers and mechanics. Shortly after the thirty-year-old Elick eloped from Evergreen, Alabama, his owner, Y. M. Rabb, divulged, "When last heard from was at Big Escambia Bridge making his way for Pensacola Navy Yard."[66] When Monroe and Galen absconded from a mill on the Alabama River about thirty miles north of Mobile, their owner, Jacob Magee, offered one hundred dollars for the capture of both men and fifty dollars for either. Magee urged interested parties in Florida to be on the alert, for "they are supposed to be in the neighborhood of Pensacola or the Navy Yard, Monroe having worked at the Navy Yard several years."[67] When Isaac Taylor ran away from James Gonzalez's brickyard, Samuel Gonzalez offered twenty-five dollars for the runaway, noting, "He is supposed to be lurking about the Pensacola Navy Yard." The advertisement led to Taylor's capture, but the bondsman persevered. According to a report

published several months later, Isaac "again made his escape and is now
at large."[68]

Accounts of fugitive slaves wearing the uniforms of the U.S. armed
services less than a decade after the War of 1812 confirms Gene Allen
Smith's finding that during this conflict "black participants—slaves
and freemen—chose sides, and those choices ultimately decided their
future."[69] Several months after Andrew Jackson accepted the transfer
of Florida from Spanish control to the United States, William Champlin
committed a black man to jail who claimed to belong to Henry Lucas
of Hancock, Georgia. According to the city marshal, the twenty-five-
year-old bondsman "had with him a common half stock Shot Gun,
Powder Horn and Pouch, and a Free Masons Apron of the most beautiful description—had on a United States uniform coat."[70] The following
year, "a negro man named LAWYER" ran away from Thomas English,
who described the bondsman as approximately thirty years old, five
feet and five inches tall, with a dark complexion, and missing a front
tooth. Even more distinguishing was what "the said negro had on when
he went from home, a blue roundabout sailors jacket; United States
Soldier's white double wove pantaloons, woolen."[71]

The United States' staunch pro-slavery and Great Britain's strong anti-
slavery stance during the War of 1812 helps explain why there are no
extant accounts of fugitive slaves in Pensacola wearing the uniform of His
Majesty's service in the aftermath of the campaign. That being said, possession of a soldier's uniform did not prove military service, especially in
a military town like Pensacola where bondspeople stole soldiers' clothing
and in other ways had access to government-issued wear.[72] Nevertheless,
slaveowners' comments remove any doubt that former American soldiers counted among the fugitive slaves who passed through antebellum Pensacola. A decade after the start of the War of 1812, a thirty-five-
year-old "negro man called Jim," who worked as a painter, glazier, and
ship carpenter, absconded from Robert Sterling, a prominent lawyer
in Monroe, Louisiana. Sterling placed an advertisement in a Pensacola
newspaper asking residents to be on the lookout for the Georgia-born
runaway, "a drummer in the army during the late war."[73] Five years later,
Pensacola constable Foster Chapman took up "a Negro fellow about 35
years of age, five feet one inch high and stout built—says that his name
is PETER, and that he belongs to John Caffey and Jacob Brassil, who live
near Montgomery, Alabama." The only distinguishing mark on Peter's

body was "a large scar on the right side, which he says was occasioned by a bayonet wound received on board the Frigate Chesapeake."[74] After the Second Seminole War, a brief report on Pensacola appeared in William Lloyd Garrison's abolitionist newspaper, *Liberator,* which read, "There is a colored man at present in the jail in this city, whom his master hired to the government to fight in Florida, against the Indians. The poor fellow did the fighting, while his master drew the pay."[75]

In addition to the accounts of enslaved veterans running away in the attire they once used to defend their country, the militancy of bonds-people in Pensacola revealed itself in reports of serial runaways who flatly refused to remain permanently enslaved. In their profile of more than eight thousand runaway slaves from five Southern states, John Hope Franklin and Loren Schweninger found evidence of intelligence, ingenuity, resourcefulness, and duplicitousness. "Perhaps the most salient characteristic, however, was courage, especially for those who ran away more than once despite fierce punishment."[76]

Courage was certainly a defining characteristic of fugitive slaves who aimed for Pensacola more than once. When Sam and Shaderick disappeared from Montgomery, Alabama, their owner, James Conyers, offered twenty dollars for their capture, noting, the "Negroes will no doubt try to get to Pensacola as Sam was once there as runaway."[77] Ranson managed to avoid capture during the several-hundred-mile journey from Winchester, Mississippi, to Pensacola, but shortly after reaching his destination found himself incarcerated in the city jail. Evidence suggests Ranson found the accommodations unacceptable, for he soon escaped from the insecure building, prompting city officials to offer a reward that remained unclaimed three months later.[78] Serial runaways in Pensacola and the local area demonstrated as much courage as those who came to the city from great distances. Shortly after Thomas Cooper, a ferry operator on the Escambia River, published an advertisement offering a ten-dollar reward for the capture of "A negro fellow named MIKE, well known in Pensacola," he quickly regained possession of the bonds-man.[79] But two years later Mike absconded again, leading Cooper to place another advertisement offering twenty dollars for the runaway's return.[80] Though Mike's fate is unknown, the second advertisement appeared in print only one time, which might suggest his capture.

While the number of times an advertisement ran in a newspaper does not prove the fate of the fugitive or fugitives described therein conclusively, it does in some cases give an indication. Over a three-year span in the 1840s, for example, "a small mulatto man" named Thornton twice fled from "Slaback's Brick Yard" along Pensacola Bay and headed east in the direction of Tallahassee. In both instances, Thornton's owner placed an advertisement offering a ten-dollar reward for the bondsman's capture. The first ad ran for three weeks, indicating Thornton's liberty was short-lived; the second ad ran for six months, suggesting the opposite.[81]

No bondsman in antebellum Pensacola proved more determined to run away than Smart. The aptly named twenty-five-year-old mulatto belonged to George Willis, a navy agent who along with his father built a small government contracting empire leasing bondsmen to the navy and other Pensacola businesses. Over a four-year period, Smart ran away from his employer at least four times. Among the worksites he abandoned were the Navy Yard, Willis's "woodyard on Santa Rosa Sound," and the "Wood Yard of Weaver, Davis & Co., on East Bay." To reclaim his possession, Willis placed nearly thirty advertisements in the *Pensacola Gazette* and offered as much as fifty dollars for Smart's capture; he eventually reduced the reward to ten dollars, however, as he may have become resigned to the bondsman's escape. Smart's determination is made more remarkable by the fact that he was "lame in the left leg, having had his thigh broken."[82]

Willis's use of the passive voice leaves little doubt as to the cause of the exceptional injury to Smart's leg, and it serves as an important reminder of the type of punishment bondspeople faced potentially when they failed in their efforts to escape from their owners and employers. In antebellum Pensacola, one case in particular stands out for its brutality. While visiting the city one summer, Peter Williamson of Jackson County, Florida, sold a bondswoman named Katy and her children to a local doctor. But upon learning of the sale, Katy absconded with her youngest child until "she was sought after by Williamson and found." Back in the possession of her owner, Katy refused to disclose the child's location and when pressed, "she named a place where the child might be but it was searched and the child wasn't found." At this juncture, Williamson, who was drunk, endeavored to teach the bondswoman a lesson. Using a leather rope, he tied Katy's hands behind her back and attached her neck to the axle of a wagon and unleashed a flurry of blows with his fists and a whip on the body of the helpless woman, who began to bleed "copiously." Williamson then ordered the wagon driver to "cut" the horses and advance. Katy's body "jerked in a frightful way" as the vehicle dragged her along the city's waterlogged streets. Only the intervention of the mayor and a group of horrified onlookers stopped the gruesome spectacle and denied Williamson the pleasure of killing the woman.[83]

Despite residents' claims in the aftermath of the chastisement, the brutal public beating of a recalcitrant bondswoman was more the rule than the exception in Pensacola and for that matter the entire South. Indeed, the scarred bodies of bondspeople who aimed for Pensacola signaled a widespread regional culture in which white men and women marked and mutilated the bodies of black people routinely. In January 1828, Richard Legon of Mount Meigs, Alabama, offered six hundred dollars for six bondsmen whose bodies testified to slavery's cruelty. Among them was Buckner, with "a scar between the nose and the upper lip"; Mason, with "a scar projecting from the upper lip to the right cheek"; and Moses, who had "several large gashes on the head." The anomalousness of Toby's back prompted the following description: "smooth, and clear of scars."[84]

The lash was the preferred weapon of slaveowners, who applied the device to the bare backs of enslaved men and women equally. One bondswoman who fled to Pensacola from central Alabama had a small scar on her left elbow, "which has the appearance of having been burnt or scalded." The only other exceptional physical characteristic was a series of "marks about the left shoulder blade, caused by the whip, and about the size of a man's thumb nail which rises above the level of the skin."[85] Eli Townsend of Pike County, Alabama, sought the return of Ben, his wife, Fillis, and their six-month-old son. In addition to the "large scars on his back and hips," Ben bore an additional distinctive mark, "a scar on his right hand his thumb and fore finger being injured by being shot last fall, a part of the bones came out of his finger and thumb and has caused his thumb more particularly to shrink."[86] Ben's mutilated appendage may have resulted from a hunting accident or a violent outburst among friends, family, or coworkers, but it was just as likely the consequence of a violent encounter with an owner or overseer.

Either way, fugitive slaves who fled to Pensacola after surviving the amputation of body parts proved slavery's depravity. J. H. McCreary of Conecuh County, Alabama, sought the capture of "a negro boy named

SANFORD, aged 20 or 21 years, about 5 feet 8 or 10 inches high—spare made, rather knockneed, has a down look when spoken to, very thick lips—broad white teeth—the fore finger of his left hand is off at the middle joint."[87] When Pensacola's jailer locked up a bondsman named Martin, who had absconded from a plantation along the Alabama River somewhere between Cahawba and Selma, he described the fugitive as "about 25 years of age, six feet high, stout built, has the first joint of the forefinger of his right hand cut off."[88] William Villard of Edgefield, South Carolina, warned the citizens of nearly every Deep South state to be on the lookout for "a Negro Woman named AGGY, about 30 or 35 years of age, of tolerable size, has a film on one of her eyes, some of her teeth out, and one of her toes next to the great toe is cut off."[89]

Bondspeoples' ears were a favorite target of sadistic slaveowners, who, by amputating the appendage, sent a powerful message without jeopardizing the lives of their valuable investments. Three months after Leonard ran away from his owner in Dooly County, Georgia, he arrived in Pensacola's jail wearing several badges of resistance. He was, according to the deputy marshal, "aged about 38 years, five feet three inches high, of black complexion, and a Taylor by trade, with a scar near each eye and two scars upon his head, and a part of his right ear cut off."[90] The "Dark Mulatto Fellow, who calls himself Adam," likewise failed in his bid to escape from servitude and instead turned up in the Pensacola jail several weeks after fleeing from his home in Mobile. The city constable reported, "Said Mulatto is about 28 or 29 years old, 5 feet 8 or 9 inches high, and has both his ears cropped."[91]

In one extraordinary case, a bondsman who aimed for Pensacola proved the sadism that underlay chattel slavery. Abraham was an "American negro" who fled from the plantation of Francoise Haydel Marmillion about twenty miles north of New Orleans on the eastern side of the Mississippi River. As the twenty-eight-year-old bondsman could read and write, his owners suspected he "may have made a false certificate of liberty." Abraham's body was intact, but something else set him apart from other bondspeople. The advertisement for his capture explained, "He is supposed to be marked on the breast with the letters V. B. M."—the initials of Marmillon's grandson Volsey B. Marmillion.[92]

Whether Abraham ever reached Pensacola is unknown; several decades later, however, the public learned how those three letters landed on the bondsman's chest when photographers published several illustrations of fugitive slaves from Louisiana in *Harper's Weekly* and an accompanying series of *cartes de visite*.[93] In one image, a group of eight slaves of varying ages and skin color face the camera in what appears to be a peculiar family portrait. Meant to show the absurdity of racial slavery, several of the children are well dressed and extraordinarily light-skinned—in fact, they are white. Behind them is a tall dark-skinned man named Wilson Chinn, who wears a thick, heavy coat and holds a hat in his right arm, which lies relaxed along his side. In another image, Chinn stands alone amid some of the "instruments of torture" slaveowners and overseers resorted to regularly. A large chain wrapped tightly around his left ankle anchors him to the floor while an iron bar that extends from his thigh down to his foot eliminates his ability to walk or run. A collared contraption surrounding Chinn's neck serves as a base for three long metallic spikes that shoot into the air several inches above his head. The purpose of this devise was to seize the heads of runaways on tree and bush branches when they took flight. The most shocking detail of the two photographs is the large, thick letters branded across Chinn's forehead. The magazine informed readers of Chinn's owner, "This man was accustomed to brand his negroes, and Wilson has on his forehead the letters 'V. B. M.'" During the Civil War, 105 bondspeople, including Chinn, escaped from Marmillion's plantation and found safety behind Union lines. Of them, "thirty had been branded like cattle with a hot iron, four of them on the forehead, and the others on the breast or arm."[94]

The ever-present fear of having one's body beaten, mutilated, or in other ways violated by another human being made some bondspeople the unfortunate victims of "soul murder," what psychologists describe as an irreversible mental trauma that renders victims socially and psychologically damaged;[95] others, however, transformed their despondency into a homicidal rage when they fled from their owners and overseers and refused to return to slavery without a fight. A bondsman named Jim demonstrated the inherent danger in any attempt to re-enslave a fugitive slave in or around Pensacola. After fleeing from James Gonzalez's brickyard, Jim headed west "on the road to Mobile" across the Florida–Alabama border. By midnight, the bondsman reached a toll station a dozen miles from Pensacola and asked a road employee named Reckard "for something to eat." Reckard suspected the weary traveler was a runaway and tried to take him into custody; before he could, however, Jim grabbed an ax on the floor of the station and "gave several strokes upon the head and back of the white man." Reckard tried to escape his assailant by fleeing to a nearby creek, but "he was overtaken by the negro and was severely cut on the throat, which wound is supposed to be very dangerous." Several days later, local papers reported that Jim had turned himself into his owner and now sat in the city jail awaiting his trial. "We hope that such a crime will be punished," the article concluded, "in a way to give an example that may prevent the perpetration of such diabolical conduct for the future."[96]

Reckard appears to have survived the violent assault, but in another instance a fugitive slave benefiting from the assistance of a notorious frontier outlaw took the life of the man who stood between him and freedom. John B. Harden was a large white man of "Herculean strength," a Mississippi native who moved to the eastern side of Pensacola Bay, where he "carried on a little traffic in liquor" with "darkies as well as the weary and idler."[97] After stealing a "roll of money" worth more than five hundred dollars, a buggy, a horse, and a double-barrel shotgun from several Pensacola residents, he fled to Alabama with his "paramour," their illegitimate child, and Jack, "a valuable negro boy," who belonged to the Pensacola firm of Forsyth & Simpson.[98] After a long pursuit, lawmen eventually caught up with Harden, whom some considered "the most enterprising, and daring villain now in the southern country," and his enslaved associate Jack in Mississippi.[99] An Alabama sheriff offered to deliver the two prisoners to the proper authorities in Florida and after placing Harden securely in irons aboard a small carriage, began the long journey toward Pensacola. Because Jack "seemed anxious to return" to his owner, the sheriff left the bondsman unchained and allowed him to follow the carriage alone on horseback.[100] It was a fateful mistake. As the party neared the Florida border, Jack climbed aboard the carriage and with a massive dagger known as an "Arkansas toothpick," wrapped his arm around the sheriff's head and sliced the unsuspecting man's neck open, killing him instantly.[101] After freeing Harden, the two fugitives emptied the sheriff's pockets and deposited his lifeless body on the side of the road. It took authorities several months to finally capture Jack and Harden, and when they did they brought the two men to a small village north of Pensacola where a furious mob exacted justice. In a rare interracial Southern lynching, Harden and Jack "were both hung to one tree and buried in one grave."[102]

The skeletons that remain buried together underneath the soil near Pensacola are a reminder of the types of interracial relationships that developed among marginalized people on the Southern frontier. Formed among enslaved African Americans and the free European Americans they lived and worked beside, these relationships lack the romance and sentimentality of the more celebrated interracial relationships formed in Northern cities and towns by middle- and upper-class reformers contemporaneously. In most cases, the interracial relationships forged on the Southern frontier were casual and often ephemeral associations that lacked any sort of ideological basis. They are significant, nonetheless, for they undermined the racial and social order that slaveowners and other white elites imposed on the region.[103]

This was the case whenever and for whatever reason white Southerners helped their enslaved black friends, coworkers, and acquaintances run away. George Willis knew little of the villainous individual who "enticed" a bondsman to escape from his lumberyard, but in order to recover his property offered fifteen dollars for the apprehension of the "worthless white man."[104] Robert Carr Lane warned ship captains in Pensacola to be on the lookout for Betsey, a bondswoman "about 20 years old, of a light black, thin visage, slender made, very likely, dresses very neat, and of a genteel appearance." The Mobile attorney believed Betsey was "enticed away from some person, probably white, and will pass as free." There was, he continued, "no doubt but she has, or will endeavor to get off by water."[105] Dennis may have been of Native American ancestry, given his "reddish cast" and "remarkably kinky hair for [a] mulatto." But this made no difference to his owner, who offered twenty-five dollars for his apprehension in the Florida territory and fifty dollars if it occurred outside of it. Because Dennis was "enticed away by some white man," Jacob Stroman also offered "100 dollars for the ruffian who assisted in his absconding."[106]

At times, slaveowners were just as eager to capture fugitive slaves' accomplices as the runaways themselves. The case of the bondsman George, a valuable servant "who always had charge of his masters affairs," provides an example. George was a dedicated family man, which explains why when he ran away from his owner just beneath the Florida–Georgia border, he went with his wife, "LETTUS, a negro woman about 45 years of age, very black, a very coarse voice in speaking, her son ADAM, about 9 years old, SUSAN, her daughter about 19 years old a very likely woman and her child a boy about one year old, BENY, a son of Lettus about 12 years old, dark complexioned, and LIZ, a girl about 10 years old, also very dark complexioned." W. C. Smith and R. J. Roberts reported the large family was "backed by some white man, who will try to carry the negroes out of the Country." The presumed owners offered $250 for the capture of the entire family, adding, "Should they be found in the possession of a white man, we will also give a liberal reward to any one, who will place him in Jail or give us such information as will lead to his detection."[107]

Even the vaguest references to mysterious individuals who assisted runaway slaves confirm interracialism's persistence on the Southern frontier. Tuscaloosa's James Sneed offered a fifty-dollar reward for the capture of the "Negro Boy" Burrell and the white man who provided the runaway with a written pass. Burrell "was seduced away," Sneed declared, "and is yet under the protection of a man named David Street." The two men came "from Demopolis to Blakely on board of a pirogue and they both left the place together."[108] The Mobile, Alabama, bondsman Ruben was an intelligent and exceptional craftsman, "not to be surpassed by any other as a carriage smith." After absconding, his owner reported that the bondsman "went off with a man by the name of David McDowel, an Irishman, is very tall, with large whiskers and dark hair—supposed to be about forty years of age."[109] When the "mulatto fellow" Jesse ran away from William B. McCall in Quincy, Florida, with a "variety of good clothing," he was not alone. He traveled with "a white man who calls himself William Sitzar, who is a blacksmith by trade, and has been in Quincy for some time past, but left the place about the time that Jesse absconded."[110]

Given the diversity of Pensacola's population, which derived primarily from the city's proximity to the water, it is expected that Northerners figured among fugitive slaves' allies. James T. De Jarnett offered the extraordinary sum of one thousand dollars for the apprehension of his bondswoman Celia and her husband, who helped her run away from Autauga County, Alabama. The husband's name was Jonathan H. Coolidge, and he was "a yankee" who lived in Alabama "for 10 or 15 years, as a Merchant, and Grocer." De Jarnett described Celia as a "bright or copper coloured negro, fine figure and very smart." Coolidge was "a man of small size, say 5 feet or 5 feet and six inches high, red complexion with dark sandy or brown hair, and sometimes wears large whiskers." De Jarnett believed the interracial couple was headed for the Florida coast, where, after changing their names and clothes, they would attempt to pass for a slaveowner and a "servant boy." De Jarnett suspected that Coolidge and Celia would try to get to the North and thus warned, "All masters and owners of vessels are cautioned against taking said negro off."[111]

It is anticipated that soldiers and military veterans also figured among the aiders and abettors of fugitive slaves because the U.S. military brought diverse people to Pensacola and the vicinity, including a great many who had no stake in the region's peculiar institution. After Deputy Marshal Joseph Sierra committed "a certain runaway slave named BILLY" into his custody, the twenty-five-year-old-bondsman confessed he belonged to Charles Abercrombie, who lived near Fort Mitchell on the Alabama–Georgia border. Billy came to Pensacola with a man who claimed his name was John Clark. Upon further investigation, however, the conspirator confessed his real name was Joseph C. Wheeler and he was "formerly an enlisted soldier."[112] Thomas Scott of Montgomery, Alabama, suspected the bondsman Carter would "aim for Pensacola" in an effort to find "work at the trade of carpenter, in which capacity he is capable of giving satisfaction to any one." Carter was a reliable servant, who "had but one flogging in his life," but he was a serial runaway who may have been trying to return ultimately to his native Virginia. In this instance, Carter fled from Scott's plantation with a "brass-barrel pocket pistol" and a free pass supplied by a white man named Black, who witnesses saw in the neighborhood with Carter shortly after the bondsman absconded. Black was distinguished "by one side of his face and nose, which is of a dark red colour; loose made, and walks parrot-toed." That he may have been headed for a military town like Pensacola wearing a military-style leather hat "with the figures 1823 or 1824 painted on it" suggested a soldier's life.[113]

For those who dared to assist fugitive slaves, the result was often arrest and incarceration followed by prosecution. Extant court records, which provide few details about the accused besides name and race, prove the existence of a small group of white and black Southerners who—like the more familiar and in some cases famous Northern conductors of the Underground Railroad—at great personal risk tried to spirit bondspeople to freedom. According to the Escambia County Circuit Court, Francis Decordy, a white "yeoman" residing in Escambia

County, "did aid and abet and assist a certain negro man slave, the property of one James Herron to runaway."[114] Ellie, alias Alexander, was "a free man of color," who "falsely, maliciously, and unlawfully" incited the bondsman Jim, alias James, to run away from Thomas Cooper, "against the form of the statue in such case made and provided as against the peace and dignity of the Territory of Florida."[115] In a similar fashion, the "free man of color" Lewis "falsely, wickedly, and unlawfully did solicit and incite one Catherine, a servant and slave of one George Willis to runaway."[116] The case of William Crosby was extraordinary. The white "yeoman," according to court records, "did entice to run away certain slaves the property of one James Gonzalez." The large group consisted of "Sandy, Jack, Washington, Scott, George, Abraham, Beverly, Kelsey, Sill, and Roy."[117]

Public officials recorded the motives of slave liberators only rarely; therefore, incidents of free citizens going to great lengths to liberate enslaved people often leave more questions than answers. The case of *State of Florida v. Charles H. Brightly* provides an example. After authorities arrested the bondsman Elvin Taylor for "willfully feloniously and maliciously" killing a hog that belonged to James Jones, a justice of the peace convened a hearing that led to his ordering the city constable Thomas Green to take Taylor into custody "until the law could be discharged." Shortly after the inquiry, however, a white "yeoman" named Charles Brightly happened upon Green and Taylor and seized the opportunity to set the bondsman free. According to the case file in the archives of the Escambia County Circuit Court, Brightly and Taylor "then and there did beat wound and ill treat" the constable "with force and arms." Following the constable's escape from his multiracial attackers, Brightly told Taylor to go "whither so ever he would," thus putting the bondsman "at large and out of the custody of the constable." Why the court eventually found Brightly not guilty of the charge of "rescuing a prisoner" remains a mystery—as does the fate of the slave he helped escape.[118]

Slaveowners applied the term "slave stealer" to anyone who helped separate bondspeople from their owners; however, good Samaritans like Brightly who sympathized with slaves and tried to ameliorate their condition should not be confused with the ruthless entrepreneurs who commodified slaves and tried to get rich by stealing them from their owners and selling them to the highest bidder. As Joshua Rothman has shown in his study of antebellum Mississippi, generations of slave stealers stalked the Southern frontier in a desperate effort to make their mark in a cutthroat capitalist society dominated by landed aristocrats. Yet they still remain largely absent from the historical literature for a number of reasons.[119] First, like all frontier bandits, slave stealers tried and often succeeded in concealing their identities along with their illegal activities; consequently, detailed primary evidence is sparse and often unreliable. Second, the relationship between slave stealers and the black men and women they appropriated was and remains exceedingly difficult and sometimes impossible to categorize. It is clear, for example, that slave stealers often conspired with the enslaved people they appropriated.

Several cases in Pensacola illustrate this. When Cicero and Bynam landed in the city jail after traveling several hundred miles, they informed their captors that "they were run off from South Carolina by white men, who sold them in Alabama." The deal fell through, however, and the slave stealers "were obliged to take them back and refund the money received for them." As a result of the failed transaction, the slave stealers left the bondsmen "with another white man, who brought them to Pensacola" where they made their escape. When the constables inquired how the kidnappers could have separated the bondsmen from their owners and moved them across the Southern frontier, Cicero and Bynam responded that the outlaws "offered to them one hundred dollars each to say nothing about it."[120] Another fugitive slave who landed in the Pensacola jail named Jim was more assertive than Cicero and Bynam in exploiting the slave–slave stealer relationship. Jim explained to the jailer that he lived in Augusta, Georgia, but "he was brought from that place by William Adams who enticed him away from his master." Jim must have seen his captor as a potential liberator, because the bondsman "runaway from this Adams when he got near the Chatahouchie River" and then aimed for Pensacola on his own before being apprehended.[121]

Slave stealers posed a significant threat to slaveowners everywhere, but the Southern frontier was particularly vulnerable given its inchoateness. In one instance, after a wave of slave thefts swept across the Deep South, the editors of the *Pensacola Gazette* felt the responsibility to warn readers of the threat as their city was likely to be visited by these gangs of "kidnappers." The paper declared "that the owners of young negroes should be on their guard." While every slaveholding community was vulnerable, the situation in Pensacola was dire. "From the very nature of our location on the seaboard and upon the great route of northern and southern travel, we are perhaps more exposed than almost any other place, to the visits of kidnappers, itinerant gamblers and other rogues." The editors did not intend to create unnecessary panic but felt they had a responsibility "to caution the community to be on the lookout."[122]

Despite the best efforts of local media, slaveowners failed to eliminate the plague of slave stealers as their desperate attempts to inform the public of the provenance of their human capital indicate. Elizabeth Humphyville of Mobile knew the man who stole Ann, a nineteen-year-old bondswoman who "was far advanced in pregnancy." Humphyville also knew the thief took the servant on the stage road to Pensacola; thus, she alerted the city's residents of the pair's imminent arrival. Worried about a potential sale, she added, "The public are cautioned not to trade for her as the titles to said woman is in me alone."[123] Richard Head lost the bondswoman Ailsey and her eight-month-old daughter to William W. McHahan of Irvington, Alabama. Besides Pensacola, Head suspected the bandit might attempt to sell the slaves in Georgia, Louisiana, Mississippi, or Alabama, and thus tried to alert prospective buyers in each of these locations, avowing, "The public is cautioned from trading for said woman and child, as no person but myself has, or ever had, any legal titles to said negroes."[124]

In antebellum Florida, slave stealers stayed one step ahead of authorities in a number of ways. First, with limited public funding as a result of the territory's and state's modest population, even the largest communities lacked the resources required to hunt and house criminals. In Pensacola, for example, the county jail, which was the bottom floor of the city constable's two-story home, was an insecure facility that criminals escaped from regularly.[125] In one memorable case, the deputy marshal of the West Florida Territory advertised in the *Pensacola Gazette:* "One Hundred Dollars Reward. ESCAPED from the custody of the Marshal on the night of the 29th day of March last, William Hambleton who was convicted of negro stealing and fined by the Jury the sum of seven Hundred Dollars, & costs of prosecution."[126] Second, ordinary citizens showed little enthusiasm for the pursuit and prosecution of a group of frontier bandits who posed no threat to their lives or property. In the most thorough examination of crime and punishment in antebellum Florida, John Denham found that throughout the entire antebellum era, Escambia County jurors found only two suspects guilty of slave stealing, suggesting that most of Pensacola's population was resigned to the particular crime.[127] A local writer amplified the apathy of the people after a jury found a man named Price innocent of the charge of slave stealing despite evidence to the contrary. The editorial concluded, "Under all the circumstances, the verdict of the jury, we believe, gives general satisfaction."[128]

The efforts of one of Pensacola's most dedicated lawmen to destroy a notorious gang of slave stealers on the eve of the Civil War illuminate the threat to slaveowners' property on the Southern frontier. After the disappearance of several bondsmen belonging to a contractor on the Pensacola and Montgomery Railroad, two armed vigilante groups set out from Pensacola in opposite directions. One posse headed east toward Tallahassee, while another, led by Sheriff Joseph Crosby, went to New Orleans and arrested Bernard Kending, a slave trader who had recently purchased three bondspeople in Pensacola valued at six thousand dollars. Kending denied any knowledge of having purchased stolen goods and claimed he had "no information as to the whereabouts of his negroes," but Crosby persisted. After searching the Crescent City for several weeks, he traveled on a steamboat to "one of the upper parishes and found the three boys alive and kicking."[129] Eventually, Crosby and his men jailed eight suspects in Pensacola for slave stealing, "proving that there has existed for the last two years, in our very midst, an organized gang of negro stealers." Estimates varied, though some claimed that as many as thirty men belonged to the "well drilled and disciplined" criminal syndicate that stretched from Texas to Florida.[130]

Any sense of security derived from the sheriff's heroic efforts was short-lived, for several days after their incarceration the eight suspects escaped. When it happened, eyewitnesses reported "a mighty noise, like the roaring of a fierce lion," coming from the city jail as the prisoners smashed the jail door and took to the streets. Bystanders watched as "a number of broad rimmed hats were seen flying back from the heads of an innumerable throng of the male sex, revealing faces whose every feature betrayed the greatest possible amount of excitement. With arms outstretched, and mouths wide open, onward they came, gaining speed every moment." Residents reacted to the news of the jailbreak passively. Because Sheriff Crosby was ill and unable to pursue the escapees, he beseeched the city's inhabitants to pursue the outlaws in his stead, but the plea fell on deaf ears. The *Pensacola Gazette* reported days later that no attention "has been paid to his message, and no steps taken to catch the runaways."[131]

The insouciance of Pensacola's citizens toward slave stealers just before the South seceded from the United States largely to protect the institution of slavery proves that on the Southern frontier slaveowners' hegemony was incomplete. As runaway slave advertisements and other evidence attest, enslaved people and their free allies continued to resist slavery in the decades after the United States' acquisition of Florida. As a result, antebellum slaveowners, like their colonial predecessors, failed to stem the tide of fugitive slaves to and from the city. To be sure, the number of bondspeople who made their way to Pensacola or escaped from it represents only a fraction of the number of enslaved people in the city and vicinity, and the number of fugitive slaves who actually won their freedom must represent an even much smaller percentage; nevertheless, the efforts of these insurgents were not made in vain. In several high-profile cases, fugitive slaves from Pensacola joined the acrimonious sectional debate on slavery and helped move the republic closer to a referendum on the institution when they climbed aboard the Underground Railroad and with the assistance of Northern abolitionists and a variety of Southern allies made a heroic bid for freedom.

◄ 5 ►

╢ UNDERGROUND RAILROAD ╟

IN JUNE 1850, after discovering a fugitive slave from Pensacola named Adam hiding aboard the *Mary Farrow*, Captain Warren prepared for a keelhauling, an archaic punishment performed by throwing victims overboard and dragging them by a rope underneath the boat's keel. The crew, which seems to have played a part in Adam's concealment, stopped the chastisement from taking place, however, "and the slave remained on board unmolested during the remainder of the passage."[1] When the vessel reached its destination at Portsmouth, New Hampshire, several weeks later, Captain Warren went ashore for the authorities. In his absence, a group of abolitionists climbed aboard the brig and in an effort to locate the stowaway conversed with the crew and several passengers, "some of whom sympathized deeply with the slave."[2] Led by Benjamin Cheever, a "local manager of the celebrated underground railroad," the abolitionists made their intentions clear.[3] They had come to rescue the black captive.

What happened next is difficult to determine exactly, though it was the type of altercation that became increasingly common across the United States in the middle of the nineteenth century. Captain Warren returned to his ship, and Adam, fearing a return to slavery, "sprang with all the desperate energy of the flying fugitive," leaping overboard into the abolitionists' boat waiting below. The "friends of freedom" then raced to the shore until they were overtaken by another small craft carrying Captain Warren. In an instant, "Adam was seized, and after receiving a stunning blow on the head from Capt. W., was dragged back into the vessel."[4] The abolitionists rushed to the city and enlisted the services of a sympathetic local official, who served a writ upon the captain affecting the prisoner's release. Moments later, Adam disembarked from the

Mary Farrow and with the assistance of his new friends made his way to "the free dominions of Queen Victoria in the North."[5]

Adam's story is truly extraordinary. Just days before, the twenty-one-year-old bondsman was bending iron and steel on the dry dock at the Pensacola Navy Yard. An enslaved blacksmith who lived and worked apart from his owner, some considered him "nearly 'free,'" but Adam surely took umbrage at the fact that the government paid his daily wage of one dollar to his owner.[6] Like countless brave bondspeople before him, Adam exploited Pensacola's proximity to the water and its transient population of sailors and seamen to abscond from the city. Two things, however, separate him from nearly every other slave who ran away from Pensacola in the decades before the Civil War. First, he reached freedom successfully in Canada several thousands of miles away. Second, he did so by riding the rails of the legendary Underground Railroad.

As is now well known, by the 1830s groups of radical abolitionists had begun coordinating efforts to assist fugitive slaves who were en route from the South to the North, Canada, and other places that outlawed slavery. This clandestine network—which earned its nickname because of its success in spiriting bondspeople away from their unsuspecting owners with the speed of a train—was a relatively modest venture until the fall of 1850 when the U.S. Congress passed the Fugitive Slave Act in an effort to stem the tide of runaways from the South. For abolitionists, the federal directive was a declaration of war against slavery's enemies, but instead of backing down, they continued at great personal risk to defy local, state, and federal laws in order to deliver slaves to freedom.[7]

Because of Pensacola's distance from the major axes of abolitionism, fugitive slaves from the city rode the Underground Railroad less frequently than their counterparts in the politically divided borderlands between the North and South; nevertheless, in two separate incidents, fugitive slaves from Pensacola who did ride the Underground Railroad had a powerful impact on the United States in the two decades before the Civil War. In the first incident, seven bondsmen from the Pensacola Navy Yard fled to the British West Indies with the assistance of their friend and former employer Jonathan Walker, a pious and impoverished ship captain from New Bedford, Massachusetts. In the second incident, an enslaved laborer and serial runaway known as Columbus Jones stowed away on a ship headed for New England, where upon his arrival he became one of the most famous fugitive slaves in the United States during the late antebellum period. In each of these celebrated cases, fugitive slaves from Pensacola failed to obtain their freedom despite having gained passage aboard the Underground Railroad; nevertheless, by upholding the long tradition of slave flight on the Southern frontier, they and their allies amplified the cross-sectional interracial attack on slavery and thus brought the nation closer to a day or reckoning for having sanctioned and supported the institution.

With emerald-green waves that roll softly along the Pensacola shore, the Gulf of Mexico was an inviting space for enslaved people in search of a gateway to freedom; it was, however, like every other body of water that bordered the antebellum South, an exceedingly dangerous place for fugitive slaves. Slaveowners and their associates kept a watchful eye on the black men and women who put out to sea; therefore, even for those slaves who managed to stow away on an oceangoing vessel and remain undetected for a considerable amount of time after pulling up anchor, it was nearly impossible to escape from any part of the antebellum South—including its frontier.

There are numerous examples of failed slave escapes from Pensacola that demonstrate just how far beyond the Gulf Coast slaveowners' power extended. In 1856, the British ship *Sarah* departed Pensacola for Barcelona, Spain, with nearly half a million feet of lumber, but about one hundred miles from the Florida shore, Captain Alfred Martin "discovered" a black stowaway and ordered the vessel to return to the port.[8] Slaveowners rejoiced at the news, calling Martin's actions "noble and praiseworthy," but they admitted his pro-slavery sentiments were seldom shared by "some of our Northern Captains who have visited this port."[9] Four months later, a bondsman belonging to Captain Walter Cozzens absconded from the Pensacola waterfront and for several weeks "all attempts to ascertain his whereabouts or the direction of his flight, were unavailing." In December, Cozzens received a letter from Captain George Murray of the brig *Amonoosuck*. He wrote from Panama, "I found a negro stowed away in my brig four days after I left Pensacola, and I believe he belongs to you, or, at all, events, to somebody in Pensacola. But, unfortunately for the negro, I was not imbued with Abolition principles, so that I made his freedom of short duration, and put him aboard of the U.S. sloop-of-war Cyane, to be returned to Pensacola." Again, slaveowners celebrated the news. One editorialist mocked abolitionists' efforts to aid and abet fugitive slaves, suggesting the case was proof of the existence of "an 'underground railway' running in the wrong direction—with a conductor of the wrong stripe."[10]

The arrest and rendition of fugitive slaves on the high seas was a routine occurrence in the antebellum South, which explains why the incidents involving the *Sarah* and *Amonoosuck* failed to attract national attention. In the middle of the nineteenth century, what captured the glare of the public spotlight and infused public debate were extraordinary cases of slave flight in which enslaved Southerners received the assistance of free Northerners.[11] These dramatic tales appealed to a mass audience in both sections as they provided pro-slavery and antislavery forces with ammunition to use in their escalating war of words over slavery.[12] Among them were separate instances involving fugitive slaves from Pensacola, which centered on the actions of two of the city's most notorious residents, the free white abolitionist Jonathan Walker and the enslaved black freedom fighter Columbus Jones.

Besides providing great drama, these two episodes are instructive as they demonstrate how the Underground Railroad functioned in Southern communities like Pensacola that produced fugitive slaves regularly. According to Keith Griffler, the Underground Railroad functioned in two different ways. "Frontline struggles" were extraordinarily dangerous interactions involving abolitionists and enslaved people that took place inside or along the edges of the South, while "support operations" occurred much farther away in the North. Though contrasting, each type of activity represented a threat to slavery that was cross-sectional, interracial, and, as the following cases attest, existential.[13]

Jonathan Walker was a citizen of the world, having traveled extensively throughout Europe, Asia, and the Americas, but he identified himself primarily as a Northerner.[14] The son of a Cape Cod mill operator, Walker received little formal education and decided early on a life at sea. Between long-distance ocean voyages, Walker worked as a shipwright in New Bedford, Massachusetts, which, besides serving as the whaling capital of the world for much of the nineteenth century, was a well-known asylum for fugitive slaves. In the decades before the Civil War, the city's residents provided sanctuary for countless runaways, including Frederick Douglass.[15] Shortly after arriving in New Bedford a local businessman, who would provide Douglass with his new surname, informed the bondsman that no slaveowner would ever lay their hands upon Douglass again as the people of New Bedford "would lay down their lives, before such an outrage could be perpetrated."[16]

Inhabiting a multiracial community that displayed great hostility toward slavery explains in part why Walker devoted much of his life to its destruction. Undoubtedly, one of the first significant steps in this direction came in 1831 when Walker purchased a subscription to William Lloyd's Garrison's *Liberator,* the first newspaper in the United States that called for the immediate abolition of slavery.[17] Another came in the fall of 1835, when after opening a correspondence with Benjamin Lundy, Garrison's mentor and a leading proponent of African American emigration, Walker sailed to Mexico's Gulf Coast to evaluate its potential as a colony for freed slaves. Hopeful of finding a peaceful resort, what he found instead was a country in turmoil as a result of Texas's War of Independence. Widespread hatred of U.S. citizens may have played a part in a violent assault on Walker, his eldest son, and a friend by a gang of armed robbers who left Walker with musket balls in his wrist and stomach. Penniless and thousands of miles away from home, Walker and his son headed for the southern coast of the United States, stopping briefly in Pensacola, before returning to Massachusetts; however, a growing demand for labor along the Gulf Coast brought Walker, his wife, and their seven children back to the region several years later.[18]

In Pensacola, Walker endeared himself to some of the city's most prominent residents; they turned against him, however, after learning he "was on good terms with the colored people." Public officials twice met with Walker, who years later recalled of the ensuing conversations, "It was intimated that there was danger in regard to my peace and safety, for should the people be excited in consequence of my discountenance of some of their rules and customs respecting the association of white with colored men, it would be out of their power to shield me from *violence.*"[19] Fearful for his family's safety, Walker relocated his wife and children back to Massachusetts, but he soon returned to the Gulf Coast, splitting his time between Pensacola and Mobile while working as a shipwright and shipwreck salvager.[20]

Despite the threats on his life, Walker continued to associate with African Americans and on several occasions came to their defense. In the spring of 1840, for example, a black sailor named William Cook landed in Pensacola's jail shortly after disembarking from a schooner on suspicion of being a runaway.[21] Six months later, because no one stepped forward to claim ownership of the prisoner, jailer Peter Woodbine moved Cook into his own house and for nearly a year "confined him in a garret by a chain." Sick and near death, Cook eventually received his release from Woodbine's custody at which time he arrived on Walker's doorstep in desperate need of medical attention. Walker nursed Cook back to "tolerable good health" and implored him to leave the city immediately; however, Woodbine barred Cook's departure, claiming the former prisoner owed more than two hundred dollars in court costs and "for being advertized in the Pensacola Gazette." To collect the debt, Woodbine leased Cook to the U.S. government, which put him to work alongside the hundreds of enslaved black laborers and mechanics at the Navy Yard. The episode infuriated Walker, who saw his friend and fellow seaman "bound with irons one year, his health nearly destroyed—burdened with lawyer's, doctor's, printer's, kidnappers' bills and jail fees; and then compelled by the administration of these laws, to work for the government to pay the cost!" Worst of all, this was no isolated incident. It was, Walker avowed, "one of the many occurrences of a similar character which are constantly taking place."[22]

Outraged with what he witnessed on a daily basis, Walker volunteered as a stationmaster on the Florida line of the Underground Railroad, and in doing so revealed the ad hoc and informal nature of the subversive network. Whereas pioneering Underground Railroad historian Larry Gara revealed abolitionists who late in life exaggerated their roles in assisting fugitive slaves, Walker's humility and the obvious need to protect the identity of the people he helped kept him from detailing his activities fully;[23] nevertheless, he admitted that while living in Pensacola, "he had for a long time been of the opinion that he would aid slaves to secure their liberty, if opportunity offered." A local paper confirmed Walker's subversive activities when it reported his role in helping two bondspeople escape on board a vessel several years before becoming a prominent national figure.[24]

In the summer of 1844, irrefutable proof of Walker's work on the Underground Railroad became public when several bondsmen approached the egalitarian ship captain and asked if he would help them escape to the North. Walker answered affirmatively, though he insisted the group sail instead to the Bahamas, a small group of islands off the East Florida coast where the British government had abolished slavery a decade earlier. Besides its proximity to Pensacola, Walker knew the Bahamas offered another significant advantage to fugitive slaves. Because "fleeing from slavery was not a crime under British law," write two historians of slave flight in antebellum South Florida, "escaped slaves arriving in British territories like Canada and the Bahamas could not be claimed by their masters."[25]

The dangerous journey began late in the evening on July 22 when the bondsmen fled from the Navy Yard and, after making their way to Pensacola, boarded Walker's thirty-foot-long whaleboat and set sail. The vessel traveled southward, rounding the western edge of Santa Rosa Island, before heading into the Gulf of Mexico. The voyage started auspiciously, but by the fifth day Walker succumbed to extreme heat exhaustion and fell in and out of consciousness while his passengers began suffering from the lack of adequate supplies. Still, the group persisted, and a week later Walker's distinctive green-and-gray schooner approached the southern tip of Florida, bringing the vessel within a day of its destination. At the same time handbills appeared throughout Pensacola offering rewards of up to one hundred dollars for the capture of each of the bondsmen and one thousand dollars for Walker—the supposed ringleader.[26]

Like runaway slave advertisements, the large posters provided detailed descriptions of the escaped bondsmen, who represented a cross section of Pensacola's enslaved labor force.[27] The brief semibiographical sketches began with the following: "MOSES JOHNSON is very black, with a full round face and pleasing expression—is stout built and about five feet four inches in height, talks rather rapidly and a little indistinctly—is fond of tobacco and occasionally drinks too much whiskey, is about 35 years of age, is a Blacksmith, basket maker and a great chopper." Charles, Phil, and Leonard Johnson were "excellent labourers" who resembled their older brother Moses except they were "younger-looking." Silas Scott was a short, "very muscular and considerably bow-legged" twenty-five-year-old who worked as a fisherman and dining room servant, while his younger brother, Harry, who was slightly taller and of a darker complexion, worked as a drayman. Anthony Catlett was a "well-built" thirty-year-old mulatto who, like the others, had a reputation as "an excellent labourer."[28]

The description of Walker was similarly subjective. The placard described him as a native of Cape Cod, Massachusetts, "where he has a wife and several children from whom he is said to have been absent

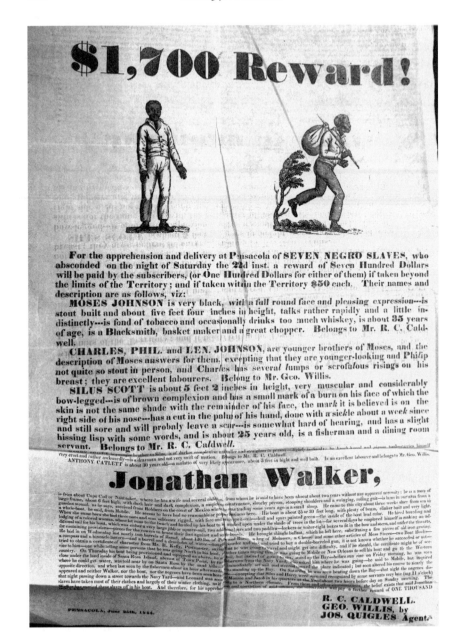

Copies of this large handbill appeared throughout Pensacola in the summer of 1844 after seven bondsmen fled to the Bahamas with the radical abolitionist Jonathan Walker. Courtesy of the National Archives.

almost two years without any apparent necessity." Walker was "a man of large frame, about 6 feet high, with dark hair and dark complexion, a suspicious countenance, slouchy person, stooping shoulders and a swinging, rolling gait." Before the disappearance of the seven bondsmen, witnesses saw Walker preparing for a long-distance trip. In addition to making an additional sail and gathering extra oars and paddles for his boat, he loaded the craft with "two barrels of Bread, about 120 lbs. of Pork and Bacon, a keg of Molasses, a Cheese and some other articles of Mess Stores—two Boat Hooks—a compass and a binnacle lantern—and a barrel and a demijohn of water—bought powder and shot and tried to buy a double-barrel gun." Whether he succeeded in actually purchasing the weapon was "not known."[29]

Local media assumed Walker's guilt because of his reputation as a radical. "The most daring and impudent outrage upon the peace and dignity of the Territory is thought to have been perpetrated," the first editorial to address the incident in the *Pensacola Gazette* began, "by the abduction of seven negro slaves on the night of Saturday last." Walker was the only suspect in the case, and, as far as most city residents were concerned, the evidence was damning. While working as a superintendent at the city's railroad depot, Walker "had frequent occasions to have negroes to work for him, and he associated with them on terms of equality and intimacy, seating them with him at his table whilst his daughter (half-grown girls) waited on the table." What is more, Walker "took lodgings with a quatroon woman" and attended an integrated church where he "preached to the negroes and exhorted them with great brotherly affection—telling them that they were just as good as he was, and that the difference of colour was a mere shadow, &c." If that was not enough, witnesses saw Moses Johnson with Walker the week before the escape, "lying under the trees in the lot, where he was working on his boat nearly all of the day."[30]

To arrest Walker and recover the men they considered valuable commodities, the three men who claimed ownership of the missing bondsmen—Byrd C. Willis, George Willis, and Marine Corps Second Lieutenant Robert C. Caldwell—looked to the federal government, and given their close ties to the Pensacola Navy Yard there was every reason to expect an accommodating response.[31] They were, however, mistaken. The three men asked the commander of the Navy Yard to help them "rescue their property," going so far as to offer to provide the fuel for any federal vessels deployed on their behalf. But the Commandant of the Navy Yard, Captain E. A. F. Lavallette, affirmed "that he had no authority—that under no circumstances whatsoever could he employ any part of the public force for such a purpose." Outraged, the slaveowners fired off a series of letters to the president of the United States, John Tyler, and the secretary of state, John C. Calhoun, demanding clarification of the federal government's policy regarding the capture of fugitive slaves. The slaveowners considered their failure to receive "public aid" immediately an issue of great magnitude as it affected "the interest and safety of the whole South."[32]

Captain Lavallette's refusal to assist in the recovery of seven fugitive slaves and their abolitionist accomplice is significant for two separate reasons. First, it is another reminder of the federal government's complicated relationship with slavery in the antebellum era. As Don Fehrenbacher and other historians have shown convincingly, the U.S. government from its inception actively promoted slavery's expansion and in other ways protected the rights of slaveowners;[33] yet, individual federal agents and representatives—including sailors, soldiers, commissioners, and even Navy Yard commanders—had the ability to undermine slavery and often did when they were positioned in slaveholding territories. Second, it adds another dimension to the history of the Underground Railroad. Regardless of Lavallette's motivations, which remain unknown, he aided and abetted Walker and the seven bondsmen when he refused the request of three important and influential slaveowners. In the antebellum South, it was often relatively simple and mundane actions taken by anonymous or obscure people like Lavallette who time and again, regardless of intent, allowed fugitive slaves to try to, and in some cases, win their freedom.

Alas, this was not the case in the summer of 1844, for while Pensacola's slaveowners waited for a response from either the White House or the Department of State regarding Lavallette's conduct, another federal official had already intervened on their behalf. On the morning of July 8, Commander Eben Farrand of the U.S. steamer *Gen. Taylor* brought the full resources of the U.S. Navy to bear on the fugitives after their abduction by the captain of a civilian wrecker near the southern tip of Florida at Key West. Without hesitation, Farrand detained Walker and the suspected runaways and then sent them on separate vessels to Pensacola, where federal marshals took custody of each of the prisoners.[34]

From this point the lives of the captives took radically different turns. For the bondsmen a return to bondage was inevitable. Caldwell was the first to reclaim his property. Awaiting the arrival of Moses, Silas, and Harry at the Navy Yard, he took possession of each of them immediately after their disembarkation from the sloop *Reform*. Because Byrd and George Willis were away or otherwise indisposed, Deputy Marshal James Gonzalez locked Anthony Catlett and the three brothers Charles, Phil, and Leonard, in the city jail. During their incarceration, the city constable subjected each of the prisoners to such a brutal beating that when George Willis arrived to take custody of the three men several weeks later they limped from the building still "being very sore."[35]

Only Silas avoided a long life of servitude—though his freedom came at great cost. In September 1844, less than two months after running away with Walker, the short and heavily scarred bondsman returned to the city jail when, despite his reputation as "a trust-worthy, respectful and obedient servant in the Navy Yard," officials arrested him on suspicion of stealing.[36] Unwilling to submit to a jailhouse beating for a second time, Silas took his life in a gruesome fashion.[37] There were no eyewitnesses to the act, but Walker, who sat in an adjacent cell at the time and later caught a glimpse of the gory crime scene, remembered, "On one side of the room, much of the floor was stained with the blood of a slave, who had three days before committed suicide by cutting open his belly and throat with a razor." Walker added, "This was one of the seven slaves whom I had vainly endeavored to save from bondage, and on whose account I was now imprisoned."[38]

Unlike the runaways who suffered in silence and faded quickly from the limelight, Walker's fate was determined in the public eye and thus contributed to his becoming the focus of local, national, and international attention. "When the prisoner landed on the wharf the crowd was immense," read one account, and as soon as a deputy took Walker to the local magistrate a "crowd thronged the streets and side-walks, and the court-room was filled to overflowing with a highly excited mass of people."[39] For the next four months, Walker sat chained to the floor of a tiny jail cell awaiting his trial before the U.S. District Court. In November, a jury took just a few hours to convict him on four counts of stealing "goods and chattels" from their owners. The punishment handed down by the federal court included the following: paying a one-hundred-fifty dollar fine and additional court costs; standing in the pillory in front of the courthouse on the corner of the town square for one hour; and having the letters S. S., which stood for Slave Stealer, branded into the palm of his right hand.[40]

Given the subaltern population of the Southern frontier, it is expected that Pensacola's authorities faced public opposition when they attempted to carry out the branding of a lowly seaman for having assisted fugitive slaves. On the morning of November 16, 1844, the day scheduled for the chastisement, officials needed to manufacture a special brand for the occasion, but "it was no easy task to get one made." They asked a local blacksmith whose shop stood adjacent to the courthouse; however, he "indignantly refused to do such work," declaring that brands were for "cattle and hogs, but not for men." The officials then asked the artisan if they could use his furnace to heat the iron they intended for the brand, "but even this too he denied to the Government of the United States." It was an act of defiance, one that belies any notion that in the antebellum South slaveowners' hegemony went unchallenged.[41]

Still, despite the actions of one defiant citizen, Walker's punishment took place after authorities found another blacksmith willing to fabricate the brand in a makeshift furnace built inside the courthouse. After securing Walker's right hand to a railing inside the "prisoner's box," U.S. Marshal Ebenezer Dorr pulled a red-hot iron from the fire and pressed it deep into Walker's palm, creating "a splattering noise, like a handful of salt in the fire." The branding was over within seconds. Walker's punishment, however, had only just begun. After returning to his cell, Walker learned that Byrd C. Willis, George Willis, and Robert C. Caldwell were now seeking damages of more than one hundred thousand dollars from Walker for depriving them of their laborers. It was an astronomical sum meant to keep the Underground Railroad activist behind bars for the rest of his life.[42]

Though facing a potential life sentence, Walker was encouraged on two accounts. First, his lengthy incarceration resulted in an outpouring of sympathy from many of Pensacola's residents. Among Walker's greatest allies were the city's Creoles. Walker informed readers that in Pensacola, "A large part of the inhabitants were Creoles (descendants of French and Spanish parents) and not generally so irresistibly devoted to the system of slavery as the American-born and bred citizens were." Consequently, during his incarceration, "this Creole population manifested more sympathy for me than the rest of the community did."[43]

Sailors were equally sympathetic, and Walker, an old salt himself, explained why. Men who spent their entire lives on the water at the mercy of tyrannical ship captains, murderous pirates, and deadly storms were, like bondspeople, a subject class that society threw "most shamefully into the scale of oppression, wrong, and neglect." Consequently, sailors identified with all oppressed people and demonstrated a willingness "to run any risk or make any sacrifice in aid of their suffering fellow-beings." Walker learned of their extraordinary generosity during his incarceration, as sailors and at least one naval officer who resided locally visited him to express their sympathy, while others from distant ports sent letters of support and cash donations for his family and his defense fund. Walker recalled of the seamen who reached out to one of their own while behind bars, "To such I am indebted, more than others, for their active and manifest sympathies toward me when in prison and in chains."[44]

The second reason for Walker to remain hopeful was that shortly after his incarceration a local defender began forwarding the details of Walker's case to William Lloyd Garrison's *Liberator*, which transformed "the hero of Pensacola" into a cause célèbre of the transatlantic abolitionist movement.[45] In the coming months, Walker's name appeared in newspapers, journals, and pamphlets across the United States, making him, like other "slave rescuers" described by Steven Lubet and Stanley Harrold, one of the most recognizable figures in American abolitionist culture.[46] At first, most of the accounts offered readers biographical information of Walker and his family while providing a play-by-play of his trial and imprisonment. Increasingly, however, the articles focused on describing the fund-raising rallies abolitionists held throughout the North in support of Walker and other suffering abolitionists, including Charles Torrey, another Massachusetts native who, like Walker, was imprisoned in the South for assisting fugitive slaves.[47]

In one memorable gathering the renowned abolitionist orator Wendell Phillips addressed a massive crowd at a downtown Boston church just days before Walker's branding. The lecture began with Phillips urging his audience not to take for granted the liberty they enjoyed, for in the South several of the "sons of New-England" had lost their freedom while spreading "the genius of liberty" throughout the land. He then launched into an assault against both the church and state as neither institution offered a "remedy for slavery." Phillips rebuked the Christian church for tolerating bondage and "thus sanctioning concubinage, trampling on the marriage institution, and striking hands with the oppressors." He vilified American Christians for "the sentiment that was prevalent in the land, that it is better to obey man than God—that legislative enactments are paramount to the Christian precepts, and should be obeyed." Phillips offered Walker as the rare individual who responded to a higher authority. As for the state, Walker's captivity exposed its debasement, because "it was in the hold of a national vessel that he was confined and carried to Pensacola—it was within the walls of a national prison that he was incarcerated—it was a national brand that was on his fetters." Phillips closed by renouncing rhetorically his citizenship in a nation dedicated to the defense of slavery and then roared defiantly, "I hail and am proud to unite with those whose rallying-cry is, 'NO UNION WITH SLAVEHOLDERS!'"[48]

Support for Walker stretched across the Atlantic as some of the world's leading abolitionists rallied to his cause. At a meeting of the British and Foreign Anti-Slavery Society in London, the organization's president Thomas Clarkson—who spearheaded the decades-long movement to abolish the slave trade across the Atlantic and slavery in the British West Indies—led a public rally in support of Walker. The group issued a resolution expressing their sympathy with the American abolitionist "for having aided or attempted to aid some of their countrymen in their escape from bondage" and denouncing the pro-slavery laws that sanctioned his imprisonment "as utterly disgraceful to a civilized community, and in the highest degree repugnant to the spirit and precepts of the gospel." The organization's secretary John Scoble forwarded a copy of the resolution to Walker, informing him that his efforts to "deliver some of your fellow-men from the sufferings and degradation of slavery" were not "unknown to the Abolitionists in Great Britain" who trusted "that the efforts which are to be made for your deliverance from the power of evil men and evil laws, will be succeeded by the divine blessing." Shocked by the international attention his case received, Walker wrote from his cell to the British and Foreign Anti-Slavery Society thanking its members for their support, though he admitted the impossibility of expressing "the feelings which the reception of the letter and resolution excited."[49]

Walker's lionization infuriated slavery's defenders, who considered it proof of the widening gap between Northern extremists and

Southern moderates. One Southern commentator explained, "To deny to the people of the north the right to entertain and to express opinions unfavorable and unfriendly to the institution of the south, would be to be unreasonable and unkind, as they have too unfrequently shown themselves towards us; erroneous opinion should be met with facts and argument, not with angry denunciation." The writer then asserted that Northern newspapers like the *Liberator* spread falsehoods about Walker's case, especially regarding his treatment when in custody; in reality, the suspect had a trial "as fair and impartial a trial as ever was accorded to a person accused; was found guilty upon the clearest and most satisfactory of evidence, upon four separate indictments, and was sentenced to nearly the lightest punishment which the law would permit."[50] Another Southern sympathizer concurred, avowing that Walker should "'thank his stars' for having got off so lightly." The findings of the Pensacola jury were "an instance of mercy and forbearance unparalleled in the history of judicial proceedings," considering they were reached "in the face of all the vituperation and malignant abuse that has been showered upon the South, in abolition meetings at Boston, and elsewhere at the North."[51]

International support for Walker was particularly troubling for Floridians who remembered Great Britain's role in establishing Negro Fort during the War of 1812. Shortly after learning of Walker's communication with British abolitionists, Florida's Territorial Legislative Council in a widely circulated protest decried the intervention of "foreign states" in domestic concerns. The council's members regarded the right of passing laws and punishing the violators of those laws "as amongst the clearest and most valuable rights of a free people, and the interference of foreign states with the exercise of that right, as insulting and unwarrantable and that it should be repelled promptly and indignantly." Walker's relationship with foreign abolitionists confirmed that conspirators were still plotting the overthrow of slavery in the South. "It can no longer be denied that systematic and powerful influences are at work throughout a large portion of Europe and many parts of our own country," the diatribe continued, "to involve ourselves and the unconscious objects of this false philanthropy in one common ruin." The international reaction to Walker's incarceration was further proof that "a vicious fanaticism, clothed in the garb of religion, is prowling around our borders, and by means of its more reckless and abandoned instruments, invading our in-most sanctuaries, whose direct purposes, scarcely concealed, are to deluge our very hearth-stones in blood, and to rear an altar to its false principles upon the ruin of all that is precious to us as freemen and dear to us as men." The only justifiable response was to defend the lives of slaveowners by any means necessary: "Self-protection is the primary law, and we shall stand justified, in the eyes of God and of man, in defending ourselves from unjust aggressions, though the means of safety may bring punishment and suffering where it is not most deserved."[52]

Though few predicted it at the time, Walker's greatest attack on slavery came after abolitionists secured his release from the Pensacola jail and published several autobiographical accounts of his experiences while in Florida. The first and most popular was *Trial and Imprisonment of Jonathan Walker, at Pensacola, Florida, for Aiding Slaves to Escape from Bondage*. Published by the American Anti-Slavery Society in Boston, the 119-page tract went through four editions between 1845 and 1850 and appeared in serial form widely in both the United States and England.[53] The book shared much in common with the *Narrative of the Life of Frederick Douglass, an American Slave*, which the American Anti-Slavery Society also published for the first time in 1845. But while Frederick Douglass's narrative illuminated the horrors of slavery from the point of view of an enslaved black Southerner, Walker's offered readers the perspective of a free white Northerner.[54] In the words of Maria Weston Chapman, an executive member of the American Anti-Slavery Society who, after referring to the United States Constitution as "an eternal wrong" for supporting slavery, added, "The narrative of Frederick Douglass gives a picture of the condition of a slave in the land that their folly and their fear betrayed. That of Jonathan Walker shows the condition of the freeman whose lot is cast in the same land, little more than half a century only after the perpetration of that treason to humanity."[55]

In addition to documenting the terrible fate that awaited any free citizen who dared enter the South and subvert its peculiar institution, *Trial and Imprisonment* demonstrated the extraordinary length slaveowners and local authorities went to discipline bondspeople who ran away or in other ways refused to accept their status. According to Walker, the small two-story brick public jail located just beyond the city's northeast perimeter provided a number of important services. It was a holding cell for many of the sailors and other scoundrels who drank, gambled, and fought in excess; it also served as a temporary home of more serious offenders—thieves, robbers, rapists, and murderers—who awaited

trial, or, in rare cases, execution. But it functioned primarily as a public space where marshals, sheriffs, jailers, and other law enforcement
officials employed violence daily to discipline intractable black men
and women.[56] The viciousness with which jail authorities punished
bondspeople shocked Walker, who in spite of the harsh treatment he
received, admitted it was "better than that which fell to the lot of the
other prisoners."[57]

During his eleven-month incarceration Walker witnessed the corporal punishment of some two dozen bondspeople, most of whom
received a peculiar punishment known as paddling. In the cruel ritual,
a jail official tied black prisoners at the wrists and forced them to lie
on the ground in the fetal position. With the prisoners' knees forced
through the opening between their arms, the officer inserted either a
stick or broom handle behind the knees and over the arms of the prisoner, leaving them "in a doubled and helpless condition." The officer
then stripped the prisoners of their clothing from the waist down and
rolled them onto their side and applied a long flat wooden paddle—or
board—forcefully to their backsides as many as fifty times, "stopping
at short intervals to allow the sufferer to answer such questions as are
asked, or make such promises as it thought best to exhort; and to give
the numbness which has been excited by repeated blows, time to sub-
side, which renders the next blows more acute and painful." After the
paddling, the jailor often applied the "raw-hide switch" to the "bruised
and blistered parts, with as many or more blows laid on." The jailer
usually worked in the presence of slaveowners who ordered and often
directed the castigation. There was, Walker concluded, "no precise rule
to be observed in regard to punishment, but the masters and mistresses
are the sole judges as to method and quantity; and whenever the paddle
is brought in requisition, it means that the raw-hide (more commonly
called cow-hide) is not equal to the offence."[58]

The case of one fugitive slave described in Walker's narrative proved
how jailhouse beatings not only failed as a deterrent but at times had
the opposite effect. In the winter of 1845, Walker noted the imprisonment of an older bondsman two separate times over the course of three
months. During each stint in the jail, the constable flogged the prisoner with both the paddle and cowhide, leaving the prisoner sick for
days. Through jailhouse conversations, Walker learned that over the
Christmas holiday, the bondsman had visited his family on a farm thirty

miles north of Pensacola with his owner's permission; he was late in
returning, however, which landed him behind bars for the first time.
After several weeks the owner removed him from the jail and sent him
to New Orleans for sale. "But being too old to meet with a ready sale in
that market, he was returned again the 1st of April, and lodged in jail
until the 12th, when his mistress came there in a rage, under the influence of liquor, and caused him to be flogged." During the "performance"
that followed, the mistress "stood by and gave directions to the operator, yelping all the while at the mangled victim of her anger." In spite
of the concerted efforts of the slaveowners and jailer, neither incarceration nor violent retribution had the desired effect. To the contrary, both
seemed to steel the bondsman's resolve to escape a life of bondage, for
subsequent to the jailhouse thrashing his owners took him to Mobile
and again offered him for sale. "He did not meet with a market, and was
sent back," Walker informed, "but soon after his return escaped from his
tormentors, and I have since heard no more of him."[59]

Like published slave narratives, *Trial and Imprisonment* brought fame,
if not fortune, to its author, but it was the visual image included on the
publication's frontispiece that provided the abolitionist movement with
one of its most recognizable icons.[60] In August 1845, just weeks after
his release from jail, Walker entered a popular Boston studio where a
professional photographer made a daguerreotype of his branded hand,
with the capital letters "S. S. clearly demarcated, that local printers committed immediately to an engraving."[61] The image exploded across abolitionist print culture, appearing on the cover of *Trial and Imprisonment*
and in a wide variety of publications, including newspapers, broadsides,
and even a children's book. The *Liberator* introduced the image with the
sort of hyperbole that became typical: "Ponder it, fellow citizens, and
as you burn, and blush, and weep, at the disgrace of our country, the
indignity done to a worthy neighbor, and the misery of the poor slaves,
let the fire burn until your soul is enkindled in the high resolve, that the
letters on Jonathan Walker's hand shall be made to read—SALVATION
TO THE SLAVE." Below the icon, the *Liberator* published fifty-two lines
by the poet laureate John G. Whittier, assuring Walker's ascension into
the pantheon of abolitionist martyrs.[62]

Walker's iconic appendage made him a prominent albeit unusual
fixture on the abolitionist lecture circuit. While large crowds gathered
in public spaces typically to hear the voices of some of the nation's

TRIAL AND IMPRISONMENT

OF

JONATHAN WALKER,

AT PENSACOLA, FLORIDA,

FOR

AIDING SLAVES TO ESCAPE FROM BONDAGE.

WITH AN

APPENDIX,

CONTAINING A SKETCH OF HIS LIFE.

"All things whatsoever ye would that men should do unto you, do ye even so unto them. For this is the law and the prophets."

BOSTON:

PUBLISHED AT THE ANTI-SLAVERY OFFICE,
25 Cornhill.
1845.

The frontispiece reproduces an engraving of Jonathan Walker's branded hand that later appeared widely in abolitionist print culture. Jonathan Walker, *Trial and Imprisonment of Jonathan Walker, at Pensacola, Florida, for Aiding Slaves to Escape from Bondage* (1845). Courtesy of the Library of Congress.

greatest orators speak of the injustice of slavery, those that greeted Walker came to see his hand. A flawed public speaker, Walker rarely spoke to audiences for more than a few moments before descending from the podium and wading through the crowd with his outstretched hand so that attendees could get a closer look at the one-of-a-kind relic.[63] The effect on the assembly was profound. Frederick Douglass, who was among those affected, recalled years later, "I well remember the sensation produced by the exhibition of his branded hand. It was one of the few atrocities of slavery that roused the justice and humanity of the North to a death struggle with slavery."[64] Fergus Bordewich provides a more objective appraisal, concluding, "Walker's callused seaman's palm became an emblem of the entire abolitionist movement and, perhaps inevitably, of the Underground Railroad, the most riveting symbol both of the sacrifice that was demanded of men who dared to assist fugitive slaves, and of the punishment that awaited them if they were caught."[65]

For his part, Walker rejected his role as an historical artifact and quietly resumed his work on the Underground Railroad after returning to the North. In the spring of 1851, he alerted the readers of the *Liberator* of the arrival in Plymouth, Massachusetts, of two bondsmen and their families, including several small children. After escaping from an undisclosed part of the South, the fugitives had fled across the Mason-Dixon Line to Lancaster, Pennsylvania, but the constant fear of being kidnapped by slave catchers led them to seek refuge farther north in New England. It infuriated Walker that his Massachusetts neighbors offered little assistance to the desperate fugitives, who were unable to secure housing in Plymouth "solely because they are guilty of the unpardonable sin of being a fraction darker than most of our neighbors." Walker wondered, "Is there no escape—is there no avoiding—is there to be no end to this dastardly, cruel and infernal prejudice, in the vicinity of the *Puritan Rock?*" The "half-dozen" refugees eventually took up residence in Walker's small cabin alongside his wife and children, but the lack of food and heating made their stay a short one. Despite his best efforts, Walker's impoverishment hindered his abolitionist activities severely. "Others have come here," he lamented, "and gone away for the same reason."[66]

Walker never again set foot in Pensacola; nevertheless, the tracks of the Underground Railroad he helped lay along Florida's Gulf Coast continued to operate. Another famous case occurred on the eve of the Civil

War when a daring and defiant bondsman from Pensacola stowed away on a ship headed to Massachusetts. Apprehended and jailed shortly after disembarking at Hyannis Port, he became, like Walker before him, the touchstone of a sensational public trial that galvanized abolitionists to continue their war against slavery. "Of the unsuccessful attempts to escape," declared the American Anti-Slavery Society during the first year of the Civil War, "none became more notorious, or excited more attention, by reason of the issues coming to be involved in it, than that of COLUMBUS JONES, who left Pensacola on the 1st of May, 1859, on board a brig bound for Boston."[67]

Before fleeing to the North, Columbus Jones was notorious in Pensacola and the vicinity because of his involvement with one of the largest slave stealing syndicates to ever operate across the Deep South. As is often the case with fugitive slaves on the Southern frontier, whether Columbus was a victim of, or accomplice to, his own theft is difficult to determine. The *Pensacola Observer* argued for the latter, announcing in October 1857, "The negro boy Columbus, advertised by Mrs. S. A. Jones, agent for the heirs of Ambrose Jones has, after a long, troublesome and circumlatory process been recovered. This negro, it seems, was stolen while in the employ of Mr. Milner, on the Railroad about the 1st of August last.—Since then it appears he has been touring quite extensively under the protection of the thief, one Leonard Singletary." Available evidence suggested that the "peregrinations," or wanderings, of Columbus and Singletary lasted several months and stretched across the Florida border into Alabama and Georgia until "the negro was found in the possession of Wm. H. Hendley, near Cambleton, Jackson County Florida, who had purchased him of Judge Yelverton, of Elba, Coffee county, Ala., whose only title was derived from a bill of sale from Singletary—who had sold him for sundries amounting to $1,100." Singletary had a number of criminal associates who managed to avoid capture, which proved the existence of "a negro stealing organization hereabouts, and owners of such property cannot be too vigilant."[68]

Undeterred by his capture and re-enslavement, Columbus turned away from the Southern interior and instead headed toward the water. Upon arrival at the shore he climbed aboard the *Rolerson*, a swift-moving brig headed for Massachusetts, with a multiracial crew of freemen and at least one woman. Columbus remained hidden for several days in the ship's cargo, where crew members provided him with food and sustenance. When first mate John Orlando discovered Columbus on board, the bondsman confessed he was a runaway but avowed "he would never go back to slavery again alive." As the vessel continued north, Columbus disappeared below the deck, where "he was supplied with food as before by some of the crew." Orlando then ordered the closing of all hatches to cut off communication between Columbus and his co-conspirators. The strategy worked. After going without food or water for nearly twenty-four hours, Columbus landed in Orlando's custody for a second time. Still, he remained defiant. Throughout the remainder of the journey, Columbus "broke three sets of handcuffs, and was at last again ironed and chained in a caboose."[69]

When the *Rolerson* finally sailed into Hyannis Port, Columbus made one last desperate attempt at freedom—this time with the assistance of members of the crew, who made the impromptu decision to join the ranks of what Jonathan Shectman calls the Underground Railroad's "operational workforce."[70] Likely among them was a former slave from Pensacola named Thomas Walkins, a free black cook who worked on the *Rolerson* and admitted having known Columbus for several years. While Orlando disembarked from the brig to seek the counsel of the vessel's captain, Gorham Crowell, Columbus freed himself yet again, and "the crew not being at all opposed to his escape, was about making a raft to float himself to the shore, when he discovered a man in a boat some little distance from the brig, whom he hailed, and bargained with for a passage to the shore."[71] The crew watched Columbus leap from the brig "but pretended not to observe it, as their sympathies were with the runaway."[72] Columbus and his new companion sped toward land, but they were overtaken by a boat carrying Crowell and Orlando, who again detained the fugitive. Aware that the schooner *Elizabeth B.* was headed south, Crowell and Orlando paid the ship's captain, Edward Bacon, five hundred dollars to return Columbus to his owner in Pensacola. Soon the steamer set sail "with the slave chained to the capstan, and got off before the citizens of Hyannis had learned of the affair."[73]

By the time local abolitionists became aware of Columbus's attempt to reach the shore they were too late; nevertheless, they immediately pursued legal action against the men responsible for Columbus's rendition. Led by Francis W. Bird, the abolitionists complained to local authorities, who issued warrants for Crowell and Orlando and arrested both. Police also detained the owner of the *Rolerson*, John W. Baker, along with Captain Bacon, when he returned to Boston several weeks later. In September, the grand jury of Barnstable County indicted the four men on various counts of kidnapping and conspiracy. During the trial before the Suffolk County Superior Court, which took place over four long days in November 1859, the opposing sides took contrary positions regarding states' rights. Massachusetts prosecutor Baylies Sanford argued that state laws protecting individual liberty trumped federal laws protecting slavery. Columbus was a freeman, the prosecution insisted; therefore, his abduction and rendition violated the state law passed recently by the commonwealth's legislature that subjected those found guilty of kidnapping to ten years in prison and a one-thousand-dollar fine. The defendants' counsel, Caleb Cushing and H. A. Scudder, countered by asserting the supremacy of the U.S. Constitution over state laws in cases regarding slaveowners' property. It was, they maintained, the duty of citizens to recognize slaveowners' power over their bondspeople across state lines as the Constitution mandated.[74]

Much of the evidentiary portion of the trial that centered on Columbus's status as either a free or enslaved person derived from two primary sources. First was courtroom testimony provided by some two dozen witnesses, including Walkins; his mother, Eliza Mitchell, who also traveled on the brig from Pensacola to Massachusetts; and Andrew J. Jones, a representative of the family in Pensacola that claimed ownership of Columbus. The second source of testimony was a series of depositions recorded in Florida that arrived in Massachusetts just days before the trial began. Among the deponents were several additional members of Andrew Jones's family and the family's legal representative, as well as one of Columbus's former employers.

Like Walker's *Trial and Imprisonment*, the published accounts of the testimony provided a rare look at slavery on the Southern frontier. Born in Macon, Georgia, to Caswell and Annie Jones around 1840, Columbus and his mother were brought to Pensacola by their owner, Ambrose Jones, before his death in 1853, at which time his widow, Shada Ann Jones, inherited both Columbus and Annie. Over the course of several years, Shada Ann and her family leased Columbus and his mother to various employers in Pensacola. Eventually, the Jones family agreed on an arrangement with Columbus and Annie that "when they had time to themselves, they can work where they please." Annie worked as a "cook, washer, and ironer" in several homes, while Columbus was a jack-of-all-trades. In addition to working on vessels on the Pensacola dock, he toiled as a "common laborer" at the Pensacola Navy Yard and the Pensacola branch of the Alabama and Florida Railroad. According to Andrew Jones, "The wages earned by Columbus were paid to my father while he lived, since his death to my mother or to myself." Forced to forfeit his hard-earned wages, Columbus rebelled. Members of the Jones family often "saw him in the streets of Pensacola doing nothing" and in general considered him "a rather bad character." Several distinguishing scars across Columbus's back confirm his contemptuousness.[75]

The Jones family was fortunate to recover Columbus after he absconded from Pensacola with the area's most notorious gang of slave stealers, and, following his second escape attempt, they again demonstrated great determination to reclaim their property. After the *Rolerson* left Pensacola for Massachusetts and the family learned that Columbus was on board, they placed numerous advertisements in the local papers and "stuck up hand-bills all around the county." They also contacted legal representatives who dispatched a letter to the U.S. Marshal in Boston warning of the imminent arrival of the bondsman. The concerted efforts to reclaim their precious commodity paid off. In mid-May, roughly one month after Columbus embarked from the Gulf Coast, Andrew Jones traveled to Norfolk, where he "found" the runaway and then returned him to Pensacola.[76]

Like most fugitive slaves from Pensacola reclaimed by their owners or employers, the record is silent on Columbus's life following his return to the city. It is likely that he remained enslaved until the abolition of slavery during the Civil War several years later; nevertheless, his impact on the escalating national dialogue on slavery continued. Abolitionists added Columbus to the pantheon of antislavery martyrs when they invoked his name in widely read tracts and pamphlets they published in the years leading up to the Civil War.

Meanwhile back in Boston, Superior Court Chief Justice Charles Allen instructed the jury on the application of the law in respect to the two central issues in the case. The first concerned whether Columbus's rendition occurred within the boundaries of Barnstable County. The second focused on the process in which the defendants returned Columbus to the South. Allen affirmed the constitutional provision that allowed slaveowners to reclaim bondspeople across state lines but noted the state legislature "does not recognize it as a duty of citizens to take back an escaped slave into servitude." Several hours later the jury offered its verdict before a tense courtroom in which "every seat was occupied, and every inch of standing room was taken up." Insisting the prosecution failed to prove their argument that Columbus's seizure had occurred within county lines, it acquitted the four defendants. A final insult to the fugitive slave from Pensacola, sympathetic crew members, and abolitionist allies came when the announcement of the jury "was received with great applause, which the Court promptly checked."[77]

The reaction to the verdict underscores how in the middle of the nineteenth century abolitionism remained an extraordinarily unpopular sentiment throughout the entire United States. Even in Boston—the home of William Lloyd Garrison, the *Liberator,* and the New England Anti-Slavery Society, the precursor of the American Anti-Slavery Society—abolitionists represented only a fraction of the population. This meant that for bondspeople and those who sympathized with their plight the future was bleak. Slavery was a powerful institution protected by the law and supported by the majority of the people. Still, all was not lost.

As the cases of Jonathan Walker and Columbus Jones make clear, resistance to slavery was both extensive and enduring. On the Southern frontier in particular, enslaved people continued to walk, run, swim, and sail toward freedom, often with free people providing a variety of assistance. Because of the actions of fugitive slaves and their allies in seaports like Pensacola and countless other small towns and large cities across the United States, by the middle of the nineteenth century war clouds loomed on the nation's horizon. Casting an ominous dark shadow over the entire republic from the New England shore to Florida's Gulf Coast, they portended that the United States would no longer remain, in Abraham Lincoln's famous words, "permanently half slave and half free."[78]

Given the long tradition of slave flight in Pensacola, it is not surprising that the first fugitive slaves to seek refuge behind Union lines at the outbreak of the Civil War fled across Pensacola Bay to the Federal-occupied Fort Pickens on Santa Rosa Island in March 1861. They were, however, not the last. Over the next several weeks and months, Fort Pickens became a refuge for hundreds of runaways in search of food, shelter, and freedom. When Union forces stationed at the fort regained control over Pensacola and the surrounding areas in the second year of the war, the enduring interracial assault on slavery that had always existed on the Southern frontier reached a dramatic conclusion, as Northern soldiers joined Southern slaves in destroying both the Confederate army and the peculiar institution the Confederacy had been created to protect and defend.

CIVIL WAR

ACCORDING TO THE *Official Records of the Union and Confederate Armies,* the massive 128-volume collection of documents from the American Civil War, the first fugitive slaves from the Confederacy to seek refuge behind Union lines crossed Pensacola Bay and arrived at Fort Pickens in March 1861 approximately one month before the firing on Fort Sumter.[1] The four runaways, who were part of a larger group that disappeared into the muddy and mosquito-infested swamps and bayous surrounding Pensacola, were "under the delusion" that if they reached the Union-controlled fort, "they would be gladly received, their services accepted, and themselves eventually sent to the North, free citizens of a free country."[2] But they were mistaken. When the garrison's commander, Adam J. Slemmer, learned they were "entertaining the idea that we were placed here to protect them and grant them their freedom," he determined "to teach them the contrary."[3] The U.S. Army lieutenant placed the bondsmen in irons and delivered them to the Pensacola Navy Yard, where their owners whipped them "unmercifully." According to an eyewitness, the brutal punishment was necessary "in order to frighten the rest, for it was clearly proven that if they had succeeded, a gang of a hundred more were in readiness to follow."[4] Despite their efforts, Federal officials and local slaveowners failed to stop the flow of runaways to Fort Pickens. "That same night four more made their appearance," Slemmer grumbled, and "they were also turned over to the authorities next morning."[5]

Over the next several months, the stream of fugitive slaves from Pensacola became a flood as Fort Pickens became a destination of hundreds of bondspeople who offered their services to the invading Northern army. Among them was a "negro deserter" who was "for several years employed by his master as a pilot of this harbor." Eager to assist the

Federal forces, the absconded slave provided crucial intelligence on Confederate actions in Pensacola and the adjacent Navy Yard, including the location of rebel troops, guns, and ships. Colonel Harvey Brown, who replaced Slemmer as the fort's commander shortly after the start of the war, described the valuable informer thusly: "the man is intelligent and has given me considerable information." In an effort to secure the black mariner's services permanently, Brown requested the assistant adjutant-general in Washington provide him "secret-service money, to be expended at his discretion." Brown then announced his intentions regarding the growing number of refugees at Fort Pickens: "I shall not send the negroes back, as I will never be voluntarily instrumental in returning a poor wretch to slavery."[6] Brown was not an abolitionist; nevertheless, the West Point graduate took an uncompromising stance against slavery.[7] And he was not alone.

Throughout the Civil War, fugitive slaves en route to Fort Pickens encountered soldiers and civilians who joined their full-scale assault on slavery. There were Union troops like Brown who came to Pensacola with no intention of freeing enslaved people but who developed a fierce commitment to the black men and women who greeted the Union army as liberators. There were also soldiers from the North and Europe with strong abolitionist convictions who while stationed in Pensacola seized the opportunity to liberate bondspeople and establish their equality. Perhaps more surprising is that runaway slaves also found allies among the free population of farmers, laborers, and sailors who had inhabited Pensacola and the vicinity since before the war. Like the invading Federal forces, these free white Southerners demonstrated great hostility toward slavery and solidarity with enslaved black people.

Fugitive slaves had always challenged the hegemony of slaveowners and other white elites on the Southern frontier, but the Civil War amplified this challenge by providing a revolutionary opportunity to destroy the institution of slavery entirely. Even before the first arrival of Union forces on Pensacola's shore, bondspeople in the city and the surrounding areas interpreted the drumbeats of sectional war as the death knell of slavery, and when the war came to Florida's Gulf Coast they, in numbers not seen since the British invasion of Florida during the War of 1812, fled from homes, shops, and mills throughout the city as well as small farms and large plantations in the immediate and surrounding areas. Seizing upon the chaos and confusion of civil war, these fugitive slaves—or, as they became known, contrabands—precipitated the war's transformation into a war over slavery and along with their allies realized the radical potential for interracial cooperation and collaboration on the Southern frontier.[8]

In May 1861, a Southern journalist who spent the first days of the Civil War in Pensacola learned what bondspeople thought of the long-awaited clash between the Union and Confederate armies. "In this section, at least, 'profound quietness' does *not* prevail among the negroes," the writer insisted regarding slaveowners' claims that slaves reacted passively to the political and military events taking place across the nation. To the contrary, bondspeople in Pensacola displayed "the most intense anxiety on the subject of the late rupture" as dreams of freedom spread among them like a disease. "In one instance, of which I have personal knowledge, the sufferer raves continually of Lincoln, and the certainty that thro' him every 'nigger' is to be set free." Because fears of a slave insurrection spread across the city, "new stringency has been added to the regulations that govern the movements of the negroes, and a more militant watch kept over them."[9]

African Americans were not the only targets of increased vigilance. In 1860, near the site of the former Arcadia Mill just north of Pensacola, an angry mob destroyed a wax figure of the radical white abolitionist John Brown, which a local craftsman had displayed in a public exhibition alongside figures of "the Savior and Apostles."[10] On the day of the presidential election, a Pensacola mob attacked a white man named Daniel Donagan, whom eyewitnesses saw telling bondspeople "that to-day Lincoln would be elected, and the slaves of the South would be free."[11] Two days later, secessionists again took to the streets in an effort to shape public opinion in their favor, leading one among them to forward a telegram to president-elect Lincoln the following day that read, "You were last night hung in effigy in this city."[12]

As the Civil War grew closer, secessionists throughout Pensacola employed violence to eliminate political dissent. After South Carolina became the first Southern state to secede from the United States, navy lieutenant Henry Erben of the USS *Supply* arrived in Pensacola and found the city in a state of pandemonium. "Conventions had been called to secede the State; town meetings were being held every evening, where the most violent speeches were made to fire the Southern heart; men, women, and children, seemed to have gone mad." Erben watched as two officers, "strong Union men," entered a "secesh" meeting in a city hotel, where they hoped to enter a civil discussion on the "merits of secession." Instead, "they soon found it was not a free discussion at all, but that they had a free fight on their hands." The two men returned to their ships the next day "with blackened eyes and cut faces, a sorry-looking pair of defenders of the Union."[13] The situation was equally explosive at the Navy Yard, where secessionists torched images of Lincoln and took part in other wild "extravagances."[14] When A. J. Lamberton, the navy's postmaster who owned a popular liquor store near the Navy Yard, remained outspoken regarding his strong pro-Unionist stance, he was "mobbed and driven away, losing all his property."[15] Inside the Navy Yard, in a more widely reported incident, a Union man "thus avowing himself, was stabbed."[16]

Secessionists' actions in the aftermath of Lincoln's election were not random acts of violence; instead, they were a strategic response to the persistence of Unionist sentiment in Pensacola and the surrounding military installations. Indeed, votes cast in December 1860 for two delegates to represent Escambia County in the upcoming state secessionist convention illuminate the depth of support for the Union on the eve of the Civil War. By nearly a three-to-one majority, voters from Pensacola and the Navy Yard elected two Unionist candidates, A. W. Nicholson and S. H. Wright. The vote was particularly one-sided at the Navy Yard, where, on the day of the election, "the navy yard men, mechanics, laborers, and watchmen went down en masse to the precinct and nearly unanimously voted for the *Union* candidates."[17] Despite such widespread antipathy toward secession, when delegates convened in Tallahassee in January to decide Florida's fate, Nicholson and Wright bowed to overwhelming pressure and attached their names to the state's Ordinance of Secession. When news arrived in Pensacola of the momentous decision, Colonel James Armstrong surrendered the Navy Yard to rebel soldiers led by Colonel William Chase and evacuated men and supplies to Fort Pickens. That Armstrong forfeited the yard without a fight resulted in his court-martial several weeks later; however, the damage was already done.[18] For the next sixteen months, Pensacola, the Navy Yard, Fort Barrancas, and Fort McRee belonged to the Confederate States of America.[19]

Only Fort Pickens remained in possession of the United States, which led the newly elected commander in chief to order its reinforcement with men and supplies just days after his inauguration. Lincoln hoped the seceded states would fire the first shots of the war toward Fort Pickens as its distance from the epicenters of the Confederacy made it easily defensible. The same could not be said of Fort Sumter, the only other significant Federal fort in the Deep South still under Union control, which lay in the middle of Charleston Harbor at the heart of the Confederacy. Despite Lincoln's wishes, Federal officials failed to carry out his order promptly, and before the first reinforcements disembarked at Pensacola the firing on Fort Sumter had already begun. Still, the plan was not a complete failure. While Fort Sumter fell quickly to the rebels, Fort Pickens remained firmly under Union control. In fact, the frontier fortress that guarded the entrance to Pensacola Harbor remained a "conspicuous federal stronghold" for the duration of the war, making it, in the words of the leading scholar of Civil War Pensacola, "a thorn in the side of the Confederacy that it could not, or at least would not, remove."[20]

For the next four years, Fort Pickens was a beacon of freedom for bondspeople across the Southern frontier. It was, wrote Major Willoughby Babcock of the Seventy-Fifth New York Infantry Regiment, "the point to which the negroes fled after the outbreak of the war, from all surrounding districts, as it was for some time the only point in the extreme South which was held by federal troops, and where they could be safe."[21] From the Gulf Coast deep into the Southern interior, fugitive slaves walked and ran toward Pensacola Bay and its tributaries and then boarded canoes and skiffs or simply floated on wooden planks toward Fort Pickens in spite of incredible dangers. Confederate snipers and "huge bloodhounds" employed by slaveowners represented the greatest threat, though snake-infested swamps and man-eating sharks posed an equally daunting challenge.[22] Nevertheless, they came.[23] Often, they were unsuccessful. In January 1862, the *Pensacola Daily Observer* reported the drowning deaths of several runaways from Pensacola who failed to reach Fort Pickens across the bay. "A quantity of negro baggage and an empty boat had been found," the paper explained, "which lead to the supposition."[24]

Many of the bondspeople who fled to Fort Pickens embarked on their difficult and dangerous journey "alone and unaided."[25] Most were local bondsmen who only needed to cross several hundred feet of water to reach Santa Rosa Island. Among them was Van Buren, a valuable dark-skinned twenty-two-year-old, who belonged to a prominent Pensacola businessman. After absconding, his owner placed an advertisement in a local paper, offering one hundred dollars for his capture.[26] Other black fugitives traveled great distances. This included Hal, or, as he preferred to be called, William Henry Harrison. The nineteen-year-old mulatto first came to Pensacola in the spring of 1861 with his master, a Confederate volunteer who participated in the rebel capture of the Navy Yard. But after returning home to Alabama, Harrison disappeared, inducing his owner to place an advertisement seeking his capture with the following comment: "I think Hal has made his way to Pensacola, as I took him there with me when in the Warrington Marine Barracks with the Greenville Guards."[27]

Runaways from Pensacola also traveled in small groups, numbering anywhere between two and a dozen or more. Among them was a married couple that reached Fort Pickens in a skiff. Peter Dyson was "an intelligent black man, about 35 years of age." A "first-rate mason and bricklayer," he had "worked on the Government forts at Pensacola for the last twenty years." Dyson's wife, Henrietta, was "a yellow woman" who before crossing the bay had hidden in the woods for several weeks after suffering a terrible beating from her owner. While at the fort, the duo provided vital information on the Battle of Santa Rosa Island, a failed surprise attack by several hundred Confederates against more than one thousand Union troops in October 1861. Loyalty, in this case, had its benefits. In return for their assistance, Colonel Brown reserved a place for the husband and wife on the steamer *McClellan*, which carried them to the North and freedom.[28]

Brown's benevolence notwithstanding, distrust of the Union army kept many bondspeople from darting to the island. In fact, reports that the first fugitives to escape to Fort Pickens were returned to their owners and beaten to death deterred many potential runaways. A writer at Fort Pickens interviewed two contrabands who affirmed that "there are a great many more would like to run away if they could get the chance and were sure of not being sent back, as they state those that were recaptured have been killed."[29] A contraband found hiding on Santa Rosa Island testified to the level of distrust. "He had been there three weeks, living on berries and crabs, and the reason he did not report himself, was that several who had come over before him had been returned, and he was afraid he might be treated in the same way." After enjoying his first hearty meal in some time, the runaway remarked on the generous treatment he received at the hands of the Federal troops. "Golly, if my bredren ober dere only knew dis, how quickly they would come."[30]

The flood tide of fugitive slaves convinced some at Fort Pickens that the war to save the Union was fast evolving into a revolutionary contest over slavery and freedom. "There are large numbers of slaves in and about Pensacola, anxiously awaiting their opportunity to escape from bondage," wrote a journalist stationed on Santa Rosa Island alongside Union troops. "The numerous sentinels ranging along the beach, from Pensacola to Fort McCrea, are thus posted as much to head off runaways from the peculiar institution as to guard against attack from the United States troops." As yet, bondspeople had made "no systematic efforts for their freedom," which was anticipated given the fears of being returned to their owners, "but the stampede will commence sooner or later." It was clear the days of slavery were numbered, for "we are getting, every day of our lives, additional evidence that the love of liberty is irrepressible and common to all humanity." The flight of so many bondspeople, despite the likelihood of their being returned to their owners, belied the existence of a "beautiful relationship between master and servant." Indeed, "Every word that is uttered regarding the love of the negro for the man who claims to own him is the merest bosh." Like all men, bondspeople coveted freedom, and with the outbreak of civil war it was only a matter of time before they, "unchecked and unawed by the Federal arm, *will emancipate themselves*." The only question that remained was whether these newly freed people would seek vengeance for having suffered years of oppression. "It will be a fearful spectacle," the piece concluded, "if the millions of degraded and brutalized Africans in the South, having once thrown off their shackles, rise up in the majesty of brute force, and wreck a terrible vengeance upon the proud and haughty race which placed the heel on their necks, and has added year after year to its crushing weight."[31]

Published in the *New York Tribune*, the North's most popular Civil War era newspaper, the report from Fort Pickens affirms David Cecelski belief that the Civil War was a conflict "in which black southerners were the driving force behind the struggle against slavery and powerful agents of their own destiny."[32] The correspondent noted that wherever Union had forces had gained a foothold along the Confederacy's perimeter the flight of bondspeople was general. "In Missouri, in Virginia, and here in

Pensacola," he informed readers perhaps unaware of the revolution that was afoot, "wherever the 'conflict' becomes practical instead of theoretical, the inevitable tendency of the black man to escape the servitude which oppresses him is manifested."[33] Still, for bondspeople trying to take advantage of the arrival of Union forces, Pensacola offered distinct advantages for fugitive slaves.

Principal among them was a segment of the local white population that encouraged and at times made the dangerous journey alongside them. In the winter of 1862, for example, a writer at the Navy Yard noted the arrival of a dozen fugitive slaves at Fort Pickens in a small boat."There was negligence of course, or it could not have happened," he opined, adding, "a white man is under arrest upon the charge of assisting them off."[34] In another instance, a "young colored married woman" absconded from her mistress on the Perdido River, several miles west of Pensacola, with the assistance of two unidentified white men who conveyed her in a sloop toward Fort Pickens. Before arriving at the fort, the USS *Colorado* intercepted the boat, and the crew took the bondswoman "on board, and to the fort."[35] What became of her two accomplices went unrecorded. Federal troops contributed to the anonymity of the mysterious people who helped bondspeople run away, by failing to note the names of the members of interracial crews arriving at the fort whom the soldiers often met with suspicion and sometimes contempt. When General L. G. Arnold forwarded intelligence that he gathered from four such refugees, he added the following qualification to his report: "This information (indefinite, however) was derived from two stupid white men and two negroes, who came over a few days since from Milton and East Bay, some 40 miles from Pensacola."[36]

In rare cases when detailed evidence on the identity of the free people who aided and abetted fugitive slaves survives, the persistence of radical interracialism on the Southern frontier comes to light. In the spring of 1862, the commander of Confederate forces at Pensacola, Colonel Thomas Jones, tried to stem the flow of white and black refugees to the city. Desperate and out of work, these civilians and slaves were willing to do anything for food and shelter, including providing intelligence to the enemy, which led the colonel to issue an extraordinary proclamation. "There are certain lounging worthless people, white as well as black, who frequent the neighborhood of Pensacola, and have no observable occupation," the March 31 decree began. As the military commander of the city "has no use for their presence, they are warned to leave, or the consequences rest on their own heads." To deter disobedience of the order, the declaration concluded, "The gallows is erected in Pensacola and will be in constant use on and after the 3d day of April, 1862." From this point forward, "the town is under complete MARTIAL LAW."[37]

Jones proved himself a man of his word when just days after issuing the proclamation he convened a series of courts-martial that charged several "white and colored" persons of committing various crimes against the Confederacy. The first to stand trial was Ebenezer, an

This Confederate Order targeted black and white refugees in Pensacola during the Confederate occupation of the city. Courtesy of the University Archives and West Florida History Center, Bibliography of West Florida Collection, Pensacola.

urban bondsman whom rebel soldiers captured en route to Santa Rosa Island with newspapers and other documents that contained "information useful to the United States troops stationed there and injurious to the Southern Confederacy."[38] The court-martial charged Ebenezer with three separate counts of attempting to violate Article 57 of the Confederate Articles of War, a capital offense that made it illegal for anyone "holding correspondence with, or giving intelligence to, the enemy, either directly or indirectly."[39] The trial began with the judge advocate providing the defendant the opportunity to deny or accept the charges leveled against him. Ebenezer responded that he was "guilty of some and of some not guilty."[40]

Subsequent testimony revealed the plan to escape to Fort Pickens developed over the course of several weeks in conversations between Ebenezer and several coconspirators. Most influential among the coconspirators was Melmore, an "Irishman" who may have been one of the hundreds of immigrants brought to Pensacola from New York City in the decades before the Civil War to work at the Navy Yard or railroad depot.[41] This "intemperate" laborer lived less than a quarter-mile from the slave quarters owned by Richard L. Campbell, Ebenezer's owner. At the beginning of the war, when Campbell informed Ebenezer that Union troops mistreated fugitive slaves, Melmore assured Ebenezer that everything Campbell said "was a damned lie." Melmore further told Ebenezer that if he "went over to the Yankees he would be well treated that they would give him work and pay for it—and send him to New York or Liberia." Neighbors considered Melmore an intelligent man, but he was "the habitual associate of negroes—and places himself upon equality with them." Another coconspirator offered more than just encouragement to the intrepid bondsman. After convincing Ebenezer that "he was a friend," a white man named Lockey promised to provide Ebenezer with a boat and accompany him to Fort Pickens. On the day of the escape, the two men boarded the vessel and set out across the bay. A wave tossed Lockey from the boat, and as he was unable to climb aboard the craft, Ebenezer proceeded to the fort alone. That he did so with intelligence considered injurious to the Confederacy sealed his fate. The court-martial concluded the accused was "an intelligent being having the faculties of conveying information to the Enemy" and thus found him guilty on all counts and sentenced him to death.[42]

The following day a second court-martial charged five other bonds-men with violation of Article 57. Peter, William, Robert, Stephen, and George belonged to one of Florida's most influential leaders, Jackson Morton, who served as territorial representative, Florida state senator, a United States senator from Florida, and delegate to the Provisional Confederate Congress. But Morton made his fortune as a government contractor, leasing bondsmen to the federal government in Pensacola and operating a brickyard and sawmill some twenty miles north of the city. When Confederate forces destroyed his home and industries as part of a scorched-earth strategy to deprive the enemy of valuable resources, Morton prepared to move his family and slaves to southern Alabama.[43] The five bondsmen refused to go, however; after collecting "large quantities" of clothes, boots, and hats, they climbed aboard a stolen boat and makeshift raft and raced toward Fort Pickens. It was a route they had traveled before while working at the Navy Yard, but this time they meandered along the shoreline for three days before Confederate sentinels intercepted their vessels and took them into custody. Soldiers interrogated the prisoners, who remained steadfast in their desire to reach Union lines, insisting their objective was "to get over, to the Island to be free."[44]

During the three-day trial, Peter emerged as one of the ringleaders of another interracial conspiracy. "The most intelligent of the five," he at first denied being a runaway slave out of fear that such an admission "would implicate white men." But he later provided the names of three European Americans who convinced him "that if he could get to Santa Rosa Island or Fort Pickens that he would be free": Lawrence G. Mayo was a former mechanic who operated a grocery store on the Blackwater River, which earned him the reputation as a "Grogshopkeeper or whiskey seller in Millton"; Arthur Chance and a man known only as Garrett worked on the water between Milton, Pensacola, and the Navy Yard, shipping and selling logs and wooden shingles.[45]

For months, all three white men risked their livelihoods and their lives by encouraging their black associates to abscond.[46] Peter attested that "Mayo and Chance had at different times from the election of Lincoln during the year 1861 advised these boys to go to Pickens—stating that by Lincoln's election they were as free as he was and that they were fools if they did not go to Pickens as it was easily done." Both Mayo and Chance had at different times spoke "of the benefits of freedom, and every thing pertaining to it." Mayo was particularly encouraging, telling Peter that "if he could get away, that he Could go to New York or Cuba or Havannah and enjoy himself as he pleased as a free man." Garrett's role in the conspiracy was less clear, though he spoke to several of the bondsmen and told them that they were as free as he was and "if they had a mind to go to Pickens they Could do so easily."[47]

European Americans who joined African Americans' assault on slavery across the Southern frontier often elude the historical spotlight on account of their obscurity; in the case of Morton's slaves, however, the defendants' counsel highlighted the role these white men played in the slaves' escape in an effort to appeal to the members of the court-martial, who may have prescribed to the paternalist argument that enslaved people lacked the will to be free. Colonel Thomas Blount maintained that before learning of their impending move to Alabama, the bondsmen received "assurances from traitrous persons with white skins, that by deserting their master and fleeing, they would not only be well fed and cared for, but would also be invested with the inestimable blessing of freedom, and placed upon the basis of a white man." The misinformation provided "was a picture of an allurement too tempting to be resisted by human beings occupying the degraded position of these accused." It made all five bondsmen powerless to resist the temptation to try to reach Fort Pickens, "this modern Canaan, this land of refuge to their longing desires."[48]

Despite the efforts of the defense, the court-martial panel found all five runaways guilty of the three counts brought against them. It sentenced to death the ringleaders Peter and William and ordered the whipping of George, Robert, and Stephen over the course of four consecutive days. The panel acquitted Garrett, the only white man, according to extant records, ever brought before the tribunal. It did, however, offer a stern warning to all those of European descent who remained in Confederate Pensacola: "this [is] not a time for white men to be ever suspected. All loyal men have now an opportunity to show their loyalty" to the Confederacy, "disloyal ones have no business among us."[49]

As Stephanie McCurry has argued in her study of the Confederate nation, the courts-martial occasioned by Jones's proclamation left an indelible mark on the history of the Southern republic by raising a host of legal and constitutional questions regarding the place of African

Americans in the "body politic."[50] The court's panel acknowledged the anomalous nature of the proceedings but insisted they were "the only safe means to protect the lives and interest of this portion of the Confederacy."[51] Morton rejected this line of reasoning, and in a series of letters intended to save the lives of the bondsmen he claimed ownership of, excoriated Jones for overextending his authority. He called the colonel a "coxcomb and fool" before asking rhetorically, "Who ever heard before of a negro slave being arraigned before a court martial for a violation of the Articles of War?" The idea, he insisted, was "absurd and the very consummation of folly."[52] The commander of Confederate forces in Alabama and West Florida, Major General Sam Jones, came to the defense of Colonel Jones, taking full responsibility for the convening of the trials. He insisted that "so much information had been conveyed to the enemy on Santa Rosa, and so much mischief done in the Community by the tampering of bad white men with negroes and the escape of the latter to the Enemy, that I advised Col. Jones it would be necessary to make Examples of some of them."[53] Despite the taunt, it appears that the executions never took place. For at the same time officials were debating the legality of the trials, the Confederacy's control over Pensacola came to an abrupt end. With their presence required to bolster rebel forces after their defeat at the Battle of Shiloh in southern Tennessee, the Confederate army evacuated West Florida and left Pensacola and the Navy Yard to the United States in May 1862.[54]

Where Union troops in major Confederate seaports encountered hundreds and sometimes thousands of people, those who disembarked in Pensacola discovered a desolate frontier community devoid of people, institutions, and even the most basic amenities. It was a "Deserted Village," wrote one soldier who was familiar with the city prior to the war. "Grass grows green and rank in the streets, where once our troops paraded, and the old quarters appear dejected and forsaken." On the waterfront, "nothing having life could be observed—there was not even a dog, cat, pig, or anything moving about the streets." Only downtown were the "signs that humanity still dwelt in Pensacola" discernible. According to one of the few remaining residents, who called himself the "Spanish Consul" in an effort to avoid reproach, "the whole population of Pensacola, white and black, is less than forty."[55]

Absent Confederate soldiers and sympathizers, Pensacola's enslaved population demonstrated a fierce commitment to the Union cause.

Naval officer David Dixon Porter came to Pensacola "thinking what a triumph it would be to receive the surrender of this ancient burgh and figure in history in connection with so glorious an event!" Upon landing, he expected to meet a crowd of loyal citizens anxious to restore the "loyal city to its allegiance." What he found instead was "a crowd of ragged negroes grinning from ear to ear and turning somersaults to testify their delight." The black throng "shouted for Mr. Linkum's gunboats until they were hoarse."[56]

Like those already safely across the water at Fort Pickens, the contrabands arriving in Union-controlled Pensacola provided Federal troops with vital intelligence, including the identification of rebel sympathizers among the city's remaining white population. When a local doctor presented himself as a Union man, an elderly bondsman stepped forward and warned General Porter in confidence, "He's de biggest ole rebel in all dese parts." The bondsman explained that the secessionist had "fifty tousand dollars congealed in his cellar way down under de foundation to keep de rebels from gobblin' it, and to keep you from knowin' he had it. Dat's de kine ob Union man he is." Fearing for his own safety, the bondsman begged Porter for protection. The general explained to the "old Unionist" that he no longer had anything to fear and gave him a half-dollar as a token of his appreciation.[57] Some of the contrabands providing information on Confederate troop strength and movements were able to do so because they had deserted from the rebel lines. One who became the personal servant of a Union officer "had been a long time in the rebel army, and was at the battle of Corinth" before escaping on the water in a "little dug-out, about ten feet long."[58] Two others who relayed information on the number of rebel troops in the vicinity of the Navy Yard "were cooks in the Fifteenth Confederate Cavalry" and, according to one officer, "deserted last night at 10 o'clock at the Seven-Mile Station."[59]

Besides intelligence, contrabands provided Union soldiers with evidence of the horrors of slavery, including open wounds caused by bloodhounds, buckshot, and other weapons Confederates used to keep them from reaching Union lines.[60] Oral testimony of dangerous and sometimes deadly escape attempts proved effective in changing the hearts and minds of troops who came to the South with preconceived notions of the region's peculiar institution and its victims. Among the affected was Major Willoughby Babcock, who accepted an appointment as provost marshal and military governor of Pensacola after the Confederate retreat. Upon assuming command of the city, he described the contrabands his regiment first encountered in unflattering terms. "Negroes are now coming in from the country above, three on Thursday, one on Friday, and two today [Saturday]," began one letter. Among them was Robert, "a real slave genius, shrewd, cunning, clownish, black, and probably dishonest," who described the harrowing journey from his master's plantation forty miles upriver from Pensacola. Initially, Babcock and the men of the Seventy-Fifth New York Infantry Regiment responded to the personal story of loss and suffering with "a roar of laughter," until the major asked the bondsman about his wife, at which time "the poor fellow's face took a sad look in an instant which touched us all." Robert explained that his "loving wife" insisted on running away with him, and shortly after the couple "set out with bundles in hand, and ran," their owner unleashed several dogs that "soon overtook them." As the animals attacked, Robert stood motionless hoping to satisfy their rage, but they flew past him and seized his wife. Robert's instincts took over and he ran to safety. How his wife fared and where she was, "he knows not." The testimony stirred strong emotions in Babcock, who identified with this African American in a way he once thought impossible. He recorded that Robert "told this tale with such reticence, such a shrinking from details and such a quiet horror at it all, that I recognized my own kinship to his black face and distorted features."[61]

Face-to-face conversations with contrabands often transformed Union soldiers, who could be indifferent to the plight of enslaved Southerners, into abolitionists. Chandra Manning describes this transformation in her study of Northern troops who arrived in the South with no intention of waging a war against slavery. "More influential than Union soldiers' preexisting notions, or even their firsthand observations of the South," she maintains, "were their interactions with actual slaves, which led many to view slavery as a dehumanizing and evil institution that corroded the moral virtue necessary for a population to govern itself."[62] These interactions also taught Northern soldiers that the men and women of African descent who stood before them were not the racial caricatures they had been led to believe populated the South. That African Americans were, in fact, people, a realization that triggered for some Union troops the basic human instinct to help the less fortunate.

Isolated on the Southern frontier, Babcock and other soldiers aided fugitive slaves without fear of Confederate reprisal or Union rebuke.

While Federal policy recognized the freedom of contrabands who reached Fort Pickens, it did not yet do the same for those in Pensacola who were still liable to arrest and rendition. In one instance, a contraband who begged Babcock for protection received the following response: "I told him I couldn't help him, and if he didn't stop bothering me I would send him to Fort Pickens." Aware of the government's policy, the bondsman fired back, "*I wish you would Massa!*" Babcock wrote that the bondsman said it "with so much unction that I was quite disconcerted by the effect of my threat." Subsequent to the brief exchange, Major Lewis Carpenter, the regiment's quartermaster, approached the bondsman and began a conversation. Babcock watched from a distance as a broad smile stretched across the bondsman's face when Carpenter inquired, "Don't you know the way to Fort Pickens?" Within moments the bondsman disappeared. "We went to our meal and I have not seen the boy since," Babcock observed. Unafraid and perhaps even a little proud, he justified his actions, writing, "My official duties bind me not to advise any slave to run away, but in proper cases I find my conscience pliant enough to inform other officers what slaves might as well go to Fort Pickens and be free!"[63]

Assisting or even just allowing bondspeople to escape could be an exhilarating experience for soldiers who in most cases never imagined they would participate in the destruction of slavery. A naval correspondent at Fort Pickens summed up the feelings of many troops at Pensacola when he wrote, "I think we were nearer feeling like 'Abolitionists' than ever in our lives before."[64] The evidence of soldiers' new outlook was palpable late at night, when the abolitionist anthem "John Brown" rang out from the casemates inside the walls of Fort Pickens where troops fought the temptation to fall asleep.[65] The transformations that occurred in Pensacola evoke some of the findings of scholars of interracialism who have traced the rapid evolution of racial thinking following prolonged periods of contact between people of diverse racial backgrounds.[66] This was the case in Pensacola, where soldiers and slaves spent months and sometimes years in close quarters far removed from the major theaters of the war. Northern troops and contrabands encountered each other in camps established at Fort Pickens, Fort Barrancas, and on Pensacola's downtown streets, where they enjoyed whiskey and wine in addition to each other's company.[67] They also met at several integrated establishments, including a Federal hospital, church, Sabbath school, and theater.[68] Years after the war, Captain Henry A. Shorey of the Fifteenth Maine Infantry Regiment, who spent nearly two years in Pensacola and along the Gulf Coast, recalled nostalgically the "dusky refugees" who flooded the regiment's camps: "They were by no means unwelcome guests; indeed they and the soldiers soon became devoted friends."[69]

Beyond tales of the "terrible inhumanities" and the "most monstrous indecencies" committed against enslaved people, it was the eagerness with which contrabands performed any sort of labor required that first ingratiated them with Federal troops in Pensacola and across the bay at Fort Pickens. The army accepted all bondsmen willing and able to perform manual labor in the Quartermaster Department and paid them fifteen dollars per month and one ration daily as "Uncle Sam's laborers." Babcock reported that the contrabands were wonderful employees. Serving as "Boatmen, teamsters, and ordinary hands," they did "more work than any other men in the island."[70] Some contrabands worked as the personal servants of Federal officers, while others worked for the government indirectly.[71] At the start of the war, a Mobile, Alabama, merchant sent his "trusted slave" Willis to Pensacola to care for his horses and mules. But after the recapture of the city by the Union army, the bondsmen refused to return. A descendant later recalled that the bondsman had "brought the mules to Pensacola, dutifully enough, but once arrived immediately set himself up in an elaborate hauling business" that was "particularly lucrative because of the government construction going on at the time."[72]

The alliance of white soldiers and black slaves intensified in the summer of 1862 when Babcock informed four runaways from Alabama that he was raising a battalion of black men and asked them to volunteer. One refused, on account that "he shouldn't want to fight the people of Florida." But the leader of the group remarked that he "could say nothing agin that" and the others agreed. The provost marshal envisioned a small force of black men "cutting roads, building bridges, driving teams, throwing up earth works, boating, etc." In return for their services, the government would pay them a fair wage and the entire army would benefit by relieving "the soldier from all but strictly military duties, and his whole time and strength are available for war."[73] Babcock's efforts to organize bondsmen into troops for backbreaking manual labor were part of a popular strategy supported by many Northerners, including the president, to capitalize on the cheap availability of formerly enslaved slave labor. At the same time, however, abolitionists and an increasing number of officers and troops were advocating a radically different idea. They wanted to give guns and ammunition to fugitive slaves and send them into battle against their former masters.[74]

Among those pushing this second option was Brigadier General Neal Dow, a former conductor on the New England line of the Underground Railroad, who washed upon Pensacola's shores in the fall of 1862 after having already initiated such a plan in New Orleans. Before the Civil War, Dow and his father were legendary prohibitionists and abolitionists whose home in Portland, Maine, was a refuge for fugitive slaves in need of "food and temporary shelter while waiting to be escorted farther toward the north star of freedom." Later in life, Dow recalled a meeting at a local black church to celebrate the successful escape of several bondsmen through Portland to Canada. "The colored presiding officer, when he introduced me, after saying to the audience that the 'underground railroad to freedom runs through his kitchen and back-yard,' added, 'His face is white, but, God bless him, his heart is black.'"[75] There was no greater compliment paid to a European American by African Americans in the middle of the nineteenth century. John Stauffer asserts that for the enemies of slavery and racial division, "the true spiritual heart was a black heart that shared a humanity with all people and lacked the airs of superiority of a white heart."[76] Dow had long considered secessionism a desperate attempt of Southern slave-owners to preserve their way of life. So when the call for volunteers reached New England, he joined up in spite of his advanced age. Fifty-seven years old when he accepted a colonelcy in the Thirteenth Maine Infantry Regiment, Dow "felt that, in the event of a civil war, slavery ought to be abolished," and "he was quite willing to bear my part in anything that would bring to pass the desired result."[77]

As soon as Dow arrived on the Gulf Coast, he led hundreds of bondspeople who had already made their way to Federal encampments along the shore in confiscating the land and property of wealthy plant-ers. After four months, some 450 contrabands resided at Union forts near the mouth of the Mississippi River, where Dow employed as many of them as possible as servants and laborers. As costs escalated and the labor supply far outweighed the demand, he decided to act on a theory he had been pondering for several months. "I see no way of speedily solving this question without a military enrollment and employment," he reasoned. "In that way we could make them earn their keep immediately, and I am confident that we could make good soldiers of all the young negroes, at a vast saving to the government and to the consternation of the Confederates." Dow believed that nothing "would go so far as to compel the substantial men in the South into speedy submission as a vigorous and systematic enrollment, arming and training of the negroes." Unwilling to wait for President Lincoln to issue a "proclamation of emancipation," he took matters into his own hands, training several crews of contrabands as artillerists. The experiment, though brief, was a success as "some of those negroes had become fairly efficient gunners."[78] Dow sent them on foraging expeditions that in addition to freeing dozens of slaves resulted in the liberation of food, guns, livestock, silverware, and furniture from multiple coastal plantations. The radical Northern abolitionist took great pleasure in inflicting pain on white Southerners "who have always exercised boundless power over their slaves" but were now "subject to the absolute will of another."[79]

Dow's loose interpretation of the army's confiscation policy resulted in his reassignment—or banishment—to the Florida frontier, where the absence of Confederate opposition and Union oversight allowed him to continue the assault on slavery. Even after Lincoln issued the Preliminary Emancipation Proclamation in September 1862, giving most Confederate slaveowners one hundred days to end their rebellion against the United States or forfeit their human property, Dow continued working "to abolish slavery as to individuals." As a result, Dow wrote, "negroes soon learned that I was friendly to them, and manifested their appreciation of it in a great variety of ways." In one case, Dow wrote shortly after arriving in Pensacola, "A very good looking woman came here a few days ago and said she was keeping house, earning money and paying wages to her master. I told her she might or might not continue at that, as she pleased. She said her master had her two children, ten and eight years old." Dow explained that he could not interfere on behalf of her children, "but if she could get them quietly into her apartments I would protect them there." Several days later, "she came and said she had the children, but Master came and 'twitched' them away and whipped them." Enraged, Dow dispatched a soldier who retrieved the children immediately. When the master came to reclaim the slaves, which he valued at nearly fifteen hundred dollars. Dow sent him away, informing him that "that kind of property was no longer of value."[80]

For four months, Dow ruled Pensacola with an iron fist. In addition to relieving the few remaining Confederate sympathizers of anything of value, including "pianos, sofas, mirrors, and other household furniture," he banned the sale of alcohol and required every person traveling through the city to carry a pass.[81] He also required all residents—white and black—to take an oath of allegiance to the United States and threw those who refused behind bars. To maintain order and advance the impending revolution over slavery and freedom, Dow formed bondsmen into an irregular regiment that, while lacking weapons and uniforms, drilled openly in the streets. A Confederate eyewitness watched as contrabands "were carried into the office [of] General Dow while he was there, and, after being brought, were sent to the 'contraband quarters' and put to work on breast-works and the Government works, and were allowed to draw rations from the military supplies there." A bondsman named Ben served as the captain of Dow's unofficial regiment, while Vemp "was generally addressed as and understood to be a lieutenant." Others belonging to the company were: "George, who belonged to Capt. Alexander Bright; one named Caesar, generally reported to be a slave, but whose [master] I do not know; another named Bob, belonging to William H. Baker, and probably fifteen or twenty others whom I knew to be slaves, but whose name and owners' names I cannot now recollect."[82]

Besides organizing contrabands for military service, Dow delivered a series of explosive public addresses in Pensacola in front of large multiracial audiences. In one, he reminded the soldiers under his command "that these people down South have been in the habit of whipping these poor colored slaves simply because they are colored and they have been under their thumbs." Adopting the plight of the slave as his own and his soldiers, he roared defiantly, "the way we will revenge ourselves will be to lay the lash on them." Dow anticipated a new day dawning in the United States when racial distinctions disappeared alongside the institution of slavery, and before returning to Louisiana in the winter of 1863, "gave the negroes to understand that they were free, regardless of the protestations of their owners, and encouraged the negroes to disobey their masters and treat them as their equals."[83]

Dow's dream of transforming chattel slaves into soldiers became a reality when Abraham Lincoln's Emancipation Proclamation authorized the use of black soldiers in combat. In the months following the decree, obtaining recruits in Pensacola remained a simple albeit impromptu process as bondsmen continued to flock to the city. In some cases fugitives arrived alone after surviving harrowing journeys. One was particularly memorable as he "came in with a heavy iron bar on his leg" after having wandered "with it three weeks through woods and swamps."[84] In other cases the army relied on black recruiters. A soldier with the Fifteenth Maine Infantry Regiment stationed at Pensacola wrote, "A short time since one of the darkies, expressed a desire to go outside the lines and collect those of his own color, to join a brigade being raised here." After receiving permission, he ventured deep into the slave country of southern Alabama and returned soon after, "bringing thirty one others." The shouts of the bondsmen as they entered the city were deafening. "Surely they must have thought the day of jubilee had come."[85]

Flush with volunteers, army officials began the formal organization of a regiment of black soldiers from Pensacola in March 1863.[86] Known as the Fifth Regiment Infantry Corps d'Afrique, it belonged to Brigadier General Daniel Ullman's brigade, which some have considered "the first colored organization authorized by the government."[87] With little use for additional forces in Pensacola, officials began relocating the black troops from the city to Louisiana to assist in the capture of the lower Mississippi River. One reporter summed up the actions that took place in July and August, writing, "All the negroes in and near Pensacola are being sent to New Orleans to be drilled and placed in the Yankee army."[88] Bondsmen from Pensacola, who upon arrival in Louisiana enlisted in the newly formed United States Colored Troops, are difficult to identify. Few left any record of their places of origin. Army officials compounded the problem by failing to record the nativity of enlisting bondsmen. Typical was the following report from Fort Barrancas: "Several contrabands, who succeeded in reaching our lines, were added to the Fourteenth Regiment, Corps d'Afrique."[89] Still, information survives on some of the men. John Sunday was the most famous. A biracial bondsman who joined Ullman's Brigade in Pensacola in May 1863, he enlisted four months later in the Sixth Regiment Infantry Corps d'Afrique at Port Hudson, Louisiana. After earning promotion as a sergeant, Sunday served in the unit that became known as the Seventy-Eighth Regiment Infantry United States Colored Troops until the end of the war. Following the Union victory, Sunday returned to Pensacola, where he helped organize the local chapter of the Grand

Army of the Republic and served as its commander. He moreover became a prominent business and political leader, earning him distinction as "one of the wealthiest colored men in the state."[90]

The departure of the first black troops recruited locally did not spell the end of Pensacola's revolutionary experiment in black soldiery and emancipation. Instead, in the last two years of the war, the city became a base for more than a dozen black Union regiments from the North and a new home for an increasing number of contrabands. Union troops liberated a small number of bondspeople in small raids on Confederate homes and farms in Pensacola and the vicinity before the Emancipation Proclamation.[91] Beginning in August 1864, however, the pursuit of contrabands intensified as black and white troops together invaded Confederate farms and plantations in the Florida and Alabama backcountry.

Orchestrating these attacks was a European immigrant who exploited the Southern frontier's liminality to further the revolutionary democratic ideals he adopted more than a decade earlier. Brigadier General Alexander Asboth was a veteran of the Hungarian Revolution of 1848, a popular democratic uprising aimed at securing political and social reforms in the Kingdom of Hungary that metamorphosed into a bloody war of independence against the Austrian Empire.[92] The nobleman served as the "aide and factotum" of the legendary freedom fighter Louis Kossuth, and then in the aftermath of the failed insurrection fled with Kossuth to the United States, where Asboth worked as an engineer in New York and served as a member of the group that helped design Central Park. With the outbreak of the Civil War, Asboth called on his countrymen to fight for "our adopted Country," and he accepted an appointment in the Department of the West as chief of staff for his friend and mentor Major General John C. Frémont.[93] It was a perfect match. The eccentric Frémont was a celebrated soldier, explorer, and presidential candidate widely known as the Pathfinder. He was also a radical abolitionist.[94]

Asboth shared Frémont's hatred of slavery and while stationed in Pensacola assaulted the institution with Northern troops and a disparate collection of roughneck volunteers who reflected the type of men often available for military service in seaports along the Southern frontier. They were fugitive slaves from the ports and plantations along the Gulf Coast and an extraordinary cavalry unit that consisted of hundreds of "loyal Southerners" from Pensacola and the vicinity. Asboth had begun organizing the latter group into a formal regiment at Fort Barrancas in December 1863. Known eventually as the First Florida Cavalry, the "rank and file" of this outfit were, according to one volunteer, "a motley crew of as dare-devil fellows as can be collected at any seaport town, I guess. Among them were Spaniards, French creoles, half-breed Indians, Germans, a few Poles and a host of crackers and gophers—the western Floridians were derisively called gophers."[95]

The First Florida Cavalry included a young Alabama abolitionist who published a brief account of his service. Wade H. Richardson considered himself "a southerner by ancestry, birth and education;" nevertheless, he shared the beliefs of his father, a Unitarian evangelist who included "all men, black and white, good and bad, in his scheme of universal redemption." For years, these unpopular views brought scorn upon Richardson's family, especially after Lincoln's election in 1860, when "a mob of half-drunken fire-eaters" kidnapped Richardson's uncle and nearly hanged him "for being an abolitionist." When Confederate authorities began enrolling teenagers in the Alabama state militia, after the fall of Vicksburg, the then sixteen-year-old Richardson and James Summerford—a friend from another family of "strong abolitionists"— headed toward the Gulf of Mexico. Along the way, the two white runaways found allies in black slaves who informed them of the movement of Confederate sentries and shared "a bit of bread or a roasted potato or ear of corn." Richardson and Summerford traveled nearly a month before finally reaching the Pensacola Navy Yard. The joy of having reached their destination was short-lived, for soon after arriving on the Gulf Coast, Summerford contracted a "terrible disease" and perished. Undeterred, Richardson enlisted as a private in Company A of the First Florida Cavalry on January 3, 1864.[96]

Several months later, Richardson and his unit participated in a successful raid on Marianna, Florida, a small hamlet more than one hundred miles east of Pensacola. In addition to freeing Union captives, Asboth intended "to collect white and colored recruits, and secure as many horses and mules as possible."[97] On September 16, one battalion of the First Florida Cavalry, three battalions of the Second Maine Cavalry, and two companies of the Eighty-Second and Eighty-Sixth Regiments Infantry United States Colored Troops under the direction of Asboth's Hungarian compatriot L. L. Zulafsky, departed Pensacola and headed east. Within days, the mounted multiracial force of seven hundred cavalry and infantry were capturing prisoners of war, seizing arms and ammunition, and liberating scores of bondspeople, some of whom enlisted immediately. On September 27, Asboth and his men encountered Confederate Colonel Alexander Montgomery and some one hundred rebels at Marianna, and in the brief but bloody battle that followed earned a "brilliant victory." The triumph came at great personal cost to Asboth, who received several gunshots, "the first in the face, breaking the cheek bone, the other fracturing my left arm in two places." The spoils of victory consisted of eighty-one prisoners of war, including Montgomery, ninety-five guns, hundreds of horses and cattle, and six hundred contrabands, including an eight-year-old boy who years later remembered the swashbuckler in blue who brought him under the protection of the Federals.[98] "A Yankee white soldier said to me, 'Boy, does you want to go?' I said to him, 'Yes, sir.' He moved one of his feet out of the stirrup and said, 'Put your feet in there,' which I did. At the same time he reached for my hand and pulled me up on the horse, and placed me behind him and placed my hands about him, and said 'Hold on; do not fall off.'"[99] The formerly enslaved African Americans who followed these soldiers enthusiastically to Pensacola accelerated the city's transformation into a multiracial crucible, bringing the total number of black contrabands, white refugees, and soldiers of both races at Fort Pickens, Fort Barrancas, and the Navy Yard to approximately fifteen thousand.[100]

Of all the soldiers stationed at Fort Pickens, the men of the Twenty-Fifth Regiment Infantry United States Colored Troops left the most detailed record of their experiences. Organized at Camp William Penn in Philadelphia for the express purpose of recruiting black men along the Gulf Coast for military service, the regimental flag served as a reminder of the regiment's primary objective. Painted by a "colored man in Philadelphia," it depicted a bondsman with "the shackles of his bondage having just fallen from his ankles, in the act of stepping forward eagerly to receive the musket and uniform of his country's defenders which the Goddess of Liberty is presenting to him."[101] Though organized in the North, fugitive slaves filled the ranks of the Twenty-Fifth. Among them was Sergeant Lewis Buchanan, a Virginia native who "gained his liberty by a trip on the Under Ground Rail Road, April 1st, 1848, and has lived in Pennsylvania nearly ever since."[102] Another volunteer acquired freedom more recently. The body servant of a rebel captain from South Carolina, he escaped to New Jersey and then Philadelphia after his master lost his leg at the Battle of Gettysburg.[103]

UNITED STATES SOLDIERS AT CAMP "WILLIAM PENN" PHILADELPHIA, PA.

"Rally Round the Flag, boys! Rally once again,
Shouting the battle cry of FREEDOM!"

This popular recruitment poster, which lithographers copied from a photograph taken at Camp William Penn in Philadelphia, depicts members of the Twenty-Fifth Regiment Infantry United States Colored Troops, some of whom resided at Fort Pickens in the last year of the Civil War. Courtesy of the Library Company of Philadelphia.

Unlike the Union troops described by Gary Gallagher in his study of the Civil War North, the members of the Twenty-Fifth saw military service as an opportunity to destroy slavery—the restoration of the Union was a secondary concern.[104] While stationed in Pensacola, the Twenty-Fifth pursued its mission through several incursions into the plantation districts of Florida and Alabama that resulted in the liberation of hundreds of bondspeople, including at least fifty who enlisted in the regiment.[105] Between raids, men and women recently removed from bondage informed their liberators of the horrors of slavery, which reinforced the soldiers' commitment to the institution's destruction. "I am more than one year in the army, and do not wish to go home till every slave in the South is set free," began Sergeant William H. Watson in a public letter to the Philadelphia-based *Christian Recorder.* "I often sit down and hear the old mothers down here tell how they have been treated." Nevertheless, a new day was dawning. The day was near "when there will be no such thing as lashing the colored man till the blood runs down his back in streams." While at Fort Barrancas, Watson watched as contrabands disrobed to reveal "the deep marks of the cruel whip upon their backs." The sight was revolting. "Oh! is not this picture enough to curdle the blood in the veins and make the heart stand still with horror? In a Christian land—in the 19th century—a human being pinioned to a stake so tightly that the veins of his forehead and brawny arms start out and burst in his agony—lashed nigh unto death, and then dragged into the old cotton-shed, to linger and to die!" Watson wondered, "Oh, if there be a God of mercy and justice, how fearful is the crime of those who uphold slavery!" Whereas stories of African Americans tortured by their white masters might have fostered in black soldiers a hatred of all people of European descent, Watson viewed the war as an opportunity to abolish bigotry along with slavery. He pleaded with those who still believed in the superiority of one race over another to change their ways: "Come with me, ye victims of prejudice, where the grave of the white and black soldier lie side by side, and tell me which is the colored man and which is the white, and which of the two you would rather be?"[106]

Watson's message of interracial brotherhood resonated with the enlisted men of the Twenty-Fifth, who while stationed at Fort Barrancas encountered white men in positions of authority who did not abuse their power. Though some white officers treated black troops harshly, others displayed a remarkable degree of fraternity and fellowship. The enlisted men were particularly fond of General Asboth, whose reputation as a "friend of the colored man and soldier" brought him respect from soldiers outside his own command. They were equally impressed with General Joseph Bailey, a Wisconsin lumberjack and engineer "who showed no distinction of color among his soldiers."[107] Beyond these two, Sergeant Milton Harris maintained, "I must say the 25th Regiment has been blessed with good officers—as good as any colored regiment that has come from the North. They take a deep interest in the boys of the 25th, and endeavor to make every thing as pleasant and comfortable as possible." White officers' generosity toward black troops revealed itself in the establishment of schools for illiterate soldiers, who quickly attained the ability to read and write. Harris singled out Captain Chester A. Greenleaf for his contributions to the education of black troops, noting that he "is one who takes a deep interest in getting books for our men. He has already furnished quite a number."[108]

The interracial religious instruction that occurred in Union-occupied Pensacola would not have proceeded without the leadership of Colonel Frederick L. Hitchcock, a Scranton, Pennsylvania, lawyer who had fought heroically at Antietam, Maryland, before taking command of the Twenty-Fifth.[109] At Fort Barrancas, Hitchcock tasked Chaplain Miller with converting "two large hospital tents" into chapels and organizing a Sabbath school, which Hitchcock's wife helped direct. Miller explained that in addition to soldiers, instruction was open to "all of the children in the vicinity of the fort," adding proudly, "We have an attendance of sixty children, and a more eager, hungry set of children after knowledge I never saw." In only five weeks, the precocious youngsters had "learned to sing correctly several pieces of Sabbath School music, and many of them are making rapid progress in learning to read."[110] The situation was the same just south of the Navy Yard, where white refugees joined black soldiers and contrabands in receiving religious instruction from Union army ministers. At the only church left standing after the Confederate evacuation, local residents "regularly assembled, both black and white, to hear the word of life, sometimes from the lips of Lieut. Kane, of the Maria Woods, and occasionally from those of Mr. Diossy, a Methodist Protestant minister serving in the Twenty-eighth Connecticut Volunteers."[111]

Racial distinctions that blurred in the transcendent experience of frontier camp life disappeared on the battlefield almost entirely when black and white troops joined forces in the face of a common enemy. Whereas Joseph Glatthaar has documented the efforts of Union officers and the black troops under their command to set aside racial differences, in Pensacola the rank and file became an interracial band of brothers as they committed themselves fully to the Confederacy's defeat.[112] In March 1865, twelve hundred black and white troops left Pensacola and marched in heavy rain across sand and mud before arriving at Fort Blakely, Alabama, where they helped secure one of the last major victories of the United States in the Civil War. Chaplain Charles Waldron Buckley of the Forty-Seventh Regiment Infantry United States Colored Troops accompanied the soldiers from Pensacola to Alabama and on the eve of the battle described the extraordinary camaraderie he witnessed during the two-week-long march. "I have never witnessed such a friendly feeling between white and colored troops," he boasted. "During the whole march I have not heard a word of reproach cast upon a colored soldier. But on the other hand, I have seen the two divisions exchange gifts, and talk with each other with apparent equality."[113]

On April 9, 1865, Confederate troops near Mobile, Alabama, yielded to Union forces, drawing the Battle of Fort Blakely to a close, while at the same time more than one thousand miles away in Appomattox Court House, Virginia, General Robert E. Lee surrendered the Army of Northern Virginia to General Ulysses S. Grant. The Civil War was over, and across the former slave states an entire society built on human bondage and racial inequality lay in ruins. While historians will continue to debate whether bondspeople emancipated themselves during the war, or if they were the beneficiaries of an invading army that came increasingly to see the abolition of slavery as a convenient wartime strategy, it is clear that in at least one seaport on the Southern frontier both groups were responsible for the destruction of slavery. In Pensacola, fugitive slaves had long refused to accept their enslaved status, and when the Civil War multiplied the number of their allies, the institution of slavery crumbled in the face of an unprecedented interracial assault. Slavery was no more, and if events in Pensacola and at Fort Pickens were an indication, the ideology of white supremacy would soon follow in its wake.

TWO YEARS AFTER the defeat of the Confederacy, an enthusiastic crowd gathered in Pensacola's public square to further the process of organizing a new city government. During the assembly, three men who represented the emergent factions that were vying for political power throughout the South—Scalawags, Carpetbaggers, and freedmen—addressed the large integrated assembly. The first speaker was the former United States senator and Confederate secretary of war Stephen Russell Mallory, who implored all those in the audience who once supported the Confederacy to stop resisting the federal government because "further resistance would be madness." He explained why it was in the best interest of all Floridians to support the freedmen in their bid to secure voting rights, maintaining that black suffrage was the natural result of the outcome of the war. Then, to prove his unwavering support of a new era in the South, Mallory offered a comment on the freedmen that must be considered as radical as any that ever emanated from the mouth of a former Confederate cabinet member: "Let us fully and frankly acknowledge, as well by deeds as by words, their equality with us, before the law, and regard it as no less just to ourselves and them than to our State and her best interest to aid in their education, elevation and enjoyment of all the rights which follow their new condition."[1]

The next two orators directed their attention at the former slaves who stood before them now as free people. J. D. Wolfe, a former captain in the Twenty-Fifth Regiment Infantry United States Colored Troops, warned the freedmen of the danger of following those who encouraged them to align themselves along racial lines. He instead urged the freedmen to adopt "a course which would identify them with the community in which they resided." Hays Satterwhite, a former bondsman, likewise suggested the freedmen pursue a more moderate position regarding their former masters. After cautioning against the formation of two "separate societies"—one black and one white—he declared with conviction, "It was the white man's interest to protect the black man, and the black man's to make friends of the white man."[2]

The speakers' dreams of a color-blind city nearly came true. Though not immune to contention and conflict, Pensacola was, relative to the rest of the postbellum South, a paragon of interracial community following the Civil War. Indeed, while Reconstruction failed and Jim Crow triumphed throughout the rest of the South, the opportunities for African Americans in postbellum Pensacola were extraordinary. For decades, the city's leaders included black business owners, bureaucrats, policemen, and politicians. A notable example was Salvador Pons, a state legislator of African and Mexican descent, who remains Pensacola's only black mayor.[3] At the turn of the twentieth century, Booker T. Washington considered the city one of the most progressive communities in the entire South as black people enjoyed "relations of helpful co-operation with the members of the white population."[4] Several years later, a Creole of Spanish and African descent who was born in the city before the Civil War remarked of the postwar era, "White and colored worked together for the good of everyone."[5]

Things changed in the coming years, however, as Pensacola began shedding its frontier status and emerged as "an important center in the New South."[6] A thriving shipping industry and the opening of the Naval Air Station in the first decades of the twentieth century brought a flood of white Southern laborers, who migrated to the city in record numbers and implanted the prejudiced and provincial views they brought with them from nearly every corner of the former Confederacy. Soon, a bifurcated community divided along rigid racial boundaries and characterized by separate neighborhoods, workplaces, and institutions replaced the once multiracial, multiethnic, and multinational society, as both de jure and de facto racial segregation became the norm.[7] In the aftermath of this radical transformation, interracialism and the memory of it having ever existed in Pensacola disappeared from the city almost entirely.

Today, there are no memorials to the fugitive slaves who defied their masters and risked their lives to become free. Nor are there any markers commemorating the sailors, soldiers, and civilians who befriended, defended, and assisted them. Instead, public monuments suggest the unlikelihood of such collaborations having ever taken place—that Pensacola was a cornerstone of the Old South.[8] On the site of the old Fort George/Fort San Miguel, where British troops during the War of 1812 and Union soldiers during the Civil War welcomed fugitive slaves into their ranks, a thirty-foot-tall statue of Robert E. Lee peers over the downtown area. Several blocks away, a Confederate flag flies prominently above a rare racially integrated cemetery that dates back to the colonial period. Where scholars could have offered an anecdote to this obvious case of historical amnesia, the historiography is equally silent. The only monograph on Civil War Pensacola mentions African Americans only sparingly, while in a more recent study neither the words "slave," "slavery," nor any related terms appear in the index at all.[9]

Despite the silencing, evidence of Pensacola having served for more than a century as both a source of and sanctuary for fugitive slaves survives in the historical record. Though racial slavery spread across Pensacola and the rest of the Atlantic and Southern frontiers, slaveowners and other white elites struggled to subjugate enslaved people who continued to disappear into the woods or on the water that encompassed the region. That fugitive slaves often received the assistance of free people of various races and ethnicities suggests that slave opposition along the South's perimeter was more extensive and enduring than previously understood. Interracial resistance to slavery survived in Pensacola from the colonial era through the Civil War, and when that great conflict came it helped accomplish the institution's destruction both in the city and beyond.

ABBREVIATIONS

≈

NOTES

≈

ACKNOWLEDGMENTS

≈

INDEX

≈

⊰ ABBREVIATIONS ⊱

ACP	Alexander Cochrane Papers, Williams Research Center, the Historic New Orleans Collection, New Orleans
ASP	*American State Papers: Foreign Relations,* 6 vols., Washington, DC, 1833–1859
CAJ	John Spencer Bassett, ed., *Correspondence of Andrew Jackson,* 7 vols. (Washington, DC: Carnegie Institution of Washington, 1926–1935)
CCC	Clerk of the Circuit Court, Archives and Records Division, Escambia County, Pensacola
HCP	Heloise H. Cruzat Papers, PKY
JMP	James Madison Papers, LOC
JLP	Joseph Byrne Lockey Papers, PKY
LOC	Library of Congress, Washington, DC
NAGB	National Archives of Great Britain, Admiralty (ADM) and War Office (WO) records, Kew, London
NARA	National Archives and Records Administration, Washington, DC, and College Park, MD
ORA	*Official Records of the Union and Confederate Armies in the War of the Rebellion,* 128 vols., Washington, DC, 1894–1927.
PAJ	Sam B. Smith and Harriet Chappell Owsley, eds., *Papers of Andrew Jackson,* 6 vols. (Knoxville: University of Tennessee Press, 1980–2002)
PC	*Papeles de Cuba,* Archivo General de Indias, University of Florida, Gainesville
PKY	P. K. Yonge Library of Florida History, University of Florida, Gainesville
PLCC	Panton, Leslie & Company Collection, University of West Florida, University Archives and West Florida History Center, Pensacola

◀ NOTES ▶

Introduction

1. "$50. Reward," *Pensacola Gazette,* June 16, 1838.
2. "100 Dollars Reward," *Montgomery Gazette and Commercial Advertiser,* June 13, 1819; "Ranaway," *Pensacola Gazette,* August 11, 1829; "$20. Reward," *Pensacola Gazette,* October 13, 1838.
3. Eric Foner, *Gateway to Freedom: The Hidden History of the Underground Railroad* (New York: W. W. Norton, 2015); Fergus M. Bordewich, *The Underground Railroad and the War for the Soul of America* (New York: Amistad, 2005).
4. Harriet Beecher Stowe, *Uncle Tom's Cabin; or, Life among the Lowly* (Boston: John P. Jewett & Company, 1852).
5. By 1860, five Southern states contained an enslaved population approaching half a million, and only Virginia with an enslaved population of 490,865 was outside the Deep South. Historians have long granted Virginia particular significance given its massive slave population, since on the eve of the Civil War, more enslaved people resided in this than any other state. Yet the number of slaves had increased only slightly since 1820. The slave population in the Deep South experienced a different trajectory. On the eve of the Civil War, South Carolina, Mississippi, Alabama, and Georgia had slave populations exceeding 400,000, and in the four decades prior, their slave populations—unlike Virginia's—multiplied many times over. Between 1820 and 1860, Georgia's slave population increased from 149,656 to 462,198, Alabama's from 41,879 to 435,080, and Mississippi's from 32,814 to 436,631, a multiplication of well more than ten times over. Florida's slave population, though miniscule by comparison, experienced a similar rate of increase. In 1830, U.S. census takers reported a slave population of 15,501; thirty years later the number had risen to 61,745, a multiplication of nearly 300 percent. United States Bureau of the Census, *Negro Population in the United States 1790–1915* (New York: Arno Press and the New York Times, 1968), 57.
6. Sarah E. Cornell, "Citizens of Nowhere: Fugitive Slaves and Free African Americans in Mexico, 1833–1857," *Journal of American History* 100, no.

2 (September 2013): 351–374; Irvin D. S. Winsboro and Joe Knetsch, "Florida Slaves, the 'Saltwater Railroad' to the Bahamas, and Anglo-American Diplomacy," *Journal of Southern History* 79, no. 1 (February 2013): 51–78; Jane Landers, "Southern Passage: The Forgotten Route to Freedom in Florida," in *Passages to Freedom: The Underground Railroad in History and Memory*, ed. David Blight (Washington, DC: Smithsonian Books, 2004), 117–131; Jane Landers, *Black Society in Spanish Florida* (Urbana: University of Illinois Press, 1999).

7. For an introduction to the concept as well as its strengths and weaknesses, see Jack P. Greene and Philip D. Morgan, eds., *Atlantic History: A Critical Appraisal* (Oxford: Oxford University Press, 2008); Alison Games, "Atlantic History: Definitions, Challenges, Opportunities," *American Historical Review* 111, no. 3 (2006): 741–757; Alison Games, Philip J. Stern, Paul W. Mapp, and Peter Coclanis, "Forum: Beyond the Atlantic," *William and Mary Quarterly* 63, no. 4 (October 2006): 675–742; Bernard Bailyn, *Atlantic History: Concept and Contours* (Cambridge, MA: Harvard University Press, 2005), 675–776; David Eltis, "Atlantic History in Global Perspective," *Itinerario* 23, no. 2 (1999): 141–161; Bernard Bailyn, "The Idea of Atlantic History," *Itinerario* 20, no. 1 (1996): 19–44.

8. A sampling of the wide variety of works in the Black Atlantic includes Randy J. Sparks, *Where the Negroes Are Masters: An African Port in the Era of the Slave Trade* (Cambridge, MA: Harvard University Press, 2013); James H. Sweet, *Domingos Alvares, African Healing, and the Intellectual History of the Atlantic World* (Chapel Hill: University of North Carolina Press, 2011); James H. Sweet, *Recreating Africa: Culture, Kinship, and Religion in the African-Portuguese World, 1441–1770* (Chapel Hill: University of North Carolina Press, 2003); Laurent Dubois and Julius S. Scott, eds., *Origins of the Black Atlantic* (New York: Routledge Taylor & Francis Group, 2010); Linda M. Heywood, Central Africans, *Atlantic Creoles, and the Foundation of the Americas, 1585–1660* (New York: Cambridge University Press, 2007); Stephanie E. Smallwood, "African Guardians, European Slave Ships, and the Changing Dynamics of Power in the Early Modern Atlantic," *William and Mary Quarterly* 64, no. 4 (October 2007): 679–716; Kevin Dawson, "Enslaved Swimmers and Divers in the Atlantic World," *Journal of American History* 92, no. 4 (March 2006): 1327–1355; José C. Curto and Paul E. Lovejoy, eds., *Enslaving Connections: Changing Cultures of Africa and Brazil during the Era of Slavery* (Amherst, NY: Humanity Books, 2004); Toyin Falola and Matt D. Childs, eds., *The Yoruba Diaspora in the Atlantic World* (Bloomington: Indiana University Press, 2004); James Walvin, *Making the Black Atlantic: Britain and the African Diaspora* (New York: Cassell, 2000); Deborah Gray White, "'Yes,' There Is a Black Atlantic," *Itinerario* 23 (1999): 127–140; John Thornton, *Africans in the Making of the Atlantic World, 1400–1800* (New York: Cambridge University Press, 1998); Paul Gilroy, *The Black Atlantic: Modernity and Double Consciousness*

(Cambridge, MA: Harvard University Press, 1993); James Barker Farr, *Black Odyssey: The Seafaring Traditions of Afro-Americans* (New York: Lang, 1989); Peter Wood, *Black Majority: Negroes in Colonial South Carolina from 1670 through the Stono Rebellion* (New York: W. W. Norton, 1975).

9. David S. Cecelski, *The Waterman's Song: Slavery and Freedom in Maritime North Carolina* (Chapel Hill: University of North Carolina Press, 2001); Kathryn Grover, *The Fugitive's Gibraltar: Escaping Slaves and Abolitionism in New Bedford, Massachusetts* (Amherst: University of Massachusetts Press, 2001); W. Jeffrey Bolster, *Black Jacks: African American Seamen in the Age of Sail* (Cambridge, MA: Harvard University Press, 1997); Martha S. Putney, *Black Sailors: Afro-American Merchant Seamen and Whalemen Prior to the Civil War* (New York: Greenwood Press, 1987).

10. Thomas Bender, "Introduction, Historians, the Nation, and the Plentitude of Narratives," in *Rethinking American History in a Global Age*, ed. Thomas Bender (Berkeley: University of California Press, 2002), 1–21.

11. For the Southern frontier and its transformation in the century before the Civil War, see Watson W. Jennison, *Cultivating Race: The Expansion of Slavery in Georgia, 1750–1860* (Lexington: University Press of Kentucky, 2012); Adam Rothman, *Slave Country: American Expansion and the Origins of the Deep South* (Cambridge, MA: Harvard University Press, 2007); Richard F. Brown, ed., *Coastal Encounters: The Transformation of the Gulf South in the Eighteenth Century* (Lincoln: University of Nebraska Press, 2007); John Craig Hammond, *Slavery, Freedom, and Expansion in the Early American West* (Charlottesville: University of Virginia Press, 2007); David Colin Crass, Steven D. Smith, Martha A. Zierded, and Richard D. Brooks, eds., *The Southern Colonial Backcountry: Interdisciplinary Perspectives on Frontier Communities* (Knoxville: University of Tennessee Press, 1998); Thomas D. Clark and John D. W. Guice, *The Old Southwest, 1795–1830: Frontiers in Conflict* (Norman: University of Oklahoma Press, 1996); Christopher Morris, *Becoming Southern: The Evolution of a Way of Life, Warren County and Vicksburg, Mississippi, 1770–1860* (New York: Oxford University Press, 1995); John Hebron Moore, *The Emergence of the Cotton Kingdom in the Old Southwest: Mississippi, 177–1860* (Baton Rouge: Louisiana State University Press, 1988); Everett Dick, *The Dixie Frontier: A Social History of the Southern Frontier from the First Transmontane Beginnings to the Civil War* (New York: Alfred A. Knopf, 1948). For the Florida frontier specifically, refer to Paul E. Hoffman, *Florida's Frontiers* (Bloomington: Indiana University Press, 2002); Edward E. Baptist, *Creating an Old South: Middle Florida's Plantation Frontier before the Civil War* (Chapel Hill: University of North Carolina Press, 2001); Frank Lawrence Owsley, Jr., and Gene A. Smith, *Filibusters and Expansionists: Jeffersonian Manifest Destiny, 1800–1821* (Tuscaloosa: University of Alabama Press, 1997); Julia Floyd Smith, *Slavery and Plantation Growth in Antebellum Florida, 1821–1860* (Gainesville: University of Florida Press, 1973). Important works on the Indian experience along the Southern frontier include William S.

Belko, ed., *America's Hundred Years' War: U.S. Expansion to the Gulf Coast and the Fate of the Seminole, 1763–1858* (Gainesville: University Press of Florida, 2011); Angela Pulley Hudson, *Creek Paths and Federal Roads: Indians, Settlers, and Slaves and the Making of the American South* (Chapel Hill: University of North Carolina Press, 2010); Christina Snyder, *Slavery in Indian Country: The Changing Face of Captivity in Early America* (Cambridge, MA: Harvard University Press, 2010); Robbie Franklyn Ethridge, *Creek Country: The Creek Indians and Their World* (Chapel Hill: University of North Carolina Press, 2003); Claudio Saunt, *A New Order of Things: Property, Power, and the Transformation of the Creek Indians, 1733–1816* (New York: Cambridge University Press, 2003); Kathryn H. Braund, *Deerskins and Duffels: The Creek Indian Trade with Anglo-America, 1685–1815* (Lincoln: University of Nebraska Press, 1993); James W. Covington, *The Seminoles of Florida* (Gainesville: University Press of Florida, 1993); J. Leitch Wright, *Creeks and Seminoles: The Destruction and Regeneration of the Muscogulge People* (Lincoln: University of Nebraska Press, 1986); John Walton Caughey, *McGillivray of the Creeks* (Norman: University of Oklahoma Press, 1938).

12. Anthony Kaye, "The Second Slavery: Modernity in the Nineteenth Century South and the Atlantic World," *Journal of Southern History* 75, no. 3 (August 2009): 627–650; Dale Tomich, *Through the Prism of Slavery: Labor, Capital, and World Economy* (Lanham, MD: Rowman & Littlefield, 2004).

13. Pensacola is known as the City of Five Flags, for at different times over the course of five centuries, Spain, France, Great Britain, the Confederate States of America, and the United States of America all laid claim to the city. The Spanish conquest lasted approximately from 1698 to 1719, 1722 to 1763, and 1781 to 1821. France claimed the city from 1719 to 1722, while British rule lasted from 1763 to 1781.

14. Despite its small stature, Pensacola was Florida's largest urban area before the Civil War. In 1860, Pensacola's population was 2,876, followed by Key West at 2,832 and Jacksonville at 2,118. Joseph C. G. Kennedy, *Population of the United States in 1860* (Washington, DC: Government Printing Office, 1864), 54.

15. Edwin Wiley and Irving E. Rines, eds., *The United States: Its Beginnings, Progress and Modern Development, Vol. VI, Third Period: The Federal Union Under the Constitution, 1789–1865* (Washington, DC: American Educational Alliance, 1913), 63.

16. Important works include Edward Blum, *Reforging the White Republic* (Baton Rouge: Louisiana State University Press, 2007); Melvin Patrick Ely, *Israel on the Appomattox: A Southern Experiment in Black Freedom from 1790s through the Civil War* (New York: Random House, 2004); John Stauffer, *The Black Hearts of Men: Radical Abolitionists and the Transformation of Race* (Cambridge, MA: Harvard University Press, 2001); Paul Goodman, *Of One Blood: Abolitionism and the Origins of Racial Equality* (Berkeley: University of California Press, 1998).

17. Examples are Cecelski, *The Waterman's Song;* Bolster, *Black Jacks;* Peter Linebaugh and Marcus Rediker, *The Many-Headed Hydra: Sailors, Slaves, Commoners, and the Hidden History of the Revolutionary Atlantic* (Boston: Beacon Press, 2000).

Chapter 1

1. Karl Bernhard, *Travels through North America, during the Years 1825 and 1826. By His Highness, Bernhard, Duke of Saxe-Weimar Eisenach* (Philadelphia: Carey, Lea & Carey, 1828), 2:45.
2. Ibid., 49.
3. William S. Coker, "Pensacola, 1686–1821," in *Archeology of Colonial Pensacola,* ed. Judith A. Bense (Gainesville: University Press of Florida, 1999), 6.
4. Frederick W. Hodge, ed., "The Narrative of Alvar Nunez Cabeza de Vaca," in *Spanish Explorers in the Southern United States, 1528–1542* (New York: Charles Scribner's Sons, 1907), 5, 38–39; Jane E. Dysart, "Indians in Colonial Pensacola," in Bense, *Archeology of Colonial Pensacola,* 61–62.
5. Another enslaved African disappeared into Indian country with a Greek shipwright several days after leaving Pensacola. Whether the two men chose to remain among the Indians or, as some have suggested, they were killed by the Indians, remains a mystery. It is possible that this bondsman was the first fugitive slave in Pensacola's history. Coker, "Pensacola," 5; Hodge, "Narrative of Alvar Nunez Cabeza de Vaca," 40; Andrés Reséndez, *A Land So Strange: The Epic Journey of Cabeza de Vaca* (New York: Perseus Books, 2007), 124–125.
6. George P. Hammon, *Narratives of the Coronado Expedition 1540–1542* (Albuquerque: University of New Mexico Press, 1940), 43–77, 141–145, 159–160, 177–178, 197–199; Robert Goodwin, *Crossing the Continent 1527–1540: The Story of the First African-American Explorer of the American South* (New York: HarperCollins, 2008), 79–129; Rayford W. Logan, "Estevanico, Negro Discoverer of the Southwest: A Critical Reexamination," *Phylon* 1, no. 4 (1940): 305–314.
7. Herbert Ingram Priestly, trans. and ed., *The Luna Papers, 1559–1561* (Tuscaloosa: University of Alabama Press, 2010), 1:xxxiv; Charles W. Arnade, "Tristan de Luna and Ochuse (Pensacola Bay) 1559," *Florida Historical Quarterly* 37, nos. 3–4 (January–April 1959): 201–222.
8. Priestly, *Luna Papers,* 2:285. In return for the promises of salary for themselves and special privileges for their wives and children, these Aztec mercenaries fashioned their own weapons and enlisted their own servants. Years later, survivors among them petitioned the Spanish crown for the yet unpaid compensation for their services. No evidence suggests the role of Africans in the Luna expedition as soldiers, but given the role of

black auxiliary troops throughout New Spain it would be incredible if none served the expedition in a military capacity. William S. Coker and Jerrell H. Shofner, *Florida: From the Beginning to 1992* (Houston: Pioneer Publications, 1991), 12–13; Jane Landers, "Transforming Bondsmen into Vassals: Arming Slaves in Colonial Spanish America," in *Arming Slaves: From Classical Times to the Modern Age,* ed. Christopher Leslie Brown and Philip D. Morgan (Hartford, CT: Yale University Press, 2006), 120–145; Matthew Restall, "Black Conquistadors: Armed Africans in Early Spanish America," *The Americas* 57, no. 2 (October 2000): 171–205.

9. Priestly, *Luna Papers,* 1:55.
10. Michael Gannon, "First European Contacts," in *The New History of Florida,* ed. Michael Gannon (Gainesville: University Press of Florida, 1996), 35–36.
11. William S. Coker and R. Wayne Childers, "The First Permanent European Settlement on the Northern Gulf Coast, 1698–1722," in *Santa María de Galve: A Story of Survival,* ed. Virginia Parks (Pensacola: Pensacola Historical Society, 1998), 11–98.
12. An early census confirms a population that was 41 percent mestizo—a combination of Indian and Spanish—34 percent Spanish, 21 percent black and mulatto, and 4 percent zambo, or a mixture of Indian and African. Hailing from Vera Cruz, Mexico, and other parts of New Spain, this variegated population of several hundred served the garrison in various capacities as soldiers, skilled and unskilled laborers, servants, and slaves. Many were convicts. Banished to Pensacola for various crimes, they often enlisted as soldiers upon arrival. Consequently, the distinction between convict and soldiers was often indeterminable, except for "the gravity of their crimes and severity of their punishments." John James Clune, Jr., R. Wayne Childers, William S. Coker, and Brenda N. Swann, "Settlement, Settlers, and Survivors," in *Presidio Santa María de Galve: A Struggle for Survival in Colonial Spanish Pensacola,* ed. Judith A. Bense (Gainesville: University of Florida Press, 2003), 25–27, quotations on 25 and 27. The racial ordering at Pensacola mimicked that in Saint Augustine. Amy Turner Bushnell, "Republic of Spaniards, Republic of Indians," in Gannon, *The New History of Florida,* 64.
13. Dunbar Rowland, A. G. Sanders, and Patricia Kay Galloway, eds., *Mississippi Provincial Archives: English Dominion* (Nashville: Brandon Printing Company, 1911), 1:136.
14. "The Summary of Public Affairs of 1765," *Scots Magazine* 28 (February 1766): 65.
15. "A Different Account of that Province," *Gentleman's Magazine* 35 (February 1765): 77.
16. "PROCLAMATION By his Excellency George Johnstone, Esq., Captain-General, Governor and Commander in Chief in and over his Majesty's province of West Florida," *Gentleman's Magazine* 35 (February 1765): 75–77.
17. Edmund Burke, *The Annual Register; or, A View of the History, Politicks, and Literature, of the Year 1762* (London: R. and J. Dodsley, 1763), 56.

18. Cecil Johnson, *British West Florida, 1763–1783* (Hamden, CT: Archon Books, 1971), 1–23; Cecil Johnson, "Pensacola in the British Period," *Florida Historical Quarterly* 37, nos. 3–4 (January–April 1959): 264–265.

19. Peter J. Hamilton, "British West Florida," *Mississippi Historical Society* 7 (1903): 404–406. Major revisions continued with the arrival of Frederick Haldimand in 1767. Disturbed by the death rate among soldiers as the result of various diseases, the brigadier general ordered the widening of streets and the draining of swamps in addition to the construction of new barracks. Coker, "Pensacola 1686–1821," 29; Robert R. Rea, "Brigadier Frederick Haldimand—the Florida Years," *Florida Historical Quarterly* 54, no. 4 (April 1976): 515–517. For mortality rates in West Florida, see Robert R. Rea, "'Graveyard for Britons,' West Florida, 1763–1781," *Florida Historical Quarterly* 47, no. 4 (April 1969): 345–364.

20. William Bartram, *Travels of William Bartram,* ed. Mark Van Doren (New York: Dover Publications, 1955), 332.

21. There were two types of land grants made available to entice prospective settlers. The colonial government offered one hundred acres of free land to any head of household with fifty addition acres for every family member—including slaves—that accompanied them. The landowner could then purchase additional land at five shillings per acre. The Privy Council offered grants of as many as twenty-two thousand acres to friends of the king, which had the effect of putting much of the colony in the hands of speculators who had no intention of improving the land or contributing in any meaningful way to the development of the colony. Robin Fabel, *The Economy of British West Florida, 1763–1783* (Tuscaloosa: University of Alabama Press, 1988), 7–10; Charlton W. Tebeau, *A History of Florida* (Coral Gables: University of Miami Press, 1971), 80.

22. James A. Padgett, "Minutes of the Council of West Florida," *Louisiana Historical Quarterly* 23, no. 2 (April 1940): 383.

23. One contingent known as the Company of Military Adventurers stood out. Consisting of several hundred highly educated and heavily armed New Englanders, they made use of a royal directive that provided free land for revolutionary war veterans. Fabel, *Economy of British West Florida*, 6–15, 153–197.

24. Rowland, Sanders, and Galloway, *Mississippi Provincial Archives,* 1:256–257.

25. Robert R. Rea and Milo B. Howard, Jr., eds., *The Minutes, Journals, and Acts of the General Assembly of British West Florida* (Tuscaloosa: University of Alabama Press, 1979), 319–321, 364–367, 386–387, 389–391, quotations on 386.

26. "News Foreign and Domestic," *Universal Magazine* 249, no. 36 (March 1765): 163.

27. Fabel, *Economy of British West Florida*, 7–8, 15–38, 115–131.

28. Rea and Howard, *Minutes, Journals, and Acts of the General Assembly*, 330–336, 342–347. This second act repealed the Slave Act of January 1757, only to

be repealed itself by the Privy Council in January 1772, thus restoring the former law. Fabel, *Economy of British West Florida*, 26; Johnson, *British West Florida*, 173–174.

29. Rea and Howard, *Minutes, Journals, and Acts of the General Assembly*, 330–336, 342–347, quotations on 330–331.

30. Fabel, *The Economy of British West Florida*, 28.

31. Jane Landers, "Gracia Real de Santa Teresa de Mose: A Free Black Town in Spanish Colonial Florida," *American Historical Review* 95, no. 1 (February 1990): 9–30.

32. "Extract of a Letter from S. Carolina, dated October 2," *Gentleman's Magazine* 10 (March 1740): 127–130; Mark M. Smith, ed., *Stono: Documenting and Interpreting a Southern Slave Revolt* (Columbia: University of South Carolina Press, 2005); Peter H. Wood, *Black Majority: Negroes in Colonial South Carolina from 1670 through the Stono Rebellion* (New York: W. W. Norton, 1996), 308–330; John K. Thornton, "African Dimensions of the Stono Rebellion," *American Historical Review* 96, no. 4 (October 1991): 1101–1113.

33. George Rawick, ed., *The American Slave: A Composite Autobiography* (Westport, CT: Greenwood, 1977), 11:100.

34. Jane L. Landers, "Traditions of African American Freedom and Community in Spanish Colonial Florida," in *The African American Heritage of Florida*, ed. David R. Colburn and Jane L. Landers (Gainesville: University Press of Florida, 1995), 25.

35. For the distinction between "slave societies" and "societies with slaves" refer to Ira Berlin, *Generations of Captivity: A History of African-American Slaves* (Cambridge, MA: Harvard University Press, 2003), 8–12. For a discussion of fugitive slaves in British Florida generally, see Paul E. Hoffman, *Florida's Frontiers* (Bloomington: Indiana University Press, 2002), 207–242; Daniel L. Schafer, "Yellow Silk Ferret Tied Round Their Wrists: African Americans in British East Florida, 1763–1784," in Colburn and Landers, *The African American Heritage of Florida*, 71–103; Fabel, *Economy of British West Florida*, 27–28.

36. *By Frederick Haldimand Esqr., Brigadier General of His Majesty's Forces Commanding the Southern District of North America, &c. &c.* (New Orleans: Denis Braud, 1768).

37. Daniel Clark to Major Lanin, undated, PLCC.

38. "Pensacola, July 27, 1767," *South-Carolina Gazette*, September 14, 1767, 1.

39. A list of residents in 1781 mentions white carpenters, tailors, blacksmiths, and bricklayers. William S. Coker and Rodrigo Fernández Carrión, "List of the Inhabitants of Pensacola Who Were Householders at the Time of the Capitulation," *Florida Historical Quarterly* 77, no. 1 (Summer 1998): 68–72.

40. Fabel, *Economy of British West Florida*, 38–43, 214; Robert R. Rea, "Brigadier Frederick Haldimand—the Florida Years," *Florida Historical Quarterly* 54, no. 4 (April 1976): 516–517.

41. Peter Chester to Bernardo de Gálvez, [1778], *PC*, legajo 204, folio 718–720, reel 283.

42. Peter Chester to Bernardo de Gálvez, [1778], in Lawrence Kinnaird, ed., *Annual Report of the American Historical Association for the Year 1945, vol. II, Spain in the Mississippi Valley, 1765–1794 (Pt. I) The Revolutionary Period, 1765–1781* (Washington, DC: United States Government Printing Office, 1949), 247.

43. Kinnaird, *Annual Report of the American Historical Association for the Year 1945*, 247.

44. Fabel, "British Rule in the Floridas," in Gannon, *The New History of Florida*, 136; Dysart, "Indians in Colonial Pensacola," 61–89.

45. Governor Johnstone exacerbated the problem by suggesting that the various Indian peoples were organizing an intertribal army in order to exterminate the "their Common Enemies." Rowland, Sanders, and Galloway, *Mississippi Provincial Archives*, 1:184.

46. Vincent Carretta, ed., *Unchained Voices: An Anthology of Black Authors in the English-Speaking World of the 18th Century* (Lexington: University Press of Kentucky, 2004), 333–334. For the life of David George, see Kathleen Tudor, "David George: Black Loyalist," *Nova Scotia Historical Review* 3 (1983): 71–82.

47. Newton D. Mereness, ed., *Travels in the American Colonies* (New York: Macmillan, 1916), 3:525.

48. Duke de la Rochefoucault Liancourt, *Travels through the United States of North America, the Country of the Iroquois, and Upper Canada, in the Years 1795, 1796, and 1797, Second Edition* (London: T. Gillet, 1800), 2:467–468.

49. Johnson, *British West Florida*, 169.

50. "Brought from the Creek Nation," *Georgia Gazette*, January 10, 1770, 4. For a discussion of the people of Angolan and Congolese descent brought to the Gulf Coast in the late eighteenth century, see Berlin, *Generations of Captivity*, 45, 69–70; Gwendolyn Midlo Hall, *Africans in Colonial Louisiana: The Development of Afro-Creole Culture in the Eighteenth Century* (Baton Rouge: Louisiana State University Press, 1992). For the slave trade and slave imports to British West Florida, see Fabel, *Economy of British West Florida*, 32–38.

51. Lathan A. Windley, *Runaway Slave Advertisements: A Documentary History from the 1730s to 1790* (Westport, CT: Greenwood Press, 1983), 4:43–44.

52. Ibid., 4:31–32.

53. Ibid., 3:257–258.

54. Ibid., 4:88.

55. "WEST FLORIDA," *South-Carolina Gazette and American General Gazette*, January 27, 1775, 8.

56. William Dunbar, *Life, Letters and Papers of William Dunbar of Elgin, Morayshire, Scotland, and Natchez, Mississippi* (Jackson: Press of the Mississippi Historical Society, 1930), 29–30, 46–47.

57. J. Barton Starr, *Tories, Dons, and Rebels: The American Revolution in British West Florida* (Gainesville: University Press of Florida, 1976); J. Leitch Wright, Jr., *Florida in the American Revolution* (Gainesville: University Press of Florida, 1975).

58. Benjamin Franklin to Count D'Aranda, in Jared Sparks, ed., *The Works of Benjamin Franklin; Containing Several Political and Historical Tracts Not Included in Any Former Edition, and Many Letters Official and Private Not Hitherto Published; with Notes and a Life of the Author* (Boston: Tappan & Whittemore, 1839), 8:212–213.

59. In preparation of a strike against Pensacola, Gálvez dispatched Captain Jacinto Panis to evaluate the town's defenses. To gain access, Panis promised to negotiate a number of important issues with the British, including the return of fugitive slaves. Though there was some disagreement over the treatment of runaways, both sides agreed that fugitives from Spanish Louisiana and British West Florida "shall be restored upon requisition to their respective owners." Panis returned home with a detailed report of Pensacola that was consistent with previous accounts. Confident in their ability to sack the colonial capital, the Spanish moved quickly with their plans for a massive invasion by both land and sea. John Caughey, "The Panis Mission to Pensacola, 1778," *Hispanic American Historical Review* 10, no. 4 (November 1930): 480–489.

60. Bernardo de Gálvez, *Diario De Las Operaciones de la Expedicion contra la Plaza de Panzacola Concluida por las Armas de S. M. Catolica, baxo las Ordenes del Mariscal de Camp D. Bernardo de Galvez* (Tallahassee: Ashantilly Press, 1966), 34.

61. Roland C. McConnell, *Negro Troops of Antebellum Louisiana: A History of the Battalion of Free Men of Color* (Baton Rouge: Louisiana State University Press, 1968), 17–21, quotation on 17; Jack D. L. Holmes, "French and Spanish Military Units in the 1781 Pensacola Campaign," in *Anglo-Spanish Confrontation on the Gulf Coast during the American Revolution*, ed. William S. Coker and Robert R. Rea (Pensacola: Gulf Coast History and Humanities Conference, 1982), 145–157; Jack D. L. Holmes, *Honor and Fidelity: The Louisiana Infantry Regiment and the Louisiana Militia Companies, 1766–1821* (Birmingham: s.n., 1965), 54–57; Virginia Parks, ed., *Siege! Spain and Britain: Battle of Pensacola, March 9–May 8, 1781* (Pensacola: Pensacola Historical Society, 1981); Kinnaird, *Annual Report of the American Historical Association for the Year 1945*, 420–423; Albert W. Haarmann, "The Siege of Pensacola," *Florida Historical Quarterly* 44, no. 3 (January 1966): 194–199; James A. Padgett, "Bernardo de Galvez's Siege of Pensacola," *Louisiana Historical Quarterly* 26, no. 2 (April 1943): 327–329.

62. The best treatment of the Siege of Pensacola and the negotiations that followed is Starr, *Tories, Dons, and Rebels*, 193–224.

63. "Discurso Preliminar," *Mercurio Histórico y Politico* 1 (January 1782): 30.

64. "A Sketch of Pensacola," *National Intelligencer, and Washington Advertiser,* July 16, 1810, 2.

65. William S. Coker and G. Douglas Inglis, eds., *The Spanish Censuses of Pensacola, 1784–1820: A Genealogical Guide to Spanish Pensacola* (Pensacola: Perdido Bay Press, 1980); Peter Zahendra, "Spanish West Florida 1781–1821" (PhD diss., University of Michigan, 1976), 101; Duvon C. Corbitt, "The Last Spanish Census of Pensacola, 1820," *Florida Historical Quarterly* 74, no. 1 (July 1945): 30–38.

66. These backwoods settlers were, in the words of one authority, "intensely individualistic, physically tough and hardy, and resentful of all authority, including that of their own government." They cherished the ideas of self-government and "Protestant fundamentalism," while possessing an insatiable demand for land, all of which put them squarely "at odds with everything that Spain stood for in the Floridas." L. N. McAlister, "Pensacola during the Second Spanish Period," *Florida Historical Quarterly* 37, no. 3 (January–April 1959): 293.

67. Coker and Inglis, *The Spanish Censuses of Pensacola,* 31–45, 91–141; Corbitt, "The Last Spanish Census of Pensacola."

68. A starting point for the discussion of race in Latin American colonies and nations is Nancy P. Appelbaum, Anne S. McPherson, and Karin Alejandra Rosemblatt, eds., *Race and Nation in Modern Latin America* (Chapel Hill: University of North Carolina Press, 2003), and Peter Wade, *Race and Ethnicity in Latin America* (New York: Pluto Press, 1997).

69. Virginia Meacham Gould, "The Free Creoles of Color of the Antebellum Gulf Ports of Mobile and Pensacola: A Struggle for the Middle Ground," in *Creoles of Color of the Gulf South,* ed. James H. Dorman (Knoxville: University of Tennessee, 1996), 34.

70. Bondspeople comprised roughly one-third of Pensacola's St. Michael's Catholic Parish. William S. Coker, "Religious Censuses of Pensacola, 1796–1801," *Florida Historical Quarterly* 61, no. 1 (July 1982): 54–57; Coker and Inglis, *The Spanish Censuses of Pensacola, 1784–1820,* 49–76.

71. Coker, "Religious Censuses of Pensacola," 61; Eric Nelson, "Negros Y Pardos: An Introduction to Pensacola's People of Color, 1781–1821" (master's thesis, University of West Florida, 1998), 30–34.

72. C. C. Robin, *Voyage to Louisiana by C. C. Robin, 1803–186, an Abridged Translation from the Original French by Stuart O. Landry, Jr.* (New Orleans: Pelican Publishing Company, 1966), 4.

73. Corbitt, "The Last Spanish Census of Pensacola," 30–38; Coker and Inglis, *The Spanish Censuses of Pensacola,* 97–125. The authors consider whether the large number of women listed in the 1820 census records as seamstresses and laundresses were actually prostitutes (94).

74. Jack D. L. Holmes, "Pensacola: Spanish Dominion, 1781–1821," in *Colonial Pensacola: The Pensacola Series Commemorating the American Revolution,* ed. James R. McGovern (Pensacola: Tom White, 1974), 105.

75. Carolina Maude Burson, *The Stewardship of Don Esteban Miró, 1782–1792: A Study of Louisiana Based Largely on the Documents in New Orleans* (New Orleans: American Printing Company, 1940), 19, 40.

76. "Pensacola Military Orders," in McGovern, ed., *Colonial Pensacola,* 121.

77. Holmes, "Pensacola: Spanish Dominion, 1781–1821," fn. 148, 115; Jack D. L. Holmes, *Pensacola Settlers, 1781–1821* (Pensacola: Pensacola Historical Restoration and Preservation Commission, 1970), 61–63.

78. Vero Z. Amelung to Andrew Jackson, June 4, 1816, *ASP,* 4:557.

79. "Pensacola," *Louisiana Advertiser,* August 16, 1820, 1.

80. For a classic overview of coartación in Spain's American colonies in the nineteenth century, see Hubert H. S. Aimes, "Coartacion: A Spanish Institution for the Advancement of Slaves into Freedmen," *Yale Review* 17 (May 1908–February 1909): 412–431. For some of the limits and variations of the practice, see Alejandro de la Fuente, "Slaves and the Creation of Legal Rights in Cuba: *Coartación* and *Papel,*" in *Slavery and Antislavery in Spain's Atlantic Empire,* eds. Josep M. Frader and Christopher Schmidt-Nowara (New York: Berghahn Books, 2013), 101–133; Gloria García Rodríguez, *Voices of the Enslaved in Nineteenth-Century Cuba: A Documentary History,* trans. Nancy L. Westrate (Chapel Hill: University of North Carolina Press, 2011); Gwendolyn Midlo Hall, *Social Control in Slave Plantation Societies: A Comparison of St. Domingue and Cuba* (Baltimore: Johns Hopkins University Press, 1971).

81. It was, for slaveowners, a lucrative business. Rented bondspeople could earn their owners $1.50 per day or fifteen dollars per month, while the most highly skilled laborers, including the multilingual riverboat pilot who could navigate both barges and pirogues, brought twenty dollars per month. In 1814, Charles Deville offered the services of his boatman for twenty gourdes, which, along the Gulf Coast, equaled roughly twenty dollars. Charles Deville to John Innerarity, August 20, 1814, PLCC; Robin, *Voyage to Louisiana,* viii; "A Sketch of Pensacola."

82. Robin, *Voyage to Louisiana,* 10.

83. J. A. Brown, "Panton, Leslie and Company: Indian Traders of Pensacola and St. Augustine," *Florida Historical Quarterly* 37, nos. 3–4 (January–April 1959): 336.

84. The standard account of the firm is William S. Coker and Thomas D. Watson, *Indian Traders of the Southeastern Spanish Borderlands: Panton, Leslie & Company and John Forbes & Company, 1783–1847* (Pensacola: University Presses of Florida, 1986). In 1804, the firm reported $140,000 in Indian debts and total assets approaching $400,000. Arthur Preston Whitaker, *Documents Relating to the Commercial Policy of Spain in the Floridas, with Incidental Reference to Louisiana* (DeLand: Florida State Historical Society, 1931), 258.

85. Whitaker, *Documents Relating to the Commercial Policy of Spain in the Floridas,* 258. In their four-hundred-plus-page history of Panton, Leslie & Company, Coker and Watson make almost no mention of the hundreds of bondspeople

the company owned in Florida, Alabama, and the West Indies (Coker and Watson, *Indian Traders*).

86. Those who remained in Pensacola lived in either the company mansion, small company-owned cottages throughout town, or homes left vacant by the British: William Panton to El Baron de Carondelet, March 12, 1796, PLCC; El Baron de Carondelet to William Panton, April 16, 1796, PLCC; Real Estate List of Houses and Lots in Pensacola, December 16, 1799, PLCC. For some of the varieties of tasks performed by enslaved company employees, see Invoice of the Estate of Edmund Wegg, May 5, 1790, PLCC; William Panton to John Forbes, May 6, 1794, in "The Panton, Leslie Papers," *Florida Historical Quarterly* 14, no. 3 (January 1936): 217–218; John Forbes & Company Invoice, June 12, 1811, PLCC; "The Creek Nation, Debtor to John Forbes & Co., Successors to Panton, Leslie & Co: A Journal of John Innerarity, 1812," *Florida Historical Quarterly* 9, no. 2 (October 1930): 67–69; William S. Coker, *Historical Sketches of Panton, Leslie and Company* (Pensacola: University of West Florida, 1976), 30, 33.

87. Martín Navarro to Arturo O'Neill, May 22, 1782, *PC,* legajo 83A, folio 832, reel 442.

88. O'Neill to Josef de Ezpeleta, July 31, 1783, *PC,* legajo 36, folio 1244, reel 185.

89. Ibid., folio 1246, reel 185. See also Arturo O'Neill to Bernardo de Gálvez, December 11, 1781, *PC,* legajo 36, folio 373, reel 183, and; Arturo O'Neill to Martín Navarro, August 8, 1783, *PC,* legajo 614A, doc. 88, reel 211.

90. Arturo O'Neill to Bernardo de Gálvez, March 24, 1783, *PC,* legajo 36, folio 556, reel 183.

91. Christine Snyder, *Slavery in Indian Country: The Changing Face of Captivity in Early America* (Cambridge, MA: Harvard University Press, 2010), 199–200.

92. Vicente Folch to Casa Calvo, June 5, 1801, PLCC.

93. Daniel Clark to William Simpson, May 16, 1805, HCP.

94. "50 Dollars Reward," *Mobile Gazette and Commercial Advertiser,* April 19, 1820, 4.

95. Claim of John McKenzie, May 15, 1798, *Indian Depredations, 1787–1825*: Original Claims, ed. Louise Frederick Hays, 5 vols. (Atlanta: Georgia Department of Archives and History, 1938–1940), vol. 2, part 2:913.

96. McKenzie testified twenty-four years later the three bondsmen were "taken" by Creek traders who sold the captives in Pensacola "being destitute of Money." Claim of John McKenzie, January 22, 1822, "Indian Depredations, 1787–1825," vol. 2, part 1:391b–391f, quotations on 391c and 391b.

97. "Fifty Dollars Reward," *Georgia Argus,* June 8, 1814, 4.

98. "100 Dollars Reward," *Halcyon, and Tombeckbee Public Advertiser,* February 15, 1819, 4.

99. "Notice," *Halcyon, and Tombeckbee Public Advertiser,* June 7, 1819, 4.

100. Daniel Meaders, *Advertisements for Runaway Slaves in Virginia, 1801–1820* (New York: Garland Publishing, 1997), 147.

101. "100 Dollars Reward," *Mobile Gazette and Commercial Advertiser,* July 14, 1819, 2.

102. "Runaways in Jail," *Mobile Gazette and Commercial Advertiser,* June 15, 1820, 3.

103. "Ran-Away," *Mobile Gazette and Commercial Advertiser,* August 3, 1820, 3.

104. Daniel McGillivray to William Panton, July 13, 1798, PLCC.

105. Julian Carballo to Arturo O'Neill, [1791–1794], *PC,* legajo 39, folio 1635, reel 162.

106. Claudio Saunt, *A New Order of Things: Property, Power, and the Transformation of the Creek Indians, 1733–1816* (Cambridge: Cambridge University Press, 1999), 126.

107. John Walton Caughey, *McGillivray of the Creeks* (Norman: University of Oklahoma Press, 1938), 3–57.

108. A significant turning point for Indian and African American relations came after the American Revolution when McGillivray, on behalf of the Indians who remained in Spanish-occupied territory, agreed to pursue and return fugitive slaves to their masters. Article 8 of the 1784 treaty read, "We will not admit deserters, nor negroes, nor mulatto slaves, fugitives (amarones) of the provinces of Louisiana and Florida, into our establishments, and those who shall present themselves within them shall be immediately (apprehended) with us at the orders of the governor, satisfaction being made us by the corps if the person apprehended be a soldier, or by the master to whom he belongs if he be a slave." *Record in the Case of Colin Mitchell and Others, versus the United States. Supreme Court of the United States. January Term, 1831* (Washington: Duff Green, 1831), 322–323. See also Richard K. Murdoch, "The Return of Runaway Slaves 1790–1794," *Florida Historical Quarterly* 38, no. 2 (October 1859): 96–113; Jack D. L. Holmes, "Spanish Treaties with West Florida Indians, 1784–1802," *Florida Historical Quarterly* 48, no. 2 (October 1969): 140–154.

109. Alexander McGillivray to Arturo O'Neill, February 10, 1786, in Caughey, *McGillivray of the Creeks,* 103.

110. Daniel McGillivray to William Panton, September 28, 1799, PLCC. For Daniel McGillivray's origins, see Edward J. Cashin, *Lachlan McGillivray, Indian Trader: The Shaping of the Southern Colonial Frontier* (Athens: University of Georgia Press, 1992), 74.

111. Daniel McGillivray to Panton, Leslie & Company, June 18, 1796, PLCC.

112. Daniel McGillivray to John Forbes, June 23, 1803, Marie Taylor Greenslade Papers, University Archives and West Florida History Center, Pensacola.

113. Alexander McGillivray to Arturo O'Neill, October 5, 1786, *PC,* legajo 199, folio 791, reel 383. See also Martín Palao and Josef Monroy to Arturo O'Neill, November 23, 1788, *PC,* legajo 38, folio 600, reel 191; Gerald Byrne to Arturo O'Neill, December 3, 1788, *PC,* legajo 38, folio 623, reel 191; Two years later the effort to return the bondsmen to their owners continued.

McGillivray expressed to the Spanish governor the unlikelihood of any-one ever reclaiming the runaways, writing, "The Negroes of Capt. Paloa & Monroy & of Burns has been long in the Cherokees & may be now with the Americans." Alexander McGillivray to Arturo O'Neill, February 2, 1789, *PC*, legajo 202, folio 663, reel 281.

114. Alexander McGillivray to Arturo O'Neill, February 5, 1784, in Caughey, *McGillivray of the Creeks*, 69–70.

115. Arturo O'Neill to Bernardo de Gálvez, October 15, 1781, *PC*, legajo 36, folio 249, reel 183.

116. John Innerarity to James Innerarity, March 19, 1817, and April 2, 1817, PLCC.

117. William Augustus Bowles, *Authentic Memoirs of William Augustus Bowles* (New York: Arno Press and the New York Times, 1971); J. Leitch Wright, Jr., *William Augustus Bowles: Director General of the Creek Nation* (Athens: University of Georgia Press, 1967).

118. "St. Mary's, 24th June, 1800," *Charleston City Gazette and Daily Advertiser*, July 8, 1800, 2.

119. Jacobo Dubreuil to Manuel de Salcedo, January 20, 1802, *PC*, legajo 2355, folio 84, reel 381.

120. Wright, *William Augustus Bowles*, 145.

121. *Record in the Case of Colin Mitchell and Others*, 26.

122. "The Journal of Dr. John Sibley, July–October, 1802," *Louisiana Historical Society Quarterly* 10, no. 4 (October 1927): 483; "Natchez, August 11," *Centinel of Freedom*, October 19, 1802, 2.

123. William Panton to Edward Forrester and William Lawrence, May 7, 1799, PLCC.

124. From Commander of Fort San Marcos to the Muskogees, July 23, 1801, PLCC.

125. "A Plan for the Abolition of Slavery in the West Indies," *Gentleman's Magazine* 42 (July 1772): 325–326.

126. Christopher Leslie Brown, *Moral Capital: Foundations of British Abolitionism* (Chapel Hill: University of North Carolina Press, 2006), 213, 230.

127. The importation of Africans liberated from illegal slave ships after the aboli-tion of the slave trade in 1807 to the West Indian colonies of Trinidad and the Bahamas also indicates the reach of Morgann's plan. For the settlement of black refugees in Sierra Leone and throughout the British Empire, see Kevin Lowther, *The African American Odyssey of John Kizell: A South Carolina Slave Returns to Fight the Slave Trade in His African Homeland* (Columbus: University of South Carolina Press, 2011); Rosanne Marion Adderley, *"New Negroes from Africa": Slave Trade Abolition and Free African Settlement in the Nineteenth-Century Caribbean* (Bloomington: Indiana University Press, 2006); Cassandra Pybus, *Epic Journeys of Freedom: Runaway Slaves of the American Revolution and Their Global Quest for Liberty* (Boston: Beacon Press, 2006); Simon Schama, *Rough Crossings: Britain, the Slaves, and the American*

Revolution (New York: HarperCollins, 2006); James W. St. G. Walker, *The Black Loyalists: The Search for a Promised Land in Nova Scotia and Sierra Leone, 1783–1870* (Toronto: University of Toronto Press, 1992).

128. Wright, *William Augustus Bowles*, 94–95; For a contemporary account of the colony, see Zachary MaCaulay, *Life and Letters of Zachary MaCaulay: By His Granddaughter Viscountess Knutsford* (London: Edward Arnold, 1900), 26–57.

129. Dunmore's vision was not a fantasy. It was, in the words of J. Leitch Wright, Jr., "motivated both by genuine sympathy for the loyalists, black and white, and by self-interest." With Bowles's assistance, he would create "a pro-British loyalist-Indian state in the Old Southwest at the expense of Spain or the United States or both and to link it with the British in the Old Northwest and Canada." J. Leitch Wright, Jr., "Lord Dunmore's Loyalist Asylum in the Floridas," *Florida Historical Quarterly* 49, no. 4 (April 1971): 379. See also John K. Mahon, "British Strategy and Southern Indians: War of 1812," *Florida Historical Quarterly* 44, no. 4 (April 1966): 285–302.

130. James Innerarity to William Panton, July 5, 1800, PLCC.

131. Bowles lost the battle over Jack Philips, but he still hoped to win the war. The Canards avowed Bowles would never see Jack again, for they intended to return him to his owners. Despite the boast, Thompson feared Bowles would in the coming days "way-lay me and get the negroes" and thus used extreme caution transporting the bondsman to Saint Augustine. Wiley Thompson to James Seagrove, June 5, 1803, East Florida Papers, University Archives and West Florida History Center, Pensacola, reel 57, 1–5, quotations on 3–4.

132. For Bowles's capture and death, see Wright, *William Augusts Bowles*, 159–171; "A Journal of John Forbes, May, 1803: The Seizure of William Augusts Bowles," *Florida Historical Quarterly* 9, no. 4 (April 1931): 279–289.

133. Christina Snyder, "Conquered Enemies, Adopted Kin, and Owned People: The Creek Indians and Their Captives," *Journal of Southern History* 73, no. 2 (May 2007): 286.

134. For the naming and origins of the Seminole, see Saunt, *A New Order of Things,* 34–36; Snyder, *Slavery in Indian Country,* 213–215.

135. Saunt, *A New Order of Things,* 211.

136. The expression *Black Seminoles* conflates the Seminole and their black allies into a distinct people and implies a relationship between the Seminole and their black allies that did not exist. Keven Mulroy provides the clearest enunciation of the relationship between the Seminole and their black allies, writing, "Whether runaways, captives, or slaves of the Seminoles, these blacks preferred to live beyond the pale and ally with Europeans and Native Americans rather than remain enslaved on Southern plantations. Of major significance to their ethnohistory, the maroons' early and close association with the Seminoles would contribute strongly to the development of their identity. Yet these people would go on to establish a culture and history of their own and in so doing define themselves, and be defined

by others, as a separate and distinct entity." Kevin Mulroy, *Freedom on the Border* (Lubbock: Texas Tech University Press, 2003), 10–11.

137. Alexander McGillivray to Arturo O'Neill, February 10, 1786, *PC*, legajo 199, folio 769, reel 383.

Chapter 2

1. The New York media covered the visit extensively. *New York Times,* September 16, 21–25, and 27, 1852. For popular engravings based on the original photograph, see *Gleason's Pictorial,* October 23, 1852, 257; "'Billy Bowlegs' and Suite," *Illustrated London News,* May 21, 1853, 395–396.

2. Frank Lawrence Owsley, Jr., "British and Indian Activities in Spanish West Florida during the War of 1812," *Florida Historical Quarterly* 46, no. 2 (October 1967): 113–115.

3. For the British in Pensacola, see Nathaniel Millett, "Britain's 1814 Occupation of Pensacola and America's Response: An Episode of the War of 1812 in the Southeastern Borderlands," *Florida Historical Quarterly* 84, no. 2 (Fall 2005): 229–255; Frank Lawrence Owsley, Jr., *Struggle for the Gulf Borderlands: The Creek War and the Battle of New Orleans 1812–1815* (Gainesville: University Presses of Florida, 1981), 95–119; Owsley, "British and Indian Activities in Spanish West Florida during the War of 1812," 111–123.

4. Nathaniel Millett, *The Maroons of Prospect Bluff and Their Quest for Freedom in the Atlantic World* (Gainesville: University of Florida Press, 2013); Gene Allen Smith, *The Slaves' Gamble: Choosing Sides in the War of 1812* (New York: Palgrave Macmillan, 2013); Alan Taylor, *The Internal Enemy: Slavery and War in Virginia, 1772–1832* (New York: W. W. Norton, 2013), 213.

5. Taylor, *The Internal Enemy,* 213. Taylor's idea is explored thoroughly in Matthew Mason, "The Battle of the Slaveholding Liberators: Great Britain, the United States, and Slavery in the Early Nineteenth Century," *William and Mary Quarterly* 59, no. 3 (July 2002): 665–696.

6. Frank A. Cassell, "Slaves of the Chesapeake Bay Area and the War of 1812," *Journal of Negro History* 57, no. 2 (April 1972): 144.

7. Alexander Cochrane to Earl Bathurst, July 14, 1814, JLP, Box 16.

8. Alexander Cochrane, "A Proclamation," April 2, 1814, NAGB, ADM, 1/508, 579. For distribution of this and other British proclamations along the Gulf Coast, see George Woodbine to Alexander Cochrane, May 31, 1814, ACP, MS2328, reel 3, p. 14.

9. For brief biographies of Nicolls and Woodbine and the genuine abolition-ism at the root of Nicolls's actions in Florida, see Millett, *The Maroons of Prospect Bluff,* 19–27, 40–41.

10. John Innerarity, "Narrative of the Operations of the British in the Floridas," [January] 1815, HCP.

11. William H. Robertson to Harry Toulmin, October 26, 1814, accompanying a letter from William Blount to the Secretary of War, November 18, 1814, *Territorial Papers of the United States Senate, 1789–1873*, RG46, NARA, M200, reel 9.

12. Edward Nicolls, "Orders for the First Battalion of Royal Colonial Marines," [August 1814], in John W. Croker to Hamilton, April 7, 1818, JLP, Box 22. *Niles' Weekly Register* published a version of Nicolls's speech; however, the editors deleted all references to the fugitive slaves who had flocked to the British and their prospects of liberty. It was a glaring omission intended to subvert Great Britain's claim as the true beacon of freedom in America. "British Proclamations, &c.," *Niles' Weekly Register*, November 5, 1814, 133–135.

13. Andrew Jackson to Thomas Hart Benton, *PAJ*, 3:132.

14. William H. Robertson to Harry Toulmin, October 26, 1814, accompanying a letter from William Blount to the Secretary of War, November 18, 1814, *Territorial Papers of the United States Senate, 1789–1873*, RG46, NARA, M200, reel 9.

15. Reliable summaries of the battle include Owsley, *Struggle for the Gulf Borderlands*, 106–119, and William S. Coker, "The Last Battle of the War of 1812: New Orleans? No, Fort Bowyer!," *Alabama Historical Quarterly* 43, no. 1 (1981): 43–63. Nicolls remembered the deployment of an "irregular force" of 252 blacks, Indians, and Royal Marines. Edward Nicolls to Lord Melville, May 5, 1817, in Nicolls to Earl Bathurst, May 5, 1817, JLP, Box 16. The numbers are confirmed by the American opposition. See Andrew Jackson to Secretary Monroe, September 17, 1814, *CAJ*, 2:50.

16. "Por Comandante de la Florida Occidental," March 8, 1815, ACP, MS2328, reel 3, p. 154. See also Andrew Jackson to Secretary Armstrong, August 5, 1814, in Bassett, *CAJ*, 2:30–31.

17. John Innerarity, "Narrative of the Operations of the British in the Floridas," [January] 1815, HCP; John Innerarity to James Innerarity, November 10th/11th, 1814, in "Letters of John Innerarity: The Seizure of Pensacola by Andrew Jackson, November 7, 1814," *Florida Historical Quarterly* 9, no. 3 (January 1931): 129.

18. John Innerarity, "Narrative of the Operations of the British in the Floridas," [January] 1815, HCP.

19. William Lawrence to John Forbes, February 25, 1816, HCP.

20. William H. Robertson to Harry Toulmin, October 26, 1814, accompanying a letter from William Blount to the Secretary of War, November 18, 1814, *Territorial Papers of the United States Senate, 1789–1873*, RG46, NARA, M200, reel 9; "Pensacola," *Niles' Weekly Register*, Supplement to Volume VII (September 1814–March 1815), 165–167; John Innerarity to Spanish Governor, September 23, 1814, and John Forbes & Co. to Lord Castlereagh, May 20, 1815, in John W. Croker to Hamilton, April 7, 1818, JLP, Box 22.

21. "Deposition of Dougherty," October 17, 1815, and William Lawrence to John Forbes, February 25, 1816, HCP.

22. William Lawrence to John Forbes, February 25, 1816, HCP; "King George III vs. John Bennett," August 3, 1816, PLCC.

23. John Innerarity, "Narrative of the Operations of the British in the Floridas," [January] 1815, HCP.

24. "Indictment of George Woodbine for Theft of Slaves," August 3, 1816, HCP.

25. "List of Negroes," August 4, 1816, in Duncan L. Clinch to Robert Butler, August 2, 1816, JMP, reel 18, p. 3843.

26. "Debate on the Seminole War," *Niles' Weekly Register,* Supplement to Volume XV (1819), 184.

27. "Por Comandante de la Florida Occidental," March 8, 1815, ACP, MS2328, reel 3, p. 155. For the Battle of Pensacola, see Latour, *Historical Memoir of the War in West Florida and Louisiana,* 44–51; Owsley, Jr., *Struggle for the Gulf Borderlands,* 112–119.

28. Vicente Sebastián Pintado to Josef de Soto, April 29, 1815, State Archives of Florida, Tallahassee, M78–177, folder 1.

29. George Woodbine to Hugh Pigot, May 25, 1814, ACP, MS2328, reel 3, p. 12.

30. Daniel T. Patterson to William Jones, July 8, 1814, Area File of the Naval Records Collection, 1775–1910, United States Navy Department, RG45, NARA, M625, reel 200.

31. Andrew Jackson to Governor Holmes, July 21, 1814, in Bassett, *CAJ,* 2:18–19.

32. American Revolution veteran and eyewitness Chevalier Anne Louis de Tousard claimed "more than two hundred negroes" deserted with the British; U.S. Army engineer Major Arsène Lacarrière Latour provided a list of 199 runaways; and slaveowners' depositions document 163 unclaimed runaways. Norman B. Wilkinson, ed., "The Assaults on New Orleans, 1814–1815," *Louisiana History* 3, no. 1 (Winter 1962): 52; Latour, *Historical Memoir of the War in West Florida and Louisiana,* clxxxi; "Depositions Concerning Slaves Liberated by British Forces after the Battle of New Orleans," Williams Research Center, The Historic New Orleans Collection, New Orleans, MSS 199.

33. Latour, *Historical Memoir of the War in West Florida and Louisiana,* cxx.

34. Lambert wrote Jackson of his efforts to return fugitive slaves: "I have from the first . . . given every facility, and used every persuasion that they should return to their masters, and many have done so." Latour, *Historical Memoir of the War in West Florida and Louisiana,* cxxi. John Weiss has documented the arrival of eighty-eight of these fugitive slaves, the family members of bondsmen who enlisted with Britain's Colonial Marines, in Trinidad several months after departing from the Gulf Coast. John McNish Weiss, *The Merikens: Free Black American Settlers in Trinidad 1815–16. New Edition: Revised and Enlarged* (London: McNish & Weiss, 2002), 54–55. Additional

discussion of the destination of the bondspeople liberated by the British after the Battle of New Orleans can be found in the following: Latour, *Historical Memoir of the War in West Florida and Louisiana,* 222; "Depositions Concerning Slaves Liberated by British Forces after the Battle of New Orleans," Williams Research Center, the Historic New Orleans Collection, New Orleans, MSS 199; "Deposition of Samuel Jervais," *ASP,* 4:551.

35. Mateo González Manrique to Alexander Cochrane, January 25, 1815, HCP.
36. José Urcollo to Robert Henry, December 30, 1814, HCP.
37. Robert Henry to Mateo González Manrique, January 12, 1815, HCP (quotation); José Urcollo to Robert Henry, January 7, 1815.
38. Robert Henry to Mateo González Manrique, January 12, 1815, HCP.
39. John Innerarity to John Forbes, May 22, 1815, PLCC.
40. Robert Spencer to Vicente Sebastián Pintado, April 14, 1815, Vicente Sebastián Pintado Papers, PKY, reel 4.
41. Robert Spencer to Vicente Sebastián Pintado, March 30, 1815, Vicente Sebastián Pintado Papers, PKY, reel 4; Spencer was successful in convincing the British to release the Spanish troops removed from Fort Barrancas during the evacuation of Pensacola. Whether the troops left Pensacola unwillingly remains unknown. For his part, Nicolls claimed they left voluntarily. Edward Nicolls to Juan Ruiz de Apodaca, November 9, 1814, in John W. Croker to Hamilton, April 7, 1818, JLP, Box, 22. For the failed missions to reclaim the fugitive slaves from Pensacola from the British post generally, see "Por Comandante de la Florida Occidental," March 8, 1815, ACP, MS2328, reel 3, pp. 155–157; John Innerarity, "Narrative of the Operations of the British in the Floridas," [January] 1815, HCP; Mateo Gonzalez Manrique to Alexander Cochrane, January 25, 1815, HCP; Alexander Cochrane to Mateo Gonzalez Manrique, February 10, 1815, HCP; John Forbes & Co. to Lord Castlereagh, May 20, 1815, in John W. Croker to Hamilton, April 7, 1818, JLP, Box 22.
42. In the end, no more than 12 of the 128 slaves who consented to be interviewed returned. Vicente Sebastián Pintado to Josef de Soto, April 29, 1815, State Archives of Florida, Tallahassee, M78–177, folder 1; John Innerarity to John Forbes, May 22, 1815, PLCC. The various lists of fugitive slaves from Pensacola at the British post include "List of the Negroes Belonging to the Inhabitants of the Town of Pensacola Who Have Been Carried Off by the English to Appalachicola," December 30, 1814, enclosed in Report of Lieutenant Don José Urcollo to Mateo Gonzalez Manrique, January 23, 1815, PLCC; Mateo Gonzalez Manrique, "Relacion de los Negroes pertenecientes á los vecinos de esta Plaza de Panzacola que se han fugado y llevado los Ingleses á Apalachicola," March 4, 1815, ACP, MS2328, reel 3, pp. 166–178; "Relacion de los Esclavos pertenecientes a los vecinos de esta Plaza que se pudieron descubrir entre los Ingleses en el Appalachicola," in Vicente Sebastián Pintado to Josef de Soto, May 6, 1815, PLCC; "Relacion de nombre de los esclavos de la propiedad de las vecinos de Panzacola que

se hallan en Apalachicola," May 8, 1815, *PC*, legajo 1796, folio 768–776, reel 118.

43. "Relacion de los Esclavos pertenecientes a los vecinos de esta Plaza que se pudieron descubrir entre los Ingleses en el Appalachicola," in Vicente Sebastián Pintado to Josef de Soto, May 6, 1815, PLCC.

44. Colonel Nicolls to Sir John Barrow, September 11, 1843, in Great Britain. Foreign Office, *Correspondence on the Slave Trade with Foreign Powers, Parties to Treaties, under which Captured Vessels Are to Be Tried by Mixed Tribunals. Class B* (London: William Clowes and Sons, 1844), 13.

45. Vicente Sebastián Pintado to Josef de Soto, April 29, 1815, State Archives of Florida, Tallahassee, M78–177, folder 1.

46. Millett, *The Maroons of Prospect Bluff*, 8.

47. George Cockburn to Alexander Cochrane, February 28, 1815, NAGB, WO, 1/144, 23–30, quotation on 25.

48. "The Panton, Leslie Papers: James Innerarity to John Forbes," August 12, 1815, *Florida Historical Quarterly* 12, no. 3 (January 1934): 123–124.

49. Alexander Cochrane to Major General Lambert, February 3, 1815, NAGB, WO, 1/143, 23–24; "Return of Muscogee or Creek Indians under the Command of Lieut. Col. Nicolls, (1815), NAGB, WO, 1/144, 69.

50. Edward Nicolls to Alexander Cochrane, August 12, 1814, ACP, MS2328, reel 3, p. 62.

51. Colonel Nicolls to Sir John Barrow, September 11, 1843, in Great Britain. Foreign Office, *Correspondence on the Slave Trade with Foreign Powers*, 13.

52. *To the GREAT AND ILLUSTRIOUS CHIEFS of the CREEK and other INDIAN NATIONS*, December 5, 1814, NAGB, WO, 1/141, 113.

53. "Treaty of Peace," December 24, 1814, in J. Russell, Jr., ed., *The History of the War between the United States and Great Britain* (Hartford: B. & J. Russell, 1815), 368–376. For an overview of the lengthy and acrimonious debate over the recovery of American-owned slaves, see Arnett G. Lindsay, "Diplomatic Relations between the United States and Great Britain Bearing on the Return of Negro Slaves, 1783–1828," *Journal of Negro History* 5, no. 4 (October 1920): 391–419.

54. Once only a footnote among scholars, Negro Fort is today a popular subject of inquiry. Millett, *The Maroons of Prospect Bluff;* Jane Landers, *Atlantic Creoles in the Age of Revolutions* (Cambridge, MA: Harvard University Press, 2010), 121–128; Jane Landers, *Black Society in Spanish Florida* (Urbana: University of Illinois Press, 1999), 231–235; Claudio Saunt, *A New Order of Things: Property, Power, and the Transformation of the Creek Indians, 1733–1816* (Cambridge: Cambridge University Press, 1999), 273–290; Frank Lawrence Owsley, Jr., and Gene A. Smith, *Filibusters and Expansionists: Jeffersonian Manifest Destiny, 1800–1821* (Tuscaloosa: University of Alabama Press, 1997), 103–117; James W. Covington, "The Negro Fort," *Gulf Coast Historical Review* 5, no. 2 (Spring 1990): 79–91; William S. Coker and Thomas D. Watson, *Indian Traders of the Southeastern Spanish Borderlands: Panton, Leslie & Company*

and John Forbes & Company, 1783–1847 (Pensacola: University of West Florida Press, 1986) , 292–309; Mark F. Boyd, "Events at Prospect Bluff on the Apalachicola River," *Florida Historical Quarterly* 16, no. 2 (October 1937): 55–96.

55. Vicente Sebastián Pintado to Josef de Soto, April 29, 1815, State Archives of Florida, Tallahassee, M78–177, folder 1.

56. Kendal Lewis Report to Capt. Limbaugh, August 6, 1815, file H191 in Letters Received by the Secretary of War, Registered Series, 1801–1870, RG107, NARA, M221, reel 62.

57. Jarius Loomis to Commodore Daniel T. Patterson, August 13, 1816, *ASP,* 4:560.

58. Duncan L. Clinch to Robert Butler, August 2, 1816, JMP, reel 18, p. 3834; Daniel T. Patterson to Benjamin W. Crowninshield, August 15, 1816, *ASP,* 4:561.

59. Colonel Nicolls to Sir John Barrow, September 11, 1843, in Great Britain. Foreign Office, *Correspondence on the Slave Trade with Foreign Powers,* 13.

60. Duncan L. Clinch to Robert Butler, August 2, 1816, JMP, reel 18, p. 3834. Additional descriptions of the fort and the number of its residents include "Deposition of Samuel Jervais," *ASP,* 4:551; Edmund Gaines to A. J. Dallas, May 22, 1815, *ASP,* 4:552; "Statement of Ned, a Free Man of Colour," in Edmund Gaines to William H. Crawford, file G22 in February 20, 1816, Letters Received by the Secretary of War, Registered Series, 1801–1870, RG107, NARA, M221, reel 69; Benjamin Hawkins to Andrew Jackson, February 27, 1815, *PAJ,* 3:288–289; William Harris Crawford to Andrew Jackson, March 15, 1816, *PAJ,* 4:15–16; Edmund Pendleton Gaines to Andrew Jackson, May 14, 1816, *PAJ,* 4:30–31; "Appalachicola," *Niles' Weekly Register,* September 14, 1816, 37–38.

61. William McGirt to Christian Limbaugh, July 20, 1815, in Benjamin Hawkins to the Secretary of War, July 27, 1815, file H185 in Letters Received by the Secretary of War, Registered Series, 1801–1870, RG107, NARA, M221, reel 62.

62. Caso y Luengo to José de Soto, September 18, 1815, *PC,* legajo 147B, folio 568, reel 479.

63. "Relacion de nombre de los esclavos de la propiedad de las vecinos de Panzacola que se hallan en Apalachiaola," May 8, 1815, *PC,* legajo 1796, folio 770, reel 118.

64. "Statement of Ned, a Free Man of Colour," in Edmund Gaines to William H. Crawford, February 20, 1816, file G22 in Letters Received by the Secretary of War, Registered Series, 1801–1870, RG107, NARA, M221, reel 69.

65. Julius Sherrard Scott III, "The Common Wind: Currents of Afro-American Communication in the Era of the Haitian Revolution" (PhD diss., Duke University, 1986).

66. "Relacion de nombre de los esclavos de la propiedad de las vecinos de Panzacola que se hallan en Apalachiaola," May 8, 1815, *PC,* legajo 1796,

folio 770, reel 118; Benjamin Hawkins to Andrew Jackson, August 12, 1815, in C. L. Grant, ed., *Letters, Journal and Writings of Benjamin Hawkins* (Savannah: Beehive Press, 1980), 2:748.

67. Millett, *The Maroons of Prospect Bluff,* 206; Jack D. L. Holmes, *Pensacola Settlers, 1781–1821* (Pensacola: Pensacola Historical Restoration and Preservation Commission, 1970), 93.

68. "Relacion de nombre de los esclavos de la propiedad de las vecinos de Panzacola que se hallan en Apalachiaola," May 8, 1815, *PC,* legajo 1796, folio 771, reel 118.

69. "Indictment of George Woodbine for Theft of Slaves," August 3, 1816, HCP. See also John Innerarity, "Narrative of the Operations of the British in the Floridas," [January] 1815, HCP.

70. The registers reveal that Pensacola's enslaved artisans were half artisans, artisans, and master artisans, and thus brought their owners varying levels of income accordingly.

71. The most valuable bondsperson was Harry, a master craftsman who trading company partners valued at two thousand pesos, or seventy pesos per month when leased. At the other side of the spectrum was a low-level brick-layer named Sam whom Antonio Montero valued at two hundred pesos or ten pesos per month. "Relacion de nombre de los esclavos de la propiedad de las vecinos de Panzacola que se hallan en Apalachicola," May 8, 1815, *PC,*legajo 1796, folio 768–776, reel 118. See also John Innerarity to Don Matheo Gonzales, 1814, in "The War of 1812—Some Florida Episodes," *Louisiana Historical Quarterly* no. 4 (April 1918): 330–331. For a comparable listing of white artisans of various skill levels, see the testimony of Peter Gilchrest and Andres Leno, in "File of Witnesses That May Be Examined by the Commissioners in Pensacola in the Suit vs. Woodbine," [1815], HCP.

72. "Appalachicola," 37.

73. Felipe Prieto to Caso Luengo, June 17, 1815, PLCC; "Relacion de nombre de los esclavos de la propiedad de las vecinos de Panzacola que se hallan en Apalachiaola," May 8, 1815, *PC,* legajo 1796, folio 772, reel 118.

74. Mateo Gonzalez Manrique, "Relacion de los Negroes pertenecientes á los vecinos de esta Plaza de Panzacola que se han fugado y llevado los Ingleses á Apalachicola," March 4, 1815, ACP, MS2328, reel 3, p. 177.

75. Edward Nicolls to Alexander Cochrane, August 12, 1814, ACP, MS2328, reel 3, p. 60.

76. Edward Nicolls to Alexander Cochrane, December 3, 1814, ACP, MS2328, reel 3, p. 118.

77. "Report of Captain Amelung to General Jackson," June 4, 1816, *ASP,* 4:557.

78. "The Panton, Leslie Papers: James Innerarity to John Forbes," 128–129.

79. John Innerarity to John Forbes, May 22, 1815, PLCC.

80. Andrew Jackson to Mauricia de Zuñiga, April 23, 1816, *PAJ,* 4:22–23.

81. Andrew Jackson to Edmund P. Gaines, April 8, 1816, *CAJ,* 2:238–239. For further evidence of Jackson leaving the final decision to attack Negro Fort

up to Gaines, see Andrew Jackson to William Harris Crawford, April 24, 1816, *PAJ*, 4:25–26.

82. Duncan L. Clinch to Robert Butler, August 2, 1816, JMP, reel 18, pp. 3825–3837.

83. For the last days and moments of Negro Fort, see the following three letters by Duncan L. Clinch, which vary only slightly. Duncan L. Clinch to Robert Butler, August 2, 1816, JMP, reel 18, pp. 3825–3837, quotations on 3829 and 3831; "General Clinch and the Indians," *Army and Navy Chronicle*, February 25, 1836, 114–115; "Negro fort on Appalachicola," *Niles' Weekly Register*, 186–188. Another useful summary is provided in "Appalachicola," 37–38.

84. Duncan L. Clinch to Robert Butler, August 2, 1816, JMP, reel 18, pp. 3831–3832.

85. "General Clinch and the Indians," 116.

86. J. Loomis to Commodore Daniel T. Patterson, August 13, 1816, *ASP*, 4:560.

87. Duncan L. Clinch to Robert Butler, August 2, 1816, JMP, reel 18, p. 3832.

88. "General Clinch and the Indians," 116.

89. John Forbes & Co. to Lord Castlereagh, May 20, 1815, in John W. Croker to Hamilton, April 7, 1818, JLP, Box 22. Two years after the destruction of Negro Fort, Nicolls, in what appears to be a clear reference to Garçon, referred to the leader of Negro Fort in its final days as "Sergeant-Major Wilson." It is unknown whether Nicolls was misquoted in the extant typed manuscript or Garçon, as other runaways from Pensacola had done after arriving at the fort, took an Anglophonic name. In 1843, Nicolls changed his story regarding the number of survivors, stating that "a few of the women and children" survived the explosion. This included Mary Ashley, who "had the courage and sagacity to hoist and pull down the colours [of the fort] morning and evening for four days, firing the morning and evening gun, shotted, into the enemy's camp, in the hope that the absent garrison would hear it, and come to their assistance." Colonel Nicolls to Sir John Barrow, September 11, 1843, in Great Britain. Foreign Office, *Correspondence on the Slave Trade with Foreign Powers*, 13. For the adoption of American names, see Vicente Sebastián Pintado to Josef de Soto, April 29, 1815, State Archives of Florida, Tallahassee, M78–177, folder 1.

90. John Innerarity's claim of at least twenty-six survivors is consistent with supporting evidence; however, it is likely that more than many more than forty of the fort's residents lost their lives as Innerarity claimed. John Innerarity to James Innerarity, August 13, 1816, in "Letters of John Innerarity and A. H. Gordon," *Florida Historical Quarterly* 12, no. 1 (July 1933): 38.

91. "List of Negroes," August 4, 1816, in Duncan L. Clinch to Robert Butler, August 2, 1816, JMP, reel 18, pp. 3834 and 3843.

92. Duncan L. Clinch to Robert Butler, August 2, 1816, JMP, reel 18, p. 3834. For nearly a decade, John Forbes & Company sought restitution for the

enslaved employees it lost to the British during the War of 1812 and never recovered; however, the Court of King's Bench ruled against the company and in an extraordinary decision took the opportunity to denounce both the United States and slavery. Chief Justin William Best defended the rights of enslaved Americans who boarded British ships during the war, declaring, "Slavery is a local law, and therefore, if a man wishes to preserve his slaves, let him attach them to him by affection, or make fast the bars of their prison, or rivet well the chains, for the instant they get beyond the limits where slavery is recognized by the local laws, they have broken their chains, they have escaped from the prisons and are free. Those men, when on board an English ship, had all the rights belonging to Englishmen, and were subject to their liabilities." Richard Vaughan Barnewall and Cresswell Cresswell, eds., *Reports of Cases Argued and Determined in the Court of King's Bench* (Philadelphia: T. & J. W. Johnson, 1870), 2:207.

93. John Innerarity to James Innerarity, August 13, 1816, in "Letters of John Innerarity and A. H. Gordon," *Florida Historical Quarterly* 12, no. 1 (July 1933): 38.

94. Edmund Doyle to John Innerarity, June 3, 1817, in "The Panton, Leslie Papers: Letters of Edmund Doyle, Trader," *Florida Historical Quarterly* 17, no. 4 (April 1939): 313–315, quotation on 315.

95. Some of the runaways from Pensacola likely departed with the British more than a year earlier and left Florida entirely. In April 1815, Nicolls wrote from the British post with great satisfaction to Benjamin Hawkins, "On the subject of the negroes lately owned by the citizens of the United States, or Indians in hostility to the British forces, I have to acquaint you that, according to orders, I have sent them to the British colonies, where they are received as free settlers, and lands given to them." While data on the final destination of runaways from Pensacola are contradictory, various reports cite black marines, their families, and other black refugees from Pensacola joining others from East Florida and the Southern United States and embarking for England, Nova Scotia, Trinidad, Bermuda, and the Bahamas. Edward Nicolls to Benjamin Hawkins, April 28, 1815, *ASP,* 4:548. See also "Memorandum of a Gentleman of Respectability at Bermuda," [St. George], May 21, 1815, *ASP,* 4:552; Latour, *Historical Memoir of the War in West Florida and Louisiana,* 221–222; Alexander Cochrane to Pulteney Malcolm, February 17, 1815, NAGB, WO, 1/143, 15–16; Alexander Cochrane to John W. Croker, February 26, 1815, NAGB, WO, 1/143, 29–30. For a list of fifty-eight black refugees from undisclosed parts of Florida who arrived in Trinidad in July 1815, see Weiss, *The Merikens: Free Black American Settlers in Trinidad,* 57–59.

96. John Innerarity to James Innerarity, August 13, 1816, in "Letters of John Innerarity and A. H. Gordon," 38; John Quincy Adams to George W. Erving, November 28, 1818, *ASP,* 4:543; Vicente Sebastián Pintado to Josef de Soto, April 29, 1815, State Archives of Florida, Tallahassee, M78–177, folder 1.

97. Saunt, *A New Order of Things*, 284.

98. Extract of a letter from George Perryman to Lieutenant Sands, February 24, 1817, *ASP*, 4:596.

99. John Quincy Adams to George W. Erving, November 28, 1818, *ASP*, 4:543. See also "Continuation of the Minutes of the Proceedings of a Special Court, whereof Major General Gaines Is President, Convened by Order of the 26th April, 1818," *ASP*, 4:592–594.

100. Edmund Gaines to Andrew Jackson, November 21, 1817, *ASP*, 4:597.

101. For the Seminole Wars see William S. Belko, ed., *America's Hundred Years' War: U.S. Expansion to the Gulf Coast and the Fate of the Seminole, 1763–1858* (Gainesville: University of Florida Press, 2011); Joe Knetsh, *Florida's Seminole Wars: 1817–1858* (Charleston: Arcadia Publishing, 2003); Kevin Mulroy, *Freedom on the Border* (Lubbock: Texas Tech University Press, 2003); James W. Covington, *The Seminoles of Florida* (Gainesville: University Press of Florida, 1993).

102. "Relacion de los Esclavos pertenecientes a los vecinos de esta Plaza que se pudieron descubrir entre los Ingleses en el Appalachicola," in Vicente Sebastián Pintado to Josef de Soto, May 6, 1815, PLCC; "Relacion de nombre de los esclavos de la propiedad de las vecinos de Panzacola que se hallan en Apalachicola," May 8, 1815, *PC*, legajo 1796, folio 768, reel 118. Harry is also described as a "most invaluable master ship carpenter" and Abraham as "a house carpenter" in John Innerarity to Don Matheo Gonzales, 1814, "The War of 1812—Some Florida Episodes," 330. Another bondsman at the fort from Pensacola of unknown occupation named Harry belonged to Dr. Eugenio Antonio Sierra; but it is more likely the highly skilled "Harry the caulker," who belonged to John Innerarity and John Forbes & Company at the same time as Abraham, was the individual who remained close with Abraham decades later. Abraham did at one point belong to Dr. Eugenio Antonio Sierra, but John Forbes & Company claimed ownership of this exceptional slave sometime before the British occupation of Pensacola. Jane Landers suggests that Abraham may have been employed at the firm's Apalachicola store prior to escaping to Negro Fort; however, in correspondence between the store's manager and the company's leaders, Abraham's name is never mentioned along with those who worked at the store, suggesting he came to the fort with the British from Pensacola. Landers, *Atlantic Creoles in the Age of Revolutions*, 176–178. For a brief description of Abraham's early life, refer to George A. McCall, *Letters from the Frontiers: Written during a Period of Thirty Years' Service in the Army of the United States* (Philadelphia: Lippincott & Company, 1868), 302.

103. "War with the Seminoles," *Niles' Weekly Register*, January 30, 1836, 367.

104. M. C. Cohen, *Notice of Florida and the Campaigns* (Charleston: Burges & Honour, 1836), 239.

105. Registry of Negro Prisoners Captured by the Troops Commanded by Major General Thomas S. Jesup, in 1836 and 1837, and Owned by Indians, or Who Claim to Be Free, 25th Cong., 3rd sess., 1837, H. Doc. 225, 69.

106. The best biographer of Abraham remains Kenneth Wiggins Porter, "The Negro Abraham," *Florida Historical Quarterly* 25, no. 1 (July 1946): 1–42; Kenneth Wiggins Porter, "Abraham," *Phylon* 2, no. 2 (1941): 107–116. Jane Landers offers a more recent appraisal in *Atlantic Creoles in the Age of Revolutions*, 175–178.

Chapter 3

1. J. Cook v. E. Garcon, 1829–387, CCC.

2. Ibid.; see also Del. E. Jupiter, "Matilda Madrid: One Woman's Tale of Bondage and Freedom," *National Geological Society Quarterly* 91 (March 2003): 41–59; William James Wells, *Pioneering in the Panhandle: A Look at Selected Events and Families as a Part of the History of South Santa Rosa County, Florida* (Fort Walton Beach: Melvin Business Services, 1976), 5–6; *The Eighth Census of the United States, 1860*, Pensacola, Florida, 25.

3. For the rise of New Orleans and Mobile, see Walter Johnson, *River of Dark Dreams: Slavery and Empire in the Cotton Kingdom* (Cambridge: Belknap Press, 2013); Lawrence N. Powell, *The Accidental City: Improvising New Orleans* (Cambridge, MA: Harvard University Press, 2012); Thomas Ruys Smith, *Southern Queen: New Orleans in the Nineteenth Century* (New York: Continuum International Publishing Group, 20011); Ned Sublette, *The World That Made New Orleans: From Spanish Silver to Congo Square* (Chicago: Chicago Review Press, 2009); Michael V. R. Thomason, ed., *Mobile: The New History of Alabama's First City* (Tuscaloosa: University of Alabama Press, 2001); Harriet E. Amos Doss, *Cotton City: Urban Development in Antebellum Mobile* (Tuscaloosa: University of Alabama Press, 1985).

4. "Florida," *Niles' Weekly Register*, August 25, 1821, 4.

5. James Parton, *Life of Andrew Jackson* (Boston: Houghton, Mifflin, 1860), 2:603–606.

6. Herbert J. Doherty, Jr., "Ante-Bellum Pensacola: 1821–1860," *Florida Historical Quarterly* 37, nos. 3–4 (January–April 1959): 342; United States Census Bureau, *Census for 1820* (Washington, DC: Gales & Seaton, 1821), 119, 123; Joseph C. G. Kennedy, *Population of the United States in 1860* (Washington, DC: Government Printing Office, 1864), 9, 54, 195.

7. Virginia Meacham Gould, "The Free Creoles of Color of the Antebellum Gulf Ports of Mobile and Pensacola: A Struggle for the Middle Ground," in *Creoles of Color of the Gulf Coast*, ed. James H. Dorman (Knoxville: University of Tennessee Press, 1996), 37.

8. George Catlin, *Letters and Notes on the Manners, Customs, and Condition of the North American Indians* (New York: Wiley and Putnam, 1841), 2:34.

9. Oliver Peake to his father, February 14, 1843, Leora M. Sutton Papers, M2986, University Archives and West Florida History Center, Pensacola.

10. Journal, 1846, John P. Haggott Papers, University Archives and West Florida History Center, Pensacola.

11. "Pensacola," *Pensacola Gazette,* February 28, 1857, 2.

12. "Mr. Editor," *Pensacola Gazette,* February 15, 1845, 3.

13. Leslie A. Thompson, *A Manual or Digest of the Statute Law of the State of Florida* (Boston: Charles C. Little and James Brown, 1845): 507–512, 531–546. For the growing oppression of free people of color in Pensacola and Florida, see Daniel L. Schafer, "'A Class of People Neither Freemen nor Slaves'," *Journal of Southern History* 26, no. 3 (Spring 1993): 587–609; Canter Brown, Jr., "Race Relations in Territorial Florida, 1821–1845," *Florida Historical Quarterly* 73, no. 3 (January 1995): 287–307; David Y. Thomas, "The Free Negro in Florida before 1865," *South Atlantic Quarterly* 10 (October 1911): 335–345.

14. Thompson, *A Manual or Digest of the Statute Law of the State of Florida,* 539.

15. "Laws of the Territory," *Pensacola Gazette,* April 16, 1842, 1–2.

16. "Pensacola," *Pensacola Gazette,* February 28, 1857, 2, and November 19, 1842, 2.

17. Ruth B. Barr and Modeste Hargis, "The Voluntary Exile of Free Negroes of Pensacola," *Florida Historical Quarterly* 17, no. 1 (July 1938): 3–14.

18. "The Worthless Negroes," *West Florida Times,* in *Liberator,* March 27, 1857, 2.

19. "Exodus," *Pensacola Gazette,* March 7, 1857, 2; "For Tampico," *West Florida Times,* March 17, 1857, 2.

20. "The Exodus," *Pensacola Gazette,* April 4, 1857, 2.

21. The efforts to reduce or eliminate Florida's free black population were unsuccessful. Census records confirm the number of free people of color in Pensacola—which accounts for some but not all Creoles—dropped from 322 in 1855 to 130 in 1860; however, the number of free people of color in the state actually increased in the 1850s from 608 to 932. Given the ban on the immigration of free people of color, there is reason to suspect some of Pensacola's Creoles migrated in state and others returned from Tampico. An anonymous letter written after the American Civil War read, "Since the war a few individuals have returned to visit their old home." Joseph C. G. Kennedy, *Population of the United States in 1860; Compiled from the Original Returns of the Eight Census, under the Direction of the Secretary of the Interior* (Washington, DC: Government Printing Office, 1864), 1:52–54; *Senate Journal: A Journal of the Proceedings of the Senate of the General Assembly of the State of Florida at an Adjourned Session, Begun and Held in the City of Tallahassee, on Monday, Twenty-Sixth November, 1855* (Tallahassee: Florida Sentinel, 1855), 25; J. D. B. De Bow, *The Seventh Census of the United States: 1850* (Washington, DC: Robert Armstrong, 1853), ix; Julien C. Yonge

Scrapbook, University Archives and West Florida History Center, Pensacola (quotation).

22. Frederick Douglass, *Narrative of the Life of Frederick Douglass, an American Slave* (Boston: Anti-Slavery Office, 1845), 34.

23. For an introduction to industrialization in antebellum Pensacola, see Brian R. Rucker, "History of Santa Rosa, 1821–1860" (PhD diss., Florida State University, 1990); Lucius F. Ellsworth, "Raiford and Abercrombie: Pensacola's Premier Antebellum Manufacturer," *Florida Historical Quarterly* 52, no. 3 (January 1974): 247–260; John A. Eisterhold, "Lumber and Trade in Pensacola and West Florida: 1800–1860," *Florida Historical Quarterly* 52, no. 3 (January 1974): 267–280; James Knox Polk, "Pensacola Commerce and Industry" (master's thesis, University of West Florida, 1971).

24. Polk, "Pensacola Commerce and Industry," 97. For industrial slave labor in Pensacola, see Wilma Louise Handley, "'The Labourers Are All Slaves': Slavery and Hiring-Out in an Antebellum Gulf Coast Community" (master's thesis, University of West Florida, 2005), 72.

25. A case in point was John Innerarity's bondsman Thomas, who earned Innerarity a dollar per day. Frustrated with the inability to employ a reliable bondsman, James Weaver inquired of Tom's availability, informing Innerarity, "I require one that knows something of a steam engine and if at the same time is competent to do ordinary plantation work in the blacksmith shop could be made to answer both purposes. If you are willing to hire Tom by the year or to sell him on fair terms I shall be glad to know the best offer that you would make." John Innerarity to Isaac Hulse, May 30, 1850, PLCC; James Weaver to Dr. Isaac Hulse, June 27, 1853, Innerarity-Hulse Papers, University Archives and West Florida History Center, Pensacola (quotation).

26. Federal Writers' Project, *Slave Narratives: A Folk History of Slavery in the United States from Interviews with Former Slaves. Volume IV. Georgia Narratives* (Washington, DC: Library of Congress, 1936–1938), 3:47–50.

27. "From the Herald of Freedom: An Incident in Slavery," *Liberator,* November 29, 1839, 1.

28. "Escambia County," *Pensacola Gazette,* June 1, 1844, 2.

29. "Pensacola," *Pensacola Gazette,* August 15, 1846, 2. See also "Southern Manufactures," *Scientific American,* January 5, 1850, 2; "Manufactories in Florida," *Scientific American,* October 3, 1846, 5; "Cotton Manufactories in Southern States," *De Bow's Review* 4, no. 2 (October 1847): 256; "Manufactures in the South," *Pensacola Gazette,* October 10, 1846, 2; "A New Article of Export from Florida," *Florida Democrat,* May, 20, 1846, 2; "Cotton Factory in Florida," *Hunt's Merchants' Magazine* 15 (October 1846): 417; "Pensacola," *Pensacola Gazette,* February 15, 1845, 2. Reliable overviews of Arcadia Mill and cotton manufacturing in antebellum Florida include Brian R. Rucker, "Arcadia and Bagdad: Industrial Parks of Antebellum Florida," *Florida Historical Quarterly* 67, 2 (October 1988): 147–165; Richard

W. Griffin, "The Cotton Mill Campaign in Florida, 1828–1863," *Florida Historical Quarterly* 40, no. 3 (January 1962): 261–274.

30. *Pensacola Gazette,* September 13, 1845, in Griffin, "The Cotton Mill Campaign in Florida," 265.

31. "Southern Manufactures"; "Cotton Manufactories in Southern States"; Rucker, "Arcadia and Bagdad," 159.

32. "Manufactures in the South."

33. Griffin, "The Cotton Mill Campaign in Florida," 269.

34. *Pensacola Gazette,* February 15, 1845, 2.

35. "Manufactures in the South."

36. "Cotton Manufactories in Southern States."

37. "WANTED TO HIRE," *Washington Globe,* August 2, 1836, 1.

38. "Public Sale of Negroes," *Pensacola Gazette,* April 11, 1840, 3.

39. Colonel Joseph Pickens to Dr. Isaac Hulse, September 20, 1836, Innerarity-Hulse Papers, University Archives and West Florida History Center, Pensacola.

40. S. J. Gonzalez, "Pensacola: Its Early History," *Florida Historical Quarterly* 2, no. 1 (April 1909): 21–22.

41. "Pensacola," *Pensacola Gazette,* October 29, 1836, 3.

42. "Notice to Labourers & Slave Holders," *Pensacola Gazette,* April 15, 1837, 3.

43. Gregg M. Turner, *A Journey into Florida Railroad History* (Gainesville: University Press of Florida, 2008), 43–49; Charles W. Hildreth, "Railroads Out of Pensacola, 1833–1883," *Florida Historical Quarterly* 34, nos. 3–4 (January–April 1959): 397–405.

44. E. K., "Life on the Gulf of Mexico: Sketch VI—Our M.D.," *Rover: A Weekly Magazine of Tales, Poetry, and Engravings* 2, no. 5 (1843): 78.

45. Robert S. Starobin, *Industrial Slavery in the Old South* (New York: Oxford University Press, 1970), 143.

46. W. J. Rorabaugh's words apply here, when he wrote, "All men are equal before the bottle." *The Alcoholic Republic: An American Tradition* (Oxford: Oxford University Press, 1979), 151.

47. In addition to these illegal actions, Alton purchased stolen goods from customers, including bondspeople who lacked the proper license or "ticket" to buy and sell merchandise as required by law. The life of crime eventually caught up with Alton, who paid the ultimate price for accusing another man of having an affair with his wife and then beating him 'unmercifully' with his fists. Later that day, a passerby found Alton's lifeless body in a puddle of blood on the side of a street with a large gash in his ribs roughly three inches wide and six inches deep. Officials arrested the suspected paramour, who, upon entering the jail, confessed to the murder. Territory of Florida v. J. Alton, 1838–3004, 3005 (first quotation), and 3006, CCC; Territory of Florida v. Phillip Pitts, 1839–3082, CCC (second quotation).

48. Andrew and Barbary Hosler v. Gabriel LeBlanc, 1846–992, CCC.

49. For the prevalence of interracial sexual relations in the antebellum South and their significance, see Joshua D. Rothman, *Notorious in the Neighborhood: Sex and Families across the Color Line in Virginia, 1787–1861* (Chapel Hill: University of North Carolina Press, 2003); Martha Hodes, *White Women, Black Men: Illicit Sex in the Nineteenth-Century South* (New Haven, CT: Yale University Press, 1999).

50. *The Acts and Resolutions of the State of Florida, Passed at its Seventh Session* (Tallahassee: Office of the Floridian & Journal, 1855), 42–43, 62.

51. "Look Out Grogshop Keepers," *Pensacola Gazette,* April 20, 1850, 3.

52. Despite the conviction, the jury recommended the defendant "warmly to the mercy of the court." State of Florida v. Joseph Rosique, 1851–1265, CCC.

53. "The Burnt District," *Pensacola Gazette,* December 2, 1848, 3. For an analysis of how the legendary New York slum known as Five Points became synonymous with illicit sexual relationships between African Americans and Irish immigrants, see Leslie Harris, *In the Shadow of Slavery: African Americans in New York City, 1626–1863* (Chicago: University of Chicago Press, 2003), 251–252.

54. "Petty Robberies in the City," *Pensacola Gazette,* August 25, 1855, 2.

55. Territory v. William H. Baker, 1831–440, CCC. See also "Editorial Department," *Pensacola Gazette,* November 27, 1830, 3.

56. Davis escaped from the Santa Rosa County jail, prompting the offer of a one-hundred-dollar reward for his capture by Florida governor Thomas Brown. "Murder," *Pensacola Gazette,* January 17, 1852, 2; "$100. Reward," *Pensacola Gazette,* February 7, 1852, 3.

57. David Robinson Preston Journal, University Archives and West Florida History Center, Pensacola.

58. "Congo Dancing," *Pensacola Gazette,* October 28, 1848, 2.

59. "Florida," *The Floridian,* December 17, 1821, 2.

60. "Our Own City," *Pensacola Gazette,* May 16, 1840, 3.

61. Dian Lee Shelley, "Tivoli Theatre of Pensacola," *Florida Historical Quarterly* 50, no. 4 (April 1972): 343–344.

62. George A. McCall, *Letters from the Frontier: Written during a Period of Thirty Years' Service in the Army of the United States* (Philadelphia: J. B. Lippincott & Co., 1868), 80–83.

63. Territory v. Joseph Vidal, 1831–433, CCC. Vidal eventually faced charges of murder, but the jury dismissed the case for a lack of evidence.

64. Charles Rockwell, *Sketches of Foreign Travel and Life at Sea; Including a Cruise on Board a Man-of-War* (New York: Tappan and Dennet, 1842), 2:400.

65. "$120 Reward" and "TWENTY DOLLARS REWARD," *Pensacola Gazette,* September 25, 1833, 3.

66. "Deserters," *Pensacola Gazette,* September 24, 1836, 4.

67. Charles Lanman, *Adventures in the Wilds of the United States and British American Provinces* (Philadelphia: John W. Moore, 1856), 2:148. For bondspeople, work on antebellum steamships was extremely dangerous

and in most cases brought few of the benefits that came with employment on oceangoing vessels. Thomas C. Buchanan, *Black Life on the Mississippi: Slaves, Free Blacks, and the Western Steamboat World* (Chapel Hill: University of North Carolina Press, 2004).

68. "Notice," *Pensacola Gazette,* May 21, 1853, 3.

69. "Negroes Wanted," *Pensacola Gazette,* February 3, 1849, 3.

70. "Administrator's Sale," *Pensacola Gazette,* June 28, 1845, 3.

71. "Murder in Florida," *New York Daily Tribune,* February 3, 1844, 2.

72. State of Florida v. William Mercer, 1847–3395, CCC.

73. Territory of Florida v. Vincente Gomes, 1829–399, CCC.

74. United States v. John Munroe, 1840–618, CCC.

75. Miscellaneous Records of the U.S. Navy, Muster Roll, 1821–1840, *Grampus,* and Payroll, 1821–1838, *Grampus,* RG45, T829, reels 51 and 52, NARA.

76. "Twenty Dollars Reward," *Pensacola Gazette,* September 20, 1834, 2.

77. "Stop the Murderer," *Mobile Register,* March 11, 1845, 2.

78. Ibid.

79. Simon Newman, "Reading the Bodies of Early American Seafarers," *William and Mary Quarterly* 55, no. 1 (January 1998): 59–65.

80. Benjamin Franklin Riley, *History of Conecuh County, Alabama* (Blue Hill, ME: Weekly Packet, 1964), 124–125. Riley states that only one of the brothers died. Additional information on the murder comes from: "Horrid Murder," *Liberator,* April 18, 1845, 4; "The Mobile Tribune Says," *Liberator,* May 9, 1845, 4; *Mobile Register,* March 11, 1845, 2.

81. Ernest F. Dibble, *Ante-Bellum Pensacola and the Military Presence* (Pensacola: University of West Florida, 1974), 67.

82. "A Sketch of Pensacola," *National Intelligencer, and Washington Advertiser,* July 16, 1810, 2.

83. "Pensacola," *Pensacola Gazette,* January 12, 1850, 2. For the United States' selection of Pensacola as the location for the Navy Yard in 1825 and its subsequent history, see George F. Pearce, *The U.S. Navy in Pensacola: From Sailing Ships to Naval Aviation, 1825–1930* (Gainesville: University Presses of Florida, 1980), 1–64; George F. Pearce, "The United States Navy Comes to Pensacola," *Florida Historical Quarterly* 55, no. 1 (July 1976): 37–47. For contemporary descriptions of the Pensacola Navy Yard, see "The Navy Yard at Pensacola," *Army and Navy Chronicle* 4, no. 6 (February 9, 1837): 81–83; "U.S. Navy Yard at Pensacola," *Pensacola Gazette,* March 23, 1850, 2; "Laying the Corner Stone of the Permanent Wharf, at the Southeast Angle of the U.S. Navy Yard, Pensacola," *Pensacola Gazette,* May 4, 1850, 2; "A Trip to Pensacola," *Floridian & Journal,* May 12, 1849, 3; "Visit to Pensacola Bay," *New York Herald,* April 9, 1861, 1.

84. For the leasing of slaves by the military at Pensacola, see Thomas Hulse, "Military Slave Rentals, the Construction of Army Fortifications, and the Navy Yard in Pensacola, Florida, 1824–1863," *Florida Historical Quarterly* 88 (Spring 2010): 497–539; Dibble, *Ante-Bellum Pensacola.*

85. Presbyterian Church in the U.S.A., *The Home and Foreign Record of the Presbyterian Church in the United States of America: Being the Organ of the Boards of Missions, Education, Foreign Missions, and Publication* (Philadelphia: Presbyterian Church, 1850), 234.

86. Daniel Drake, S. Hanbury Smith, and Francis G. Smith, eds., *A Systematic Treatise, Historical, Etiological, and Practical, on the Principal Diseases of the Interior Valley of North America, as They Appear in the Caucasian, African, Indian, and Esquimaux Varieties of Its Population* (Philadelphia: Lippincott, Grambo, 1854), 234.

87. A typical advertisement read, "I wish to hire immediately, 38 NEGRO MEN to be employed in the Navy Yard, and amongst whom it is desirable to obtain 2 or 3 joiners. For the laborers there will be allowed 15 dollars per month, with the common Navy rations and medical attendance, and for the mechanics, the usual addition of price; proportioned to their qualifications. Sam'l R. Overton, Navy Agent." "NEGRO MEN WANTED," *Pensacola Gazette*, March 23, 1827, 4. For the number of enslaved employees at the yard, which often exceeded two hundred, see Hulse, "Military Slave Rentals," 514; Dibble, *Ante-Bellum Pensacola*, 62.

88. Hulse, "Military Slave Rentals"; Dibble, *Ante-Bellum Pensacola*.

89. "IMPORTANT TO SLAVE OWNERS. Laborers Wanted," *Pensacola Gazette*, June 11, 1836, 2. For additional details on the arrangement see "NEGRO MEN WANTED"; "Laborers Wanted," *Pensacola Gazette*, November 9, 1826, 3.

90. William S. Coker, "Tom Moreno: A Pensacola Creole," *Florida Historical Quarterly* 67, no. 3 (January 1989): 335.

91. "Mr. Editor," *Pensacola Gazette*, April 20, 1850, 2.

92. "The Navy Yard at Pensacola," 1. An advertisement confirms the boarding of bondspeople near the Navy Yard in privately run establishments: "Board for Negroes. I am prepared to Board 40 Negroes at Eight dollars per month, they will be furnished with as much good provisions as they can make use of. They will be carefully attended to as regards their duties to their masters. Thomas Conlin. Navy Yard." *Pensacola Gazette*, May 8, 1847, 3. See also Dibble, *Ante-Bellum Pensacola*, 27.

93. "Presentment of the Grand Jury," *Pensacola Gazette*, June 9, 1849, 2.

94. "Drowned," *Pensacola Gazette*, December 4, 1847, 2.

95. The State of Florida v. Robert, a Slave, 1850–1194, CCC.

96. "Liquors, Liquors," *Pensacola Gazette*, December 30, 1854, 3.

97. "Army and Navy Intelligence," *New York Times*, July 27, 1860, 3.

98. Correspondence at Pensacola, Florida, 1828–1831, Melancthon T. Woolsey Papers, University Archives and West Florida History Center, Pensacola. The court-martial convicted Clack; however, President Andrew Jackson reversed the decision and promoted Clack to Master Commandant in 1831. Andrew Jackson to the Senate of the United States, March 2, 1831, in James D. Richardson, *A Compilation of the Messages and Papers of*

the Presidents, 1789–1897 (Washington, DC: Government Printing Office, 1909), 2:543.

99. George Ballentine, *Autobiography of an English Soldier in the United States Army. Comprising Observations and Adventures in the States and Mexico* (New York: Stringer & Townsend, 1853), 88–90.

100. Edwin C. Bearss, *Fort Pickens 1821–1895: Historic Structures Report, Historic Data Section* (Washington, DC: U.S. Department of the Interior, 1983), 1–11.

101. Ballentine, *Autobiography of an English Soldier in the United States Army,* 74.

102. Hulse, "Military Slave Rentals," 529–533; Dibble, *Ante-Bellum Pensacola,* 76; Handley, "The Labourers Are All Slaves," 62–64. Unlike the situation at the Navy Yard, the Army Corps of Engineers under Chase's direction offered contracts for enslaved workers almost exclusively to two of Chase's West Point classmates, Jasper Strong and Frederick Underhill; consequently, advertisements for bondsmen to work on the forts appeared infrequently. For an exception, see "NEGROES WANTED," *Pensacola Gazette,* March 24, 1829, 2.

103. William H. Chase to Colonel R. E. DeRussey, 41st Cong., 3rd sess., December 25, 1859, S. Doc. 103, 25–26.

104. The surrounding villages of Warrington and Woolsey, which contained upward of 130 homes at midcentury, were under "the entire control" of the Commandant. "Laying the Corner Stone of the Permanent Wharf, at the Southeast Angle of the U.S. Navy Yard, Pensacola."

105. For the history of African Americans in the U.S. Army and Navy, see Barbara Tomblin, *Bluejackets and Contrabands: African Americans and the Union Navy* (Lexington: University Press of Kentucky, 2009); Steven J. Ramold, *Slaves, Sailors, Citizens: African Americans in the Union Navy* (DeKalb: Northern Illinois University Press, 2002); Bernard C. Nalty, *Strength for the Fight: A History of Black Americans in the Military* (New York: Simon and Schuster, 1989); Bernard C. Nalty and Morris J. MacGregor, eds., *Blacks in the United States Armed Forces: Basic Documents,* 13 vols. (Wilmington, DE: Scholarly Resources, 1977), 213–223; Jack D. Foner, *Blacks and the Military in American History: A New Perspective* (New York: Praeger Publishers, 1974), 20–31.

106. "A New Scheme of Abolition," *Pensacola Gazette,* February 8, 1845, 2.

107. George Livermore, *An Historical Research Respecting the Opinions of the Founders of the Republic on Negroes as Slaves, as Citizens, and as Soldiers* (Boston: John Wilson and Son, 1862), 203–204.

108. Foner, *Blacks and the Military in American History,* 27; see also Ramold, *Slaves, Sailors, Citizens,* 6–24; and Herbert Aptheker, "The Negro in the Union Navy," *Journal of Negro History* 32, no. 2 (April 1947): 170–174.

109. "Case of Lieut. Hooe—a Notable Instance of Whig Honesty," *Extra Globe,* August 19, 1840, 157–159, quotation on 157.

110. "HOUSE OF REPRESENTATIVES," *Niles' Weekly Register*, June 20, 1840, 253–254, quotation on 254. Years later Hooe exacted revenge by bringing charges against his former captain for several transgressions, including the tarring and feathering of a seaman. The ensuing court-martial resulted in Levy's temporary dismissal from the navy. Ira Dye, *Uriah Levy: Reformer of the Antebellum Navy* (Gainesville: University of Florida Press, 2006), 178–189; Donovan Fitzpatrick and Saul Saphire, *Navy Maverick: Uriah Phillips Levy* (New York: Doubleday, 1963), 156–167. The case resulted in several proposals in the United States Congress to prohibit the enlistment of any "negroes or colored persons" in the navy and army entirely; however, the measures failed. "Case of Lieut. Hooe—a Notable Instance of Whig Honesty," 159.

111. William G. Brownlow, *A Political Register: Setting Forth the Principles of the Whig and Locofoco Parties in the United States, with the Life and Public Services of Henry Clay* (Jonesborough: Jonesborough Whig, 1844), 184–190.

112. "NEGRO TESTIMONY," *Richmond Whig*, in *Southern Recorder*, August 11, 1840, 2.

113. "From the National Intelligencer," *Southern Recorder*, August 11, 1840, 2.

114. "Pensacola," *Pensacola Gazette*, September 5, 1840, 2.

115. "Naval," *Pensacola Gazette*, January 5, 1839, 2–3, quotation on 2. A Pensacola jury found Jones guilty of involuntary manslaughter and sentenced him to receive thirty-nine lashes and a year imprisonment. "Pensacola," *Pensacola Gazette*, November 24, 1838, 3; Territory of Florida v. Sam Jones, 1838–3029, CCC; Minute Book 4, November 22 and 23, 1838, CCC.

116. Parton, *Life of Andrew Jackson*, 2:600.

117. Ibid., 1:575.

Chapter 4

1. "Forty Dollars Reward," *Apalachicola Gazette*, May 10, 1838, 4; "Apalachicola," *Apalachicola Gazette*, May 11, 1839, 1.

2. "Apalachicola."

3. Ibid.

4. For further details of the case see also "Very Mysterious," *Apalachicola Gazette*, August 14, 1839, 2; "100 Dollars Reward," *Pensacola Gazette*, June 15, 1839, 4; "Notice," *Pensacola Gazette*, June 22, 1839, 3; "100 Dollars Reward," *Apalachicola Gazette*, July 17, 1839, 1; Territory of Florida v. Negro Slave (Caesar), December 8–11, 1839, State Archives of Florida, Tallahassee, RG 970, ser. 73, box 3, folder 29.

5. "Murderers Caught," *Apalachicola Gazette*, July 17, 1839, 3.

6. "$200. REWARD," *Tallahassee Floridian*, November 2, 1839, 3. Trial testimony revealed that when Herron confronted the runaways, they chased

him into the water and then "choked, suffocated, and drowned" him until he expired. Territory of Florida v. Negro Slave (Caesar), December 8–11, 1839, Florida State Archives, RG 970, ser. 73, box 3, folder 29; certificate to Nathan Baker deputy marshal of the Apalachicola district Florida, April 5, 1842, State Archives of Florida, Tallahassee, RG 352, ser. 584, box 3, folder 4; "$200. REWARD," *Tallahassee Floridian,* November 2, 1839, 3.

7. Peter Wood, *Black Majority: Negroes in Colonial South Carolina from 1670 through the Stono Rebellion* (New York: W. W. Norton, 1975), 240.

8. A review of newspapers published in Pensacola and across the Deep South establishes 271 fugitive slaves en route to, originating from, or jailed in Pensacola during the territorial and state periods. Personal correspondence and court and military records confirm another forty-one bondspeople either ran away or were "stolen" from Pensacola and the vicinity. Vague references to individuals or groups of runaways are not included in this calculation, and bondspeople who appear more than once in the records over the course of several years are counted only once. It is worth noting that especially in frontier communities like Pensacola few could afford the cost of advertising for a runaway and even fewer could pay cash rewards for their capture. In the decades before the Civil War, the *Pensacola Gazette* charged one dollar for each advertisement per fourteen lines, putting the cost of advertisement out of the reach of most residents. See "Terms," *Pensacola Gazette,* November 5, 1830, 4, and "Advertisements," *Pensacola Gazette,* January 2, 1858, 4.

9. David Waldstreicher, "Reading the Runaways: Self-Fashioning, Print Culture, and Confidence in Slavery in the Eighteenth-Century Mid-Atlantic," *William and Mary Quarterly* 56, no. 2 (April 1999): 247. For some of the most innovative use of runaway slave advertisements, see also Gad Heuman, ed., *Out of the House of Bondage: Runaways, Resistance and Marronage in Africa and the New World* (New York: Routledge, 2013); Antonio T. Bly, "A Prince among Pretending Free Men: Runaway Slaves in Colonial New England Revisited," *Massachusetts Historical Review* 14 (July 2012): 87–118; and Antonio T. Bly, "'Pretends He Can Read': Runaways and Literacy in Colonial America, 1730–1776," *Early American Studies: An Interdisciplinary Journal* 6, no. 2 (Fall 2008): 261–294; David Waldstreicher, *Runaway America: Benjamin Franklin, Slavery, and the American Revolution* (New York: Hill and Wang, 2005); John Hope Franklin and Loren Schweninger, *Runaway Slaves: Rebels on the Plantation* (Oxford: Oxford University Press, 1999); Jonathan Prude, "To Look upon the 'Lower Sort': Runaway Ads and the Appearance of Unfree Laborers in America, 1750–1800," *Journal of American History* 78, no. 1 (June 1991): 124–159; Philip D. Morgan, "Colonial South Carolina Runaways: Their Significance for Slave Culture," *Slavery and Abolition* 6, no. 3 (December 1985): 57–78; Daniel E. Meaders, "South Caroline Fugitives as Viewed through Local Colonial Newspapers with Emphasis on Runaway Notices, 1732–1801," *Journal of Negro History*

60, no. 2 (April 1975): 288–319; Gerald W. Mullin, *Flight and Rebellion: Slave Resistance in Eighteenth-Century Virginia* (Oxford: Oxford University Press, 1974); Wood, *Black Majority;* Lorenzo J. Greene, "The New England Negro as Seen in Advertisements for Runaway Slaves," *Journal of Negro History* 29, no. 2 (April 1944): 125–146.

10. In his classic treatment of the Underground Railroad, Larry Gara disputed the memory of aged white Northerners in the late nineteenth century who remembered risking their lives to help black strangers escape from slavery in the decades before the Civil War. According to Gara, "Evidence for a nation-wide conspiratorial network of underground railroad lines is completely lacking; the nationally organized railroad with its disciplined conductors, controlling directors, and planned excursions into the South did not exist." Regarding the black fugitives who enjoyed the assistance of Northerners, Gara continued, they "did so after having already completed the most difficult and dangerous phase of their journey alone and unaided." Without reducing the heroic efforts of enslaved people, recent scholarship on the Underground Railroad challenges Gara's conclusion, finding evidence of a significant and subversive network of antislavery radicals who aided fugitive slaves not only in the North but also the South. Larry Gara, *The Liberty Line: The Legend of the Underground Railroad* (Lexington: University Press of Kentucky, 1961), 18. For the more recent literature, see Eric Foner, *Gateway to Freedom: The Hidden History of the Underground Railroad* (New York: Norton, 2015); R. J. M. Blackett, *Making Freedom: The Underground Railroad and the Politics of Slavery* (Chapel Hill: University of North Carolina Press, 2013); David G. Smith, *On the Edge of Freedom: The Fugitive Slave Issue in South Central Pennsylvania, 1820–1870* (New York: Fordham University Press, 2012); Steven Lubet, *Fugitive Justice: Runaways, Rescuers, and Slavery on Trial* (Cambridge: Belknap Press, 2010); Stanley Harrold, *Border War: Fighting over Slavery before the Civil War* (Chapel Hill: University of North Carolina Press, 2010); Stanley Harrold, *Subversives: Antislavery Community in Washington, DC, 1828–1865* (Baton Rouge: Louisiana States University Press, 2003); Fergus M. Bordewich, *Bound for Canaan: The Underground Railroad and the War for the Soul of America* (New York: HarperCollins, 2005); Keith P. Griffler, *Front Line of Freedom: African Americans and the Forging of the Underground Railroad in the Ohio Valley* (Lexington: University Press of Kentucky, 2004); John R. McKivigan and Stanley Harrold, eds., *Antislavery Violence: Sectional, Racial, and Cultural Conflict in Antebellum* (Knoxville: University of Tennessee Press, 1999).

11. John P. Duval, *Compilation of the Public Acts of the Legislative Council of the Territory of Florida, Passed Prior to 1840* (Tallahassee: Samuel S. Sibley, 1839), 221.

12. "Notice," *Pensacola Gazette,* July 17, 1847, 3.

13. "Notice," *Pensacola Gazette,* July 19, 1845, 3.

14. "Taken Up," *Pensacola Gazette,* July 30, 1836, 4.

15. "Notice," *Pensacola Gazette*, March 30, 1844, 3.

16. "Notice," *Pensacola Gazette*, July 13, 1844, 3.

17. "Taken up by the Subscribers, on the 30th Inst.," *Pensacola Gazette*, April 2, 1825, 3.

18. "TAKEN UP by the Subscribers This Day," *Pensacola Gazette*, April 2, 1825, 3.

19. "Taken Up," *Pensacola Gazette*, May 6, 1826, 3.

20. "Taken Up," *Pensacola Gazette*, July 1, 1828, 3.

21. "$20 Reward," *Pensacola Gazette*, May 27, 1837, 2, and June 3, 1837, 3.

22. "Fifty Dollars Reward," *Pensacola Gazette*, September 22, 1849, 3.

23. "$10 Reward," *Pensacola Gazette*, May 29, 1852, 3.

24. "$100 Reward," *Pensacola Gazette*, August 8, 1857, 2.

25. "$50 Reward," *Pensacola Gazette*, July 19, 1840, 3.

26. "$30 Reward," *Pensacola Gazette*, March 25, 1854, 2.

27. "$5 Reward," *Pensacola Gazette*, January 11, 1845, 3.

28. "FIVE DOLLARS REWARD," *Florida Democrat*, January 23, 1846, 2.

29. "Ranaway," *Pensacola Gazette*, August 11, 1829, 2.

30. "$50 Reward," *Pensacola Gazette*, September 11, 1824, 4.

31. Despite the punishment, former slaves recalled that "within a few months, reading and writing went on on the Morten plantation." Martin Richardson, "Pensacola Ethnography," in *The Florida Negro: A Federal Writer's Project Legacy*, University Archives and West Florida History Center, Pensacola, 5–6. Antebellum slaveowners resorted to the amputation of bondspeoples' fingers frequently. For examples of fugitive slaves in Pensacola and the vicinity missing fingers possibly as the result of amputation, see: "Taken Up," *Pensacola Gazette*, November 15, 1834, 2; "50 Dollars Reward," *Pensacola Gazette*, May 12, 1838, 2.

32. "Committed to Jail," *Pensacola Gazette*, January 2, 1833, 4.

33. "Committed to Jail," *Pensacola Gazette*, February 13, 1830, 3.

34. "Notice," *Pensacola Gazette*, March 20, 1830, 3.

35. "$20 Reward," *Pensacola Gazette*, November 3, 1838, 2.

36. Henry Potts v. Charles and Thomas Beeler, 1822–98, CCC.

37. "Ranaway," *Pensacola Gazette*, February 24, 1838, 3.

38. "$20 Reward," *Pensacola Gazette*, October 22, 1836, 2.

39. "100 Reward," *Pensacola Gazette*, February 23, 1856. 2.

40. "$20 Reward," *Pensacola Floridian*, August 7, 1822, 4.

41. "$20 Reward," *Pensacola Gazette*, May 18, 1827, 3.

42. "Pensacola," *Pensacola Gazette*, November 30, 1844, 2.

43. "Communications," *Pensacola Gazette*, June 22, 1827, 2. A full account of the violent encounter and the short-lived maroon community can be found in "Mobile, June 21st," *New York Spectator*, July 17, 1827, 2.

44. Lucius F. Ellsworth and Jane E. Dysart, "West Florida's Forgotten People: The Creek Indians from 1830 until 1970," *Florida Historical Quarterly* 59, no. 4 (April 1981): 422–439.

45. Brian R. Rucker, "Forgotten Struggle: The Second Creek War in West Florida, 1837–1854," in *America's Hundred Years' War: U.S. Expansion to the Gulf Coast and the Fate of the Seminole, 1763–1858,* ed. William S. Belko (Gainesville: University of Florida Press, 2011), 254.

46. "Pensacola," *Pensacola Gazette,* June 17, 1837, 3.

47. "$25 Reward," *Pensacola Gazette,* August 29, 1840, 3.

48. "Ranaway," *Pensacola Gazette,* October 6, 1949, 3.

49. "$20 Reward," *Pensacola Gazette,* August 15, 1835, 2.

50. "Fifty Dollars Reward," *Pensacola Gazette,* July 20, 1850, 3.

51. "$50 Reward," *Pensacola Gazette,* May 2, 1828, 3.

52. "Ranaway," *Pensacola Gazette,* June 30, 1838, 4.

53. "$30 Reward," *Pensacola Gazette,* April 18, 1828, 3. Bell also advertised in the *New Bern North Carolina Sentinel,* thus indicating his conviction the three men were headed for North Carolina. "$30 Dollars Reward," *North Carolina Sentinel,* May 31, 1828, 4.

54. "Fifty Dollars Reward," *Pensacola Gazette,* March 7, 1846, 3.

55. "$100 Reward," *Pensacola Gazette,* January 30, 1830, 3.

56. "Ranaway," *Pensacola Gazette,* November 21, 1835, 2.

57. "Runaway," *Pensacola Gazette,* October 11, 1851, 3.

58. "Notice," *Pensacola Floridian,* April 13, 1822, 3.

59. "Notice," *Pensacola Gazette,* August 21, 1830, 3.

60. "Runaway Slave," *Pensacola Gazette,* May 25, 1850, 3.

61. Steven Deyle, *Carry Me Back: The Domestic Slave Trade in American Life* (New York: Oxford University Press, 2005).

62. "25 Dollars Reward," *Pensacola Gazette,* August 21, 1841, 3.

63. "Fifteen Dollars Reward," *Pensacola Gazette,* November 21, 1828, 3.

64. "Ranaway," *Pensacola Gazette,* April 21, 1849, 3.

65. Though illegal, the murder of one bondsman by another was in antebellum Florida unworthy of the death penalty, as the court sentenced Prior to a public whipping and ordered him to stand in the pillory in front of the courthouse. "Pensacola," *Pensacola Gazette,* June 19, 1852, 2; "$100 Reward," *Pensacola Gazette,* July 31, 1852, 3; "Pensacola," *Pensacola Gazette,* October 16, 1852, 2; State of Florida v. Henry Prior, 1852–1276, CCC.

66. "25 Dollars Reward," *Pensacola Gazette,* September 17, 1853, 3.

67. "One Hundred Dollars Reward," *Pensacola Gazette,* April 8, 1854, 2.

68. "$25 Reward," *Pensacola Gazette,* April 23, 1853, 3; "50 Reward," *Pensacola Gazette,* June 4, 1853, 3.

69. Gene Allen Smith, *The Slaves' Gamble: Choosing Sides in the War of 1812* (New York: Palgrave McMillan, 2013), 3.

70. "Committed to Jail," *Pensacola Floridian,* October 15, 1821, 3.

71. "Ten Dollars Reward," *Pensacola Floridian,* January 28, 1822, 1.

72. The following report appeared in the *Pensacola Gazette:* "The quarters of Dr. Macomb, at the Hospital, Cantonment Clinch, were entered by some

consummate villain early this morning, 'twixt the hours of 1 and 6 A.M. and the following articles stolen:— ONE PORTABLE WRITING DESK—ONE GOLD WATCH. The villain likewise entered the Quarters of the Hospital Matron and carried off a quantity of Soldier's clothing, consisting of Shirts, Trowsers, &c: The Robber is supposed to be a young negro named Jose of large stature and remarkably large feet, employed by Dr Macomb in the month of June as a waiter TWENTY DOLLARS REWARD is offered, for the apprehension of the Robber and recovery of the watch. "Daring Robbery," *Pensacola Gazette,* August 25, 1826, 3.

73. Ulrich Bonnell Phillips, *Plantation and Frontier Documents, 1649–1863: Illustrative of Industrial History in the Colonial & Ante-Bellum South* (Cleveland: Arthur H. Clark Company, 1909), 2:83–84.

74. "Taken Up," *Pensacola Gazette,* April 20, 1827, 3.

75. "Northern Subserviency—Slavery in the District," *Liberator,* March 31, 1843, 1.

76. Franklin and Schweninger, *Runaway Slaves,* 224.

77. "$20 Reward," *Pensacola Gazette,* October 20, 1838, 2.

78. "Taken Up," *Pensacola Gazette,* July 6, 1827, 3; "Escaped from the Jail of This City," *Pensacola Gazette,* August 17, 1827, 3.

79. "$10 Reward," *Pensacola Gazette,* January 7, 1837, 3.

80. "$20 Reward," *Pensacola Gazette,* November 16, 1839, 3.

81. "10 Dollars Reward," *Pensacola Gazette,* August 5, 12, and 19, 1843, all on 3; "Ten Dollars Reward," *Florida Democrat,* January 23, 1846, 3–July 1, 1846, 1.

82. "$30 Reward," *Pensacola Gazette,* April 15, 1837, and July 14, 1838, both on 3; "$50 Reward," *Pensacola Gazette,* August 24, 1839, and July 25, 1840, both on 3.

83. In the aftermath of the beating, authorities took Katy to a local doctor and Williamson to court. A grand jury found the defendant guilty of "cruel and unusual punishment" and fined him one hundred dollars plus court costs. In an extraordinary pronouncement, the court upbraided Williamson, declaring, "You have been convicted of cruel treatment to your slave, under circumstances of the most aggravated nature. The feelings of the inhabitants of this City were roused, to a pitch of excitement and indignation seldom witnessed, by the shocking spectacle of a female chained to the hinder part of a wagon, her arms pinioned, and driven at a trot through the street, at the imminent risk of her life. In this situation she was dragged through ponds of water, at the same time cruelly beaten, and at length, when the citizens collected, and the Mayor interfered, the wretched creature was carried in a swoon to the City Hospital. Such occurrences, I hope, for the honor of human nature, are of rare occurrence any where, and I trust may never occur again in our City." The defendant, for his part, "endeavored to prove the bad character of the slave" by accusing Katy of drunkenness. "Superior Court," *Pensacola Gazette,* March 10, 1829, 2; Territory of Florida v. P. G. Williamson, 1829–386, CCC.

84. "$600 Reward," *Pensacola Gazette,* January 18, 1828, 3.

85. "$1000 Reward," *Pensacola Gazette,* August 25, 1838, 1.

86. "Ranaway," *Pensacola Gazette,* July 22, 1837, 2.

87. "Fifty Dollars Reward," *Pensacola Gazette,* May 12, 1838, 2.

88. "Taken Up," *Pensacola Gazette,* November 15, 1834, 2.

89. "Stop the Thief," *Pensacola Gazette,* April 17, 1824, 3.

90. "Notice," *Pensacola Gazette,* February 1, 1840, 3.

91. "Taken Up," *Pensacola Gazette,* November 7, 1828, 3.

92. "$25 Reward," *Pensacola Gazette,* October 14, 1828, 3.

93. For a discussion of Chinn and the images, consult Eric Foner, *Forever Free: The Story of Emancipation and Reconstruction* (New York: Random House, 2013), 72; Jeff Rosenheim, *Photography and the Civil War* (New York: Metropolitan Museum of Art, 2013), 157–162.

94. "White and Colored Slaves," *Harper's Weekly,* January 30, 1864, 69, 71.

95. Nell Irvin Painter, "Soul Murder and Slavery: Toward a Fully-Loaded Cost Accounting," in *Southern History across the Color Line* (Chapel Hill: University of North Carolina Press, 2002), 15–39; Leonard Shengold, *Soul Murder: The Effects of Childhood Abuse and Deprivation* (New York: Ballantine Books, 1991).

96. "Attempt to Murder," *Pensacola Gazette,* May 17, 1856, 2.

97. "Mr. Editor" and "Tragedy in Green County, Miss.," *Pensacola Gazette,* April 19, 1851, both articles and quotations on 2.

98. Ibid.

99. "John B. Hardin Again!," *Jacksonville Florida News,* May 10, 1851, 2.

100. "Mr. Editor."

101. "Tragedy in Green County, Miss."

102. "Correspondence of the Mobile Tribune: Pensacola, May 31st, 1851," *Tallahassee Floridian & Journal,* June 14, 1851, 2. See also "Pensacola," *Pensacola Gazette,* May 31, 1851, 3; Dr. J. R. S. Pitts, *Life and Confession of the Noted Outlaw James Copeland* (Jackson: University Press of Mississippi, 1980), 215–216.

103. Jeff Forret, *Race Relations at the Margins: Slaves and Poor Whites in the Antebellum Southern Countryside* (Baton Rouge: Louisiana State University Press, 2006), 131–143.

104. "$30 Reward," *Pensacola Gazette,* July 14, 1838, 3.

105. "$15 Reward," *Pensacola Gazette,* March 18, 1826, 3.

106. "Runaway or Stolen," *Pensacola Gazette,* February 1, 1840, 2.

107. "250 Dollars Reward," *Pensacola Gazette,* June 8, 1839, 3.

108. "50 Dollars Reward," *Pensacola Floridian,* June 8, 1822, 3.

109. "$1000 Reward," *Pensacola Gazette,* April 2, 1836, 2.

110. "$130 Reward," *Pensacola Gazette,* July 17, 1830, 3.

111. "$1000 Reward," *Pensacola Gazette,* August 25, 1838, 1.

112. "Runaway Slave," *Pensacola Gazette,* March 25, 1834, 2.

113. "$50 Reward," *Pensacola Gazette,* June 26, 1824, 3.

114. State of Florida v. Francis Decordy, 1853–1376, CCC.
115. Territory of Florida v. Ellie, 1838–3016, CCC.
116. Territory of Florida v. Lewis, 1838–3035, CCC.
117. State of Florida v. William Crosby, 1850–1167, CCC.
118. State of Florida v. Charles J. Brightly, 1851–1243, CCC; Minute Book A, CCC, n.p.
119. Joshua D. Rothman, *Flush Times and River Dreams: A Story of Capitalism and Slavery in the Age of Jackson* (Athens: University of Georgia Press, 2012).
120. "Taken Up and Committed to Jail," *Pensacola Gazette*, July 23, 1825, 3.
121. "Taken Up," *Pensacola Gazette*, April 11, 1833, 3.
122. "Pensacola," *Pensacola Gazette*, May 26, 1838, 3.
123. "$50 Reward," *Pensacola Gazette*, March 7, 1846, 3.
124. "$150 Reward," *Pensacola Gazette*, November 3, 1838, 2.
125. Matthew J. Clavin, "'The Floor Was Stained with the Blood of a Slave': Crime and Punishment in the Old South," in *Buried Lives: Incarcerated in Early America*, ed. Michele Lise Tarter and Richard Bell (Athens: University of Georgia Press, 2012), 259–281.
126. "One Hundred Dollars Reward," *Pensacola Gazette*, April 18, 1835, 2.
127. James M. Denham, *A Rogue's Paradise: Crime and Punishment in Antebellum Florida* (Tuscaloosa: University of Alabama Press, 1997), 233.
128. "Pensacola," *Pensacola Gazette*, June 10 and 17 (quotation), 1854, both on 2.
129. "Sheriff Crosby in New Orleans—Slaves Caught," *Pensacola Gazette*, December 19, 1857, 2.
130. "Negro Stealing Organization Discovered," *Pensacola Observer*, in *San Antonio Ledger*, December 12, 1857, 1. See also "Singletary Captured," *Pensacola Gazette*, November 21, 1857, 2; "Singletary," *Pensacola Gazette*, November 28, 1857, 2; "Negro Stealers," *Pensacola Gazette*, December 5, 1857, 2; "Pensacola," *Pensacola Gazette*, December 12, 1857, 2; "Pensacola," December 19, 1857, 2; "Pensacola," *Pensacola Gazette*, December 25, 1857, 2.
131. "Pensacola," *Pensacola Gazette*, January 23, 1858, 2. Information regarding an accomplice came later when hunters in Conecuh County, Alabama, happened upon Lard, one of the slave stealers, and took him into custody. Under interrogation in Pensacola, the prisoner revealed "the files with which the prisoners severed their chains and were enabled recently to make their escape from the jail, were furnished by Mrs. Singletary, wife of one of the prisoners." Lard apparently told the truth, for subsequent to his arrest it was reported, "Lard, the only one of the Negro Thieves, who was re-captured and brought back to Pensacola after breaking out of jail, was found in the street, with his chains filed off, taking his departure." "Pensacola," *Pensacola Gazette*, January 30, 1858, 2; "Pensacola," *Pensacola Gazette*, March 13, 1858, 2. See also "Pensacola," *Pensacola Gazette*, February 6, 1858, 2; "Pensacola," *Pensacola Gazette*, February 13, 1858, 2; "Pensacola," *Pensacola Gazette*, February 27, 1858.

Chapter 5

1. "An Arrival from Florida," *New York Evangelist*, August 15, 1850, 131.

2. "The Fugitive Slave in Portsmouth," *Liberator*, August 16, 1850, 3.

3. Ezra S. Stearns, William F. Whitcher, and Edward E. Parker, *Genealogical and Family History of the State of New Hampshire* (New York: Lewis Publishing Company, 1908), 2:523.

4. "The Fugitive Slave in Portsmouth."

5. "An Arrival from Florida." Further details of the episode are described in the following: "A Fugitive Slave," *New Hampshire Patriot and State Gazette*, August 8, 1850, 2; "Pensacola," *Pensacola Gazette*, August 17, 1850, 2; "Fugitive Slave," *New-Hampshire Gazette*, August 20, 1850, 2.

6. "A Fugitive Slave."

7. For the Fugitive Slave Act and the abolitionist response, see Eric Foner, *Gateway to Freedom: The Hidden History of the Underground Railroad* (New York: W. W. Norton, 2015); R. J. M. Blackett, *Making Freedom: The Underground Railroad and the Politics of Slavery* (Chapel Hill: University of North Carolina Press, 2013); Paul Finkelman and Donald R. Kennon, eds., *Congress and the Crisis of the 1850s* (Athens: Ohio University Press, 2011); David M. Potter, *The Impending Crisis: American before the Civil War, 1848–1861* (New York: Harper Perennial, 2011); Stanley Harrold, *Border War: Fighting over Slavery before the Civil War* (Chapel Hill: University of North Carolina Press, 2010); Steven Lubet, *Fugitive Justice: Runaways, Rescuers, and Slavery on Trial* (Cambridge, MA: Harvard University Press, 2010); Earl M. Maltz, *Fugitive Slave on Trial: The Anthony Burns Case and Abolitionist Outrage* (Lawrence: University Press of Kansas, 2010). David G. Smith finds that despite the rash of famous fugitive slave cases after 1850, the fugitive slave issue actually receded by the mid-1850s. *On the Edge of Freedom: The Fugitive Slave Issue in South Central Pennsylvania, 1820–1870* (New York: Fordham University Press, 2012).

8. "The Fugitive Slave Law in Florida," *New York Herald*, August 10, 1856, 3; For the ship's cargo see "Port of Pensacola," *Pensacola Gazette*, July 19, 1856, 3.

9. "Pensacola," *Pensacola Gazette*, July 26, 1856, 2.

10. "Fugitive Slave Brought To," *Daily Picayune*, January 30, 1857, 2. For an abolitionist rejoinder, see "A Piratical Yankee Commended," *Anti-Slavery Bugle*, March 7, 1857, 3.

11. As historians are only just beginning to understand, slave resistance could be a political act with far-reaching implications. For recent articulation of the idea, see Irvin D. S. Winsboro and Joe Knetsch, "Florida Slaves, the 'Saltwater Railroad' to the Bahamas, and Anglo-American Diplomacy," *Journal of Southern History* 79, no. 1 (February 2013): 51–78; Blackett, *Making Freedom;* and Smith, *On the Edge of Freedom.* Classic accounts of the political ramifications of slave resistance include: Steven Hahn, *A Nation under Our Feet: Black Political Struggles in the Rural South from Slavery to the*

Great Migration (Cambridge, MA: Harvard University Press, 2003); James Oakes, "The Political Significance of Slave Resistance," *History Workshop Journal* 22 (Fall 1986): 89–107.

12. Among the most famous of these cases were the capture of seventy-seven slaves from Washington, DC on the schooner *Pearl* in 1848, and Anthony Burns's return to servitude in 1854 after having escaped to Boston, Massachusetts, from Richmond, Virginia, several months earlier.

13. Keith P. Griffler, *Front Line of Freedom: African Americans and the Forging of the Underground Railroad in the Ohio Valley* (Lexington: University Press of Kentucky, 2004), xii.

14. For Walker's biography, see Jonathan Walker, *Trial and Imprisonment of Jonathan Walker, at Pensacola, Florida, for Aiding Slaves to Escape from Bondage* (Boston: Anti-Slavery Office, 1845); Jonathan Walker, *A Brief View of American Chattelized Humanity, and Its Supports* (Boston: Dow and Jackson, 1846); Jonathan Walker, *A Picture of Slavery, for Youth* (Boston: J. Walker and W. R. Bliss, [1846]).

15. Kathleen Grover, *The Fugitive's Gibraltar: Escaping Slaves and Abolitionism in New Bedford, Massachusetts* (Amherst: University of Massachusetts Press, 2001).

16. Frederick Douglass, *My Bondage and My Freedom* (New York: Miller, Orton & Mulligan), 347.

17. "The Dedham and Waltham Celebrations," *Liberator,* August 15, 1845, 1.

18. Walker, *Trial and Imprisonment,* 108–110; "Waltham Pic-Nic," *Liberator,* August 8, 1845, 2; Fergus M. Bordewich, *Bound for Canaan: The Underground Railroad and the War for the Soul of America* (New York: HarperCollins, 2005), 268–271; Stanley Harrold, "John Brown's Forerunners: Slave Rescue Attempts and the Abolitionists, 1841–51," *Radical History Review* 55 (1993): 92.

19. Walker, *Trial and Imprisonment,* 9 and 63, quotations on 9. See also "Pensacola," *Pensacola Gazette,* June 29, 1844, 2; "Waltham Pic-Nic."

20. Handbill enclosed with R. C. Caldwell and George Willis to the Secretary of State, July 24, 1844, Miscellaneous Letters of the Department of State, 1789–1906, RG59, NARA.

21. "Notice," *Pensacola Gazette,* April 25, 1840, 3; "Notice," *Pensacola Gazette,* September 26, 1840, 3.

22. According to Walker, Cook's release came after "an individual of the place succeeded in obtaining his free papers at the expense of about forty dollars." Walker, *A Brief View of American Chattelized Humanity,* 8–9. The Escambia County Court eventually dismissed Woodbine's claim against Cook for five hundred dollars and set Cook free, but it initially ordered Cook, even though he regained possession of free papers and produced them to the court, to serve Woodbine for two years in order to pay the accumulated debt of three hundred dollars. CCC, Minute Book 5, 1842, Peter Woodbine v. William Cook, March 1842, n.p.

23. Larry Gara, *The Liberty Line: The Legend of the Underground Railroad* (Lexington: University Press of Kentucky, 1961), 164–194.

24. Walker, *Trial and Imprisonment,* 36. When the *Pensacola Gazette* reported Walker's connection with the earlier escape, he offered no denial. "Pensacola," *Pensacola Gazette,* June 29, 1844.

25. Winsboro and Knetsch, "Florida Slaves, the 'Saltwater Railroad' to the Bahamas, and Anglo-American Diplomacy," 54. Walker undoubtedly knew that just three years earlier in 1841 colonial authorities refused to recognize the rights of American slaveowners in the case of the slave revolt on the brig *Creole.* Walker discusses the abolition of slavery in the British West Indies briefly in *A Picture of Slavery, for Youth,* 21–23; for the *Creole* case, see Howard Jones, "The Peculiar Institution and National Honor: The Case of the *Creole* Slave Revolt," *Civil War History* 21, no. 1 (March 1975): 28–40.

26. Walker, *Trial and Imprisonment,* 10–14; handbill enclosed with R. C. Caldwell and George Willis to the Secretary of State, July 24, 1844, Miscellaneous Letters of the Department of State, 1789–1906, NARA.

27. "Young, strong, healthy, intelligent men," they fit the profile of fugitive slaves found throughout the antebellum South and described by historians John Hope Franklin and Loren Schweninger in *Runaway Slaves: Rebels on the Plantation* (Oxford: Oxford University Press, 199), 233.

28. Handbill enclosed with R. C. Caldwell and George Willis to the Secretary of State, July 24, 1844, Miscellaneous Letters of the Department of State, 1789–1906, NARA.

29. Ibid.

30. "Pensacola," *Pensacola Gazette,* June 29, 1844.

31. For the Willis family, see Byrd C. Willis, *A Sketch of the Willis Family: Fredericksburg Branch* (Richmond: Whittet & Shepperson, 1909); little is known of Caldwell besides his service in the Marine Corps: "Documents: Washington in 1834; Letter of Robert C. Caldwell," *American Historical Review* 27, no. 2 (January 1822): 271.

32. R. C. Caldwell and George Willis to the Secretary of State, July 24, 1844, Miscellaneous Letters of the Department of State, 1789–1906, NARA.

33. George Van Cleve, *A Slaveholders' Union: Slavery, Politics, and the Constitution in the Early American Republic* (Chicago: University of Chicago Press, 2011); David Ericson, *Slavery in the American Republic: Developing the Federal Government, 1791–1861* (Lawrence: University of Kansas Press, 2011); David Waldstreicher, *Slavery's Constitution: From Revolution to Ratification* (New York: Hill and Wang, 2009); Robin L. Einhorn, *American Taxation, American Slavery* (Chicago: University of Chicago Press, 2008); Don E. Fehrenbacher, *The Slaveholding Republic: An Account of the United States Government's Relations to Slavery* (New York: Oxford University Press, 2001).

34. Walker, *Trial and Imprisonment,* 14–16, 36–37, 57–59.

35. Walker, *Pensacola Gazette,* 24–25, 53, quotation on 25.

36. "Pensacola," *Pensacola Gazette,* September 7, 1844, 2.

37. Regarding the suicide, a Pensacola writer alleged, "Conjugal infidelity on the part of his [Silas's] wife is said to have caused occasional fits of melancholy and partial insanity for some time past, and it was during one of these paroxysms that he committed the rash deed." Abolitionists refuted the account, interpreting Silas's death as the final act of a great American freedom fighter: "fearing the dreadful punishment with which the vengeance of his master would visit him, and perhaps desperate with lost hope, he nearly severed his head from his body, and cut out his entrails, that he might at least be sure of liberty in death." Ibid. See also "Jonathan Walker," *National Anti-Slavery Standard,* July 24, 1845, 2.

38. Walker, *Trial and Imprisonment,* 21. Neither Walker nor the *Pensacola Gazette* mentioned Silas by name; however, Navy Yard payroll records and shipping manifests at the National Archives, as well as estate records at the Escambia County Courthouse confirm that six of the seven bondsmen who escaped with Walker remained enslaved in Pensacola through the 1850s. Only Silas disappeared from the historical record after 1844, confirming his identity as the suicide victim. Additionally, the *Pensacola Gazette* stated the deceased bondsman belonged to Byrd C. Willis, while other sources indicate that Silas belonged to Caldwell; nevertheless, the contradiction is explained easily. The bondsmen who escaped with Walker worked at different times for Caldwell, Byrd C. Willis, and his son George Willis. In antebellum Pensacola slaveowners at times owned property collectively and given the widespread practice of slave hiring the distinction between a bondsperson's owner and employer was often negligible. "PayRoll of Mechanics, Laborers, etc.," Pensacola Navy Yard, June 1855, RG71, Box 136, NARA; Slave Manifests of Coastwise Vessels Filed at New Orleans, Louisiana, 1807–1860, March 1, 1845, Records of the U.S. Customs Service, RG36, microfilm M1895, reel 10, NARA; Last Will and Testament and Appraisement of the Personal Estate of George Willis, 1862, CCC.

39. "Pensacola," *Pensacola Gazette,* July 20, 1844, 2.

40. Walker, *Trial and Imprisonment,* 34 and 39, quotation on 34.

41. "Jonathan Walker."

42. Ibid.; Walker, *Trial and Imprisonment,* 42–43.

43. Walker, *Trial and Imprisonment,* 102.

44. Ibid., 32–33, 118–19.

45. In September, for example, the informant used the alias "A SUBSCRIBER TO THE LIBERATOR." "Arrest of Jonathan Walker," *Liberator,* September 13, 1844, 3.

46. Lubet, *Fugitive Justice*; Harrold, "John Brown's Forerunners: Slave Rescue Attempts and the Abolitionists, 1841–51."

47. Arrested in Baltimore, Torrey died from tuberculosis in the Maryland State Penitentiary after almost two years of incarceration. Stanley Harrold, "On the Borders of Slavery and Race: Charles T. Torrey and the Underground Railroad," *Journal of the Early Republic* 20, no. 2 (Summer 2000): 273–292;

J. C. Lovejoy, ed., *Memoir of Rev. Charles T. Torrey, Who Died in the Penitentiary of Maryland, Where He Was Confined for Showing Mercy to the Poor* (Boston: Jon P. Jewett & Co., 1847). For references to the "Hero of Pensacola" see "Middlesex and Suffolk Counties" and "Mass Meeting in Lynn!," *Liberator,* July 25, 1845, 3.

48. "Lecture by Wendell Phillips," *Liberator,* November 8, 1844, 3; See also "Lecture by Wendell Phillips," *Liberator,* November 1, 1844, 3.

49. Walker, *Trial and Imprisonment,* 83–87.

50. "The Boston Liberator," *Pensacola Gazette,* September 12, 1846, 2.

51. "The Case of Jonathan Walker," *Daily Picayune,* November 29, 1844, 4.

52. Walker, *Trial and Imprisonment,* 87–93.

53. Walker also self-published two editions of *A Brief View of American Chattelized Humanity* and one edition of a book for young readers, *A Picture of Slavery, for Youth.* Walker's authorial success distressed Pensacola's slaveowners, who continued to see him as a common criminal. While visiting Philadelphia, George Willis "discovered a number of these pamphlets in a book store, purchased the whole collection, tore them up and scattering them upon the floor turned and walked out." Willis, *A Sketch of the Willis Family,* 83.

54. Frederick Douglass, *Narrative of the Life of an American Slave* (Boston: Anti-Slavery Office, 1845).

55. Walker, *Trial and Imprisonment,* v.

56. For the jail's function as an "engine of discipline," see Matthew J. Clavin, "'The Floor Was Stained with the Blood of a Slave': Crime and Punishment in the Old South," in *Buried Lives: Incarcerated in Early America,* ed. Michele Lise Tarter and Richard Bell (Athens: University of Georgia Press, 2012), 259–281.

57. Walker, *Trial and Imprisonment,* 70.

58. Ibid., 26–27.

59. Ibid., 45–46, 50–51.

60. Walker wrote publicly, "With but few exceptions have I received any other aid than an occasional meal or a night's lodging . . . Anti-slavery proper *don't pay,* in dollars and cents; this fact has long been abundantly experienced by those who have labored earnestly and faithfully in the cause, and consequently, 'the laborers are few.'" "Travels in Vermont," *Liberator,* February 14, 1851, 4.

61. Marcus Wood adds that the hand "literally reached out to a mass audience across the free Northern states." *Blind Memory: Visual Representation of Slavery in England and America, 1780–1865* (New York: Routledge, 2000), 249.

62. "POETRY," *Liberator,* August 15, 1845, 4.

63. "Walker Meeting in New Bedford," *Liberator,* August 22, 1845.

64. Frederick Douglass to Photius Fisk, July 15, 1878, in Frank Edward Kittredge, "The Man with the Branded Hand," *New England Magazine* 19, no. 3 (November 1898): 370–371.

65. Bordewich, *Bound for Canaan*, 292.
66. "Spiritual Knockings—Again," *Liberator,* June 6, 1851, 4.
67. American Anti-Slavery Society Executive Committee, *The Anti-Slavery History of the John-Brown Year; Being the Twenty-Seventh Annual Report of the American Anti-Slavery Society* (New York: American Anti-Slavery Society, 1861), 51–52.
68. "Columbus Discovered," *Pensacola Gazette,* October 30, 1857, 2. A Pensacola grand jury indicted Singletary for stealing Columbus, though the case may have never taken place given Singletary's escape from the jail following his arrest. State of Florida v. Leonard Singletary, 1857–1753, CCC.
69. "The Hyannis Kidnapping Case," *New York Times,* June 1, 1859, 5.
70. Jonathan Shectman, *Bound for the Future: Child Heroes of the Underground Railroad* (New York: Praeger, 2012), 199.
71. "Rev. Mr. Pope of Hyannis," *Liberator,* September 9, 1859, 3.
72. "The Hyannis Kidnapping Case."
73. Ibid. See also Samuel J. May, *The Fugitive Slave Law and Its Victims* (New York: American Anti-Slavery Society, 1861), 118–119. One of Crowell's defenders maintained that the captain tried to protect Columbus from the pro-slavery zealots who awaited his arrival at Hyannis Port, but there is no corroborating evidence to support the story. "Rev. Mr. Pope of Hyannis," *Liberator,* September 9, 1859, 3.
74. "The Hyannis Kidnapping Case," *Boston Daily Advertiser,* November 16, 1859, 1; November 17, 1859, 2; November 18, 1859, 2; November 19, 1859, 1; and November 21, 1859, 1.
75. "The Hyannis Kidnapping Case," *Boston Daily Advertiser*, November, 19, 1.
76. Ibid.
77. "The Hyannis Kidnapping Case," *Boston Daily Advertiser,* November 21, 1859, 1.
78. Roy P. Basler, ed. *Abraham Lincoln: His Speeches and Writings* (Cambridge, MA: Da Capo Press, 2001), 372.

Chapter 6

1. "Military Treatment of Captured and Fugitive Slaves," *ORA,* ser. 2, vol. 1, p. 749.
2. "The War for the Union," *New York Tribune,* April 19, 1861, 5.
3. A. J. Slemmer to Lieut. Col. L. Thomas, March 18, 1861, *ORA,* ser. I, vol. 1, p. 362.
4. "The War for the Union."
5. A. J. Slemmer to Lieut. Col. L. Thomas, March 18, 1861, *ORA,* ser. I, vol. 1, p. 362. The total number of fugitive slaves in Pensacola prior to the commencement of the war is indeterminable. Abolitionist Lydia Maria Child thought the number was thirty, while a Northern newspaper correspondent